CHATELAINE
food express

Quickies

Quickies

TEN QUICK WAYS WITH EVERYDAY FOODS

BY MONDA ROSENBERG

M&S

A SMITH SHERMAN BOOK
produced in conjunction with CHATELAINE®
and published by McCLELLAND & STEWART INC.

Canadian Cataloguing in Publication Data

Rosenberg, Monda
    Quickies: ten quick ways with everyday foods

(Chatelaine food express)
"A Smith Sherman book produced in conjunction with Chatelaine"
Includes index

ISBN 0-7710-7592-8

1. Quick and easy cookery. I. Title II. Series

TX833.5.R672 1997   641.5'55   C97-930615-9

ACKNOWLEDGEMENTS

Any chef will tell you that it is the quality of the ingredients that makes a dish – so it is the hard work, dedication and talent of many, many players that produce a cookbook. First, a special thank you to the talented team of Carol Sherman and Andrew Smith, who took an idea we've had for 12 years and made it happen. Joseph Gisini for his eagle-eyed attention to design detail. Bernice Eisenstein whose outstanding copy-editing skills caught even the tiniest errors. Lolita Osorio, who assisted in copy editing, and Debra Sherman, who meticulously input the recipes. Among the CHATELAINE crew we would especially like to thank Lucie Cousineau, who deftly negotiated through many hurdles and juggled many tasks because she believed in this book. Marilyn Crowley and Trudy Patterson, who initially tested the recipes in the CHATELAINE Test Kitchen and gave their sound advice. Rona Maynard, who was very supportive and gave constant encouragement. Anita Draycott, who cheerfully gave us the bonus of her sharp editorial eye. Lee Simpson for her caring encouragement. For the superb photographs, creative director Miriam Gee, food stylists Rosemarie Superville and Kate Bush; photographers Ed O'Neil, Michael Mahovlich and Lorella Zanetti; and art director Caren Watkins and creative associate Barbara Glazer. Alison Fryer and Jennifer Grange from The Cookbook Store for their superb marketing advice. The team at McClelland & Stewart for their expert guidance, particularly Pat Kennedy for flawless editing, Valerie Jacobs for her good-natured endurance throughout contract negotiations, and, last but by no means least, Avie Bennett and Doug Gibson for their strong commitment to this book.

MONDA ROSENBERG

COVER PHOTO: CHICKEN WITH DRIED FRUIT, *see recipe page 46*

PHOTO PAGE 2: FAST NIÇOISE FETTUCCINE, *see recipe page 198*

CREDITS: *see page 224*

An A to Z recipe book that gives delicious new meaning to choice in cooking

Quickies is designed to help you prepare fast and flavorful meals with **ingredients you already have on hand.** With the help of our alphabetic pages, it's as easy as ABC to have a meal on the table fast. Use this book like you would **a dictionary** and look up the ingredient you want to prepare. With **100 categories and 10 recipes in each** – some using less than 5 ingredients – you're sure to find more than one terrific recipe that uses exactly what you have on hand.

Make an *Instant Fish Chowder* from **a can of tuna** or *Easy Thai Chicken Salad* from **leftover chicken** and a bottle of peanut sauce. From the classic comfort of *Baked Granola Apples* to wrap-and-roll *Fiery Fajitas*, the **1,000 recipes** presented here are timeless and timely. Stir-fries, pasta sauces and salad dressings mingle with recipes using the barbecue, microwave and broiler. You'll find ethnic touches from the Orient to the Mediterranean to down-home favorites such as *Rice Pudding* and *Perfect Barbecued Ribs*.

Maybe you feel like a soup or salad or something for breakfast. Go directly to our comprehensive **Index** (pages 212 to 223) for a listing of meal occasions, including Appetizers, Breakfast, Entrées, Desserts, even Home Alone, for those days you're cooking solo. Our **Contents** (pages 6 and 7) lists the 100 ingredients from A to Z and lays out exactly what you'll find in the index. Plus our **Survival Guide** (pages 210 and 211) will help you keep your cupboards, freezer and refrigerator well-stocked. It also offers **spice equivalents for fresh and dried.**

Quickies is a book for everybody. With it at your fingertips, great meals are just a snap away.

A is for Apple...

CONTENTS

F is for Fish ...

N is for Nuts ...

O is for Oats ...

R is for Ribs ...

Z is for Zucchini.

A is for Apples...

Tender pieces of fresh asparagus add that special sophisticated taste to our CHICKEN PARMIGIANA PASTA (see recipe page 14). Simply add asparagus to the pasta for the last few minutes of cooking while the chicken is simmering in white wine and basil.

APPLES

Much more than a juicy snack, apples are a rich source of soluble fibre, which helps lower cholesterol levels. Enjoy them in a peck of healthy ways from citrusy applesauce to fibre-rich muffins.

SAUTÉED CURRIED APPLES

Melt 2 tbsp butter over medium heat.
Add 2 cups sliced peeled apples,
   2 tbsp raisins, $\frac{1}{2}$ tsp curry powder
   and pinch of sugar.
Sauté until apples are tender. Great with
   chicken. *Makes 1¼ cups.*

SOPHISTICATED CRAB SPREAD

Stir $\frac{1}{4}$ to $\frac{1}{2}$ tsp curry powder with
   $\frac{1}{4}$ cup light mayonnaise or sour cream.
Stir in 6-oz (170-g) can drained crabmeat,
   I unpeeled grated apple and
   I sliced green onion.
Serve with crisp whole-grain crackers or on
   top of cucumber rounds. *Makes 1¼ cups.*

GRILLED CHEESE & APPLE SANDWICH

Lightly spread bread with Dijon.
Cover with thin slices of apple.
Top with thick slices of Swiss or
   cheddar cheese.
Broil until cheese melts.

HOT HORSERADISH RELISH

Toss $\frac{1}{2}$ cup coarsely grated apple with
   I tsp lemon juice.
Stir in $\frac{1}{4}$ cup horseradish.
Wonderful with roast beef and pork.
   Makes ⅔ cup.

CITRUSY APPLESAUCE

In a saucepan, combine
   6 chopped peeled apples with
   $\frac{3}{4}$ cup water, $\frac{1}{4}$ cup sugar,
   $\frac{1}{2}$ tsp nutmeg and I tsp grated lemon peel.
Cook over medium heat, stirring often, until
   boiling. Reduce heat and simmer, uncovered.
   Stir often, until thick, about 20 min.
Stir in I tsp lemon juice. *Makes 3 cups.*

5-MINUTE BAKED APPLES

Remove cores from 4 unpeeled apples
   without cutting through to the bottoms.
   Pierce skins several times.
Place on a 9-in. (23-cm) pie plate.
Spoon I tsp brown sugar, I tsp butter and
   $\frac{1}{4}$ tsp vanilla into each apple hollow.
   Cover with waxed paper or clear wrap,
   venting 1 corner.
Microwave, on high, until tender, 5 to 8 min.
   Serves 4.

BAKED GRANOLA APPLES

Remove cores from 4 unpeeled apples.
   Firmly pack with $\frac{3}{4}$ cup granola.
   Arrange in a baking dish.
   Sprinkle generously with cinnamon.
Bake, uncovered, at 350°F (180°C), 30 min.,
   or until tender.
Drizzle with maple syrup and top with a dab
   of yogurt. *Serves 4.*

BAKED GRANOLA APPLES

CLASSIC APPLE CRISP

Stir ¼ cup brown sugar with
  1 tbsp flour and ¼ tsp cinnamon.
Toss with 8 chopped peeled apples.
  Place in an 8-in. (2-L) baking dish.
Stir ½ cup all-purpose flour with
  ¾ cup rolled oats and ½ cup brown sugar.
  Slowly stir in ¼ cup melted butter.
  Spread over apples.
Bake at 350°F (180°C) until apples are tender,
  about 35 min. *Serves 6.*

APPLE-CINNAMON MUFFINS

Toss 1 finely chopped apple with
  1 tsp cinnamon and ½ tsp nutmeg.
Prepare a bran muffin mix following directions
  or use your favorite muffin recipe.
Stir apples into batter and bake.
  Makes 12 large muffins.

SPICY APPLE HERMITS

Using a fork, stir 1¾ cups all-purpose flour
  with 1 cup brown sugar and
  ½ tsp each baking soda, salt,
  cinnamon and ginger.
Whisk ⅓ cup melted butter with
  ½ cup milk and 1 egg.
Stir into flour mixture. Fold in
  2 coarsely chopped peeled apples,
  1 cup raisins and
  1 cup chopped nuts.
Drop by heaping tablespoons, 2 in. (5 cm)
  apart, onto greased baking sheets.
Bake at 375°F (190°C) until golden,
  12 to 14 min. *Makes 60 cookies.*

ARTICHOKES

The smart avenue to indulging in artichokes is to open a can of perfect hearts or a jar of marinated quarters. We've also included a fast microwave way to cook fresh artichokes.

ARTICHOKE, RED PEPPER & OLIVE SALAD

Arrange 1 head Bibb lettuce over a large
   platter.
Scatter with 2 (14-oz/398-mL) cans
   drained artichoke hearts, quartered,
   1 julienned red pepper and
   $\frac{1}{3}$ cup small black olives.
Drizzle with Light Green Goddess Dressing
   (see recipe page 13) or Caesar dressing.
   Serves 8.

ARTICHOKE & PEPPER SALAD

Toss 2 (14-oz/398-mL) cans drained
   artichoke hearts, quartered, with
   $\frac{1}{2}$ cup pitted sliced black olives,
   1 julienned red pepper and
   3 sliced green onions.
Drizzle with $\frac{1}{2}$ cup Creamy Fresh Lemon
   Dressing (see recipe page 102).
Serve on a bed of greens. *Serves 4.*

ANTIPASTO SALAD

Whisk $\frac{1}{3}$ cup olive oil with
   2 tbsp lemon juice, $\frac{1}{2}$ tsp dried basil
   and $\frac{1}{2}$ tsp sugar.
Toss with 1 head leaf lettuce, torn into
   pieces, 14-oz (398-mL) can drained
   artichoke hearts, halved,
   19-oz can drained chickpeas and
   $\frac{1}{4}$ lb (125 g) julienned salami slices.
   Serves 4.

WARM PARMESAN DIP

Purée 14-oz (398-mL) can drained
   artichokes with $\frac{1}{2}$ cup sour cream
   and pinches of garlic powder and
   white pepper.
Stir in $\frac{1}{2}$ cup grated Parmesan.
Cover and bake at 350°F (180°C) until warm,
   15 min. Serve with breadsticks or crackers.
   Makes 1¾ cups.

CHERRY TOMATO SALAD

Toss 6-oz (170-mL) jar marinated artichokes,
   including dressing, with
   2 cups cherry tomatoes, sliced in half, and
   pinches of salt, sugar and pepper.
Sprinkle with chopped fresh basil and chives.
Serve on lettuce. *Makes 4 cups.*

AVOCADO, ARTICHOKE & SHRIMP SALAD

Combine 2 heads leaf lettuce, such as
   Boston, broken into pieces, with
   14-oz (398-mL) can drained
   artichoke hearts, quartered, and
   1 chopped avocado.
Top with 8 oz (250 g) cooked baby shrimp.
Whisk $\frac{1}{3}$ cup vegetable oil with
   2 tbsp lemon juice, $\frac{1}{2}$ tsp Dijon,
   $\frac{1}{4}$ tsp dried tarragon, $\frac{1}{4}$ tsp sugar and
   pinches of salt and white pepper.
Toss with salad.
Sprinkle with sliced green onions. *Serves 4.*

TEMPTING TUNA NIÇOISE

Toss 7½-oz can drained tuna with
   6-oz (170-mL) jar drained marinated
   artichokes, 1 tomato, cut into wedges,
   2 tbsp slivered black olives and
   ¼ cup vinaigrette-style Italian dressing.
Serve on greens. *Serves 2 to 3.*

LIGHT GREEN GODDESS DRESSING

In a food processor, whirl
   ½ cup fresh basil leaves with
   14-oz (398-mL) can drained artichoke
   hearts, 1 tbsp lemon juice and
   1 tbsp olive oil.
With processor running, slowly add
   ½ to ¾ cup buttermilk.
Covered and refrigerated, dressing will keep
   up to 2 days. *Makes 1⅔ cups.*

ARTICHOKE & RED ONION PIZZA

Sprinkle 1 cup grated mozzarella over
   a store-bought pizza crust.
Chop 6-oz (170-mL) jar drained marinated
   artichoke hearts.
Scatter over crust with 1 cup thinly sliced
   red onion, ¼ tsp dried thyme and
   ¼ tsp dried basil.
Top with 1 cup grated mozzarella.
Bake at 450°F (230°C) for 15 min. *Serves 4.*

MICROWAVE FRESH ARTICHOKES

Slice ⅓ off top of 4 artichokes and trim base.
   Wash, but leave clinging water.
   Wrap each in plastic wrap.
Microwave, on high, 12 to 20 min.
Dip tender ends of leaves and choke base in
   Lemon Vinaigrette Dressing (see page 103).

TEMPTING TUNA NIÇOISE

ASPARAGUS

Asparagus is always a treat. Be careful not to overcook it, and don't overpower it with robust sauces or herbs. A light sauté or sprinkle of Parmesan is all this elegant vegetable needs.

STEAMED LEMON ASPARAGUS

Diagonally slice 1 lb (500 g) asparagus into 1½-in. (3.5-cm) pieces.

Stir-fry stalk pieces in 1 tbsp butter for 2 min.

Add tip ends, ¼ cup water and sprinkling of sugar.

Cover and simmer for 3 min. Drain and serve with lemon. *Serves 2 to 4.*

SAUTÉED PARMESAN ASPARAGUS

Slice 1 lb (500 g) asparagus into 2-in. (5-cm) pieces.

Sauté in 1 tsp butter and 1 tsp olive oil until tender-crisp, about 3 min.

Toss with 2 tbsp grated Parmesan and pinches of salt. *Serves 2 to 4.*

WARM CHÈVRE ASPARAGUS ROLLS

Cut 16 cooked asparagus spears in half.

Lightly spread ⅔ cup creamy goat cheese over 16 thin ham slices.

Sprinkle with pepper.
Cut ham in half lengthwise.

Place asparagus piece at end of each slice.
Roll tightly. (Ends of asparagus will show.)

Bake at 375°F (190°C) until hot, about 5 min.

Serve hot. *Makes 32 appetizers.*

CHICKEN PARMIGIANA PASTA

Cook 1 lb (450 g) pkg penne until al dente.

Slice 1 lb (500 g) asparagus into 2-in. (5-cm) pieces. Add to pasta last 3 min. of cooking.

Meanwhile, slice 4 skinless boneless chicken breasts into strips.

Sauté in 2 tbsp butter until cooked, about 4 min.

Add 2 tbsp white wine,
½ tsp dried basil and generous pinches of salt and white pepper.

Toss with drained pasta, asparagus and ½ cup grated Parmesan. *Serves 4.*

PROVENÇAL ASPARAGUS TOSS

Boil 1 lb (500 g) asparagus, covered, until tender-crisp, 4 min.

Stir 1 tbsp melted butter with 1 tsp Dijon and 1 tsp red wine vinegar.

Toss with drained asparagus and serve warm. *Serves 2 to 4.*

SWISS BAKE

Partially cook asparagus, about 3 min.

Arrange in a baking dish and sprinkle with grated Swiss cheese and pinches of salt and pepper. Dot with butter.

Bake at 450°F (230°C), about 10 min. to melt cheese.

Mediterranean Touches

MEDITERRANEAN TOUCHES

Whisk ¼ cup olive oil with
　1½ tbsp lemon juice and
　pinches of salt and pepper.
Add 2 sliced green onions and
　¼ cup slivered black olives.
Drizzle over 1 lb (500 g) cooked hot or
　chilled asparagus.
Serve right away. *Serves 2 to 4.*

MICROWAVE FRENCH ASPARAGUS

Place 1 finely chopped onion and
　2 tbsp butter in a microwave-safe dish.
Cover and microwave, on high, 2 min.
Stir in 2 cups asparagus, cut into
　1-in. (2.5-cm) pieces.
Cook, covered, on high, 2 min.
Stir in 1 tsp Dijon.
Let stand, covered, 3 min. *Serves 2.*

BARBECUED ASPARAGUS

Brush asparagus with
　sesame or vegetable oil.
Barbecue over medium-hot coals with lid
　down, turning often, until just tender,
　6 to 8 min.

PARISIENNE TARRAGON ASPARAGUS

Boil 1 lb (500 g) asparagus, covered, until
　tender-crisp, 4 min.
Whisk ¼ cup olive oil with
　2 tbsp lemon juice,
　3 tbsp finely chopped shallots,
　1 tsp chopped fresh tarragon,
　¼ tsp salt and pinch of white pepper.
Toss with drained asparagus. Let sit no more
　than 1 hour. *Serves 2 to 4.*

AVOCADOS

*Whether you think of it as a fruit (which it is) or a vegetable, an avocado
is a powerhouse of nutrition. Along with its rich texture and nutlike flavor, it delivers
numerous vitamins, including A and E.*

SMOOTH GUACAMOLE

In a food processor, whirl pulp of
   I large avocado with I chopped garlic clove,
   2 tbsp lime juice, 2 sliced green onions,
   dash of hot pepper sauce and
   pinches of salt and pepper.
Sprinkle with chopped tomato. *Makes ¾ cup.*

CHUNKY GUACAMOLE

Mash 2 tbsp grated onion with
   3 crushed garlic cloves,
   I tbsp chopped seeded hot pepper,
   2 tbsp lemon juice and ¼ tsp salt.
Stir in 2 diced peeled avocados,
   ¼ cup finely chopped fresh coriander and
   2 diced seeded tomatoes.
Serve with tortilla chips. *Makes 1½ cups.*

COOL AVOCADO SOUP

In a food processor, whirl pulp of
   3 avocados with I cup chicken broth,
   I chopped garlic clove,
   dash of hot pepper sauce and pinch of salt.
Stir with 1½ cups chicken broth,
   I cup light sour cream and
   I to 2 tbsp lime juice.
Refrigerate until cold but serve within 3 to 4
   hours. *Serves 6.*

CURRIED AVOCADO DIP

Sauté I chopped onion, sprinkled with
   2 tsp curry powder, in I tsp olive oil
   for about 5 min. Cool.
Stir with I tsp Dijon and
   ¼ cup mayonnaise.
Cut 2 peeled avocados into chunks and mash
   with mixture.
   Add 2 tsp lemon juice if needed.
Serve right away as a dip with tacos,
   as a spread or over barbecued chicken.
   Makes 1½ cups.

CLASSY CREAMY SPREAD

Mash I ripe avocado with
   I tsp lemon juice,
   2 tbsp sour cream and
   ¼ tsp hot pepper sauce.
Spread over corn bread, focaccia or a chicken
   sandwich. *Makes ½ cup.*

TEX-MEX GREEN CHILI SPREAD

In a food processor, whirl pulp of I avocado
   with 3 tbsp chopped canned green chilies
   or chopped seeded jalapeños,
   I tbsp chopped onion, 2 tbsp lime juice
   and dash of hot pepper sauce.
Spread generously over bagels or burgers and
   top with sliced tomatoes. *Makes ¾ cup.*

AVOCADO & BLACK OLIVE SALAD

Whisk ⅓ cup olive oil with I tbsp lemon
  juice and pinches of salt and pepper.
Add ¼ cup sliced black olives.
Peel and slice 2 avocados. Cover 4 salad
  plates with lettuce. Fan avocado slices on
  top. Drizzle with dressing. *Serves 4.*

AVOCADO SALSA HALVES

Slice 3 avocados in half, remove pits.
Stir 4 finely chopped seeded tomatoes
  with 3 sliced green onions,
  ¼ cup chopped fresh coriander,
  ½ tsp dried basil, pinch of dried rosemary
  and ¼ cup Italian dressing.
Spoon over 6 avocado halves.
Serve as appetizer or with sliced chicken.
  Serves 6.

CALIFORNIA TOMATO SANDWICH

Spread pumpernickel bread with
  mashed avocado or guacamole.
Add sliced tomatoes and a drizzling of
  Caesar dressing and shredded fresh basil.
Serve open-face.

ROMA TOMATO & AVOCADO BRUSCHETTA

Stir 4 to 6 finely chopped seeded Roma or
  plum tomatoes with I finely chopped
  avocado and 2 sliced green onions.
Whisk 2 tsp olive oil with 2 tsp lemon juice,
  I crushed garlic clove, ½ tsp salt and
  pinch of pepper.
Toss with tomato mixture and 2 tbsp
  chopped fresh basil and grated Parmesan.
Serve on toasted sliced baguette.
  Makes 2¾ cups.

ROMA TOMATO & AVOCADO BRUSCHETTA

B is for Broccoli...

What an impressive beginning for your next dinner party – a beautiful ruby red borscht. Our fast REAL COOL BORSCHT (see recipe page 30) remarkably doesn't need cooking, just chilling. Finish with a swirl of sour cream and a sprig of fresh dill.

B

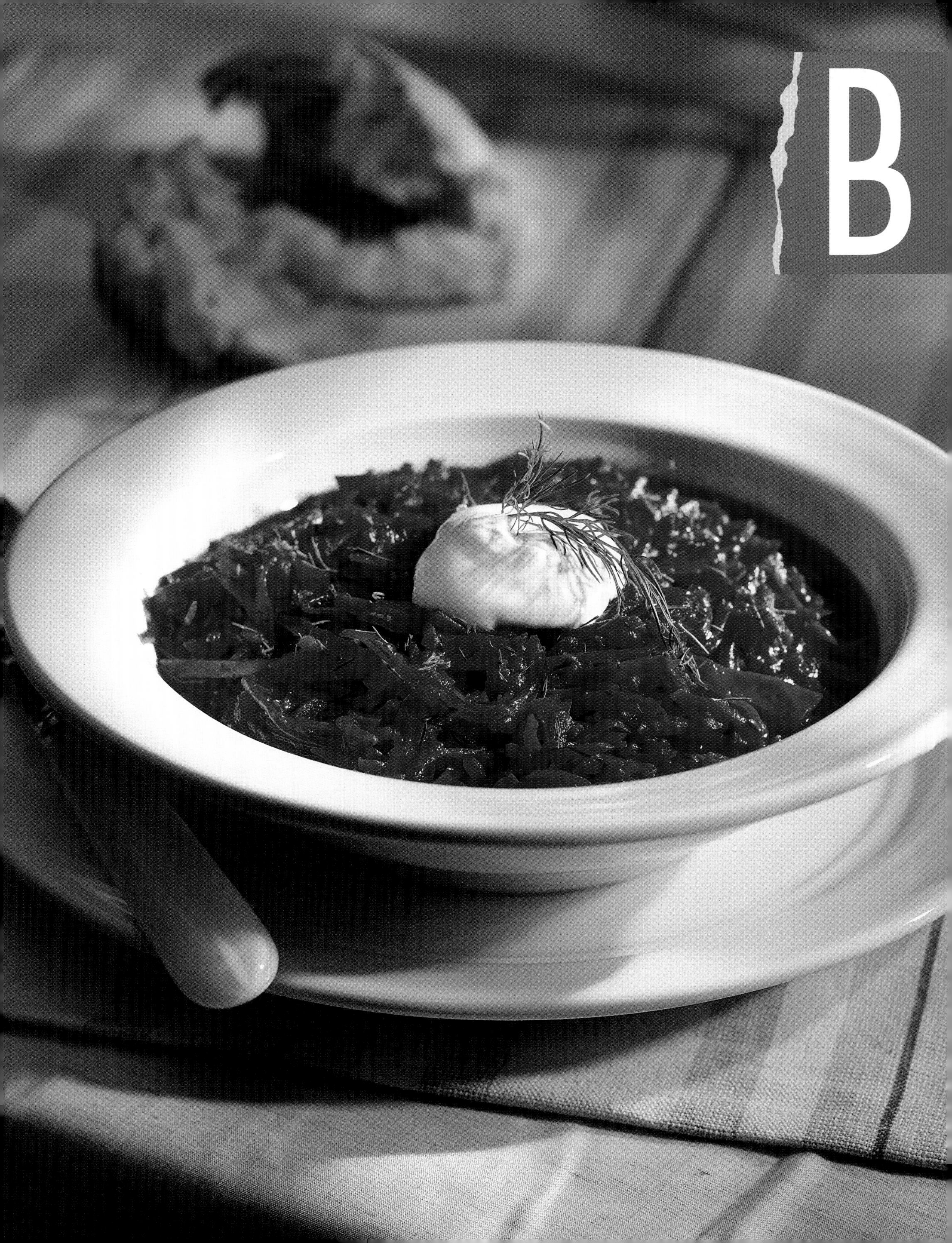

BANANAS

Bananas are a universally enjoyed fruit. An excellent source of potassium, mash, freeze or shake them up into muffins, smoothies or chocolate treats.

COFFEE-BANANA SHAKE

In a food processor, whirl 1 banana with 1 cup milk, 1 tsp instant coffee and 1 tsp brown sugar.

Great breakfast on hot summer mornings. *Makes 1½ cups.*

FROZEN BANANA-STRAWBERRY SMOOTHIE

In a food processor, whirl 2 frozen or chilled bananas with 2 cups strawberries, 2 cups yogurt or milk and pinch of nutmeg. *Makes 4 cups.*

ISLAND SHAKE-UP

In a blender, whirl ½ cup plain yogurt with ½ ripe banana and 2 tbsp sweetened flaked coconut. *Makes 1 cup.*

BANANA BREAKFAST MUFFINS

Beat 2 mashed bananas with ⅓ cup brown sugar, 1 cup buttermilk, ¼ cup vegetable oil, 1 egg and 1½ tsp vanilla.

In a separate bowl, stir 1 cup all-purpose flour with 1 cup whole wheat flour, ¾ cup natural bran, 1 tsp baking powder, ¼ tsp baking soda, ½ tsp salt and ½ cup coarsely chopped nuts.

Stir in banana mixture. Spoon into 12 greased muffin cups.

Bake at 425°F (220°C), about 14 min. *Makes 12.*

BANANA NUT BREAD

With a fork, stir 2 cups all-purpose flour with ½ cup granulated sugar, 3 tsp baking powder, ½ tsp baking soda and ½ tsp salt.

Stir in ½ cup finely chopped nuts.

Whisk 1 egg with ¾ cup milk and ¼ cup vegetable oil.

Stir in 1½ cups mashed bananas.

Pour into centre of dry ingredients and stir just until mixed. It will be lumpy. Turn into a greased 9x5-in. (23x13-cm) loaf pan.

Bake at 350°F (180°C), until a toothpick inserted in centre comes out clean, about 65 min. *Makes 12 slices.*

CHOCOLATE BANANA CAKE

Prepare 16-oz (500-g) pkg chocolate cake mix following directions, but use only 1 cup water.

Stir in ½ cup puréed banana.

Bake in 2 greased 9-in. (2.5-L) square baking pans for 30 min. *Makes 18 squares.*

HEALTHY FREEZER TREAT

Freeze an unpeeled banana. Remove from freezer and slice through peel lengthwise. Remove peel.

Slice frozen banana and toss with 1 tsp brown sugar and ¼ cup yogurt or sour cream. *Serves 1.*

Hot Saucy Bananas & Ice Cream

HOT SAUCY BANANAS & ICE CREAM

Slice **3** peeled bananas diagonally into
1-in. (2.5-cm) pieces. Arrange in an
8-in. (20-cm) greased baking pan.
Sprinkle with **2 tbsp** brown sugar,
$\frac{1}{4}$ tsp cinnamon and
generous pinch of allspice.
Bake, uncovered, at 350°F (180°C) until
bubbling, about 15 min.
Spoon over ice cream. *Serves 4.*

CHOCO-NUT BANANAS

Melt **4 oz** (112 g) semisweet chocolate in a
frying pan over low heat, stirring often.
Roll **4** bananas (one at a time) in chocolate,
covering completely. Place on a baking
sheet covered with waxed paper.
Sprinkle with $\frac{1}{4}$ cup finely chopped toasted
nuts. Insert a wooden stick about 2 in.
(5 cm) into each banana.
Freeze until firm, about 45 min. *Serves 4.*

NEW ORLEANS BANANAS & CREAM

In a food processor, purée **2** bananas
with **2 tbsp** orange juice concentrate
and **4 tbsp** rum.
Add **4 cups** softened vanilla ice cream
and whirl. Pour into dessert dishes.
Freeze, then cover with foil.
Before serving, heat $\frac{1}{4}$ cup brown sugar with
2 tbsp butter in a large frying pan.
Stir often.
Stir in **1 tbsp** orange juice concentrate and
2 sliced bananas.
When hot, stir in **2 tbsp** rum.
Spoon over frozen dessert. *Serves 6.*

BASIL

Basil is one of the world's oldest herbs, grown both for its medicinal and culinary properties. Its sweet smell and rich, aromatic taste add a unique freshness to dishes.

FRESH HERB BASTE FOR FISH

Stir 2 tbsp finely chopped fresh basil and
2 tbsp chopped fresh dill into
1/3 cup olive oil.
Brush on fish or vegetable kabobs and sliced
zucchini before and during grilling.
Makes ½ cup.

PEPPERONI 'N' BASIL APPETIZERS

In a food processor, whirl
½ cup sliced pepperoni with
½ cup lightly packed fresh basil and
½ (8-oz/250-g) pkg cream cheese.
Spread on mini bagels and top with fresh
basil leaves. Or spread over tortillas, roll up
and refrigerate until cold.
Slice into rounds as appetizers. *Makes 1 cup.*

LIVELY COLESLAW

Shred ½ cup fresh basil.
Stir into 4 cups of your favorite coleslaw
with sliced pickled peppers or finely
chopped hot peppers. *Serves 2.*

BASIL-DIJON SPREAD

Stir 2 tbsp chopped fresh basil with
3 tbsp Dijonnaise or 2 tbsp Dijon and
1 tbsp mayonnaise.
Spread generously on grilled sausages,
salmon steaks, hot dogs or burgers.
Makes ¼ cup.

BASIL-TOMATO SAUCE

Stir 4 finely chopped seeded tomatoes
with 3 sliced green onions,
3 tbsp chopped fresh basil,
2 crushed garlic cloves, 1 tsp sugar,
¼ tsp salt, ¼ tsp pepper and
3 tbsp olive oil.
Toss with 8 oz (250 g) cooked hot pasta or
generously spoon over fish steaks,
scrambled eggs or barbecued steaks.
Makes 2½ cups.

TOMATO-BASIL DIP

In a food processor, whirl
1 chopped garlic clove with
1 seeded hot pepper and ¼ cup fresh basil.
Add 19-oz can drained tomatoes and whirl
until chunky.
Great as a dip with shrimp or spooned over
grilled burgers or steaks. *Makes 2 cups.*

MUSTARD-BASIL HAM GLAZE

Whisk ½ cup Dijon with ¼ cup each
brown sugar, liquid honey, vegetable oil
and white vinegar in a saucepan.
Stir over medium heat, 5 min.
Remove from heat and stir in
2 tbsp chopped fresh basil.
Use as a glaze on ham or roast pork, basting
over meat for the last half hour of baking.
Makes 1 cup.

*BASIL-TOMATO
SAUCE ON PASTA*

FRESH BASIL DRESSING

Whisk ¼ cup olive oil with
   2 tbsp red wine vinegar, ¼ tsp salt
   and ¼ tsp pepper.
Stir in ¼ cup finely chopped fresh basil.
Drizzle over sliced tomatoes or toss with
   lettuce and tomatoes. Sprinkle with
   grated Parmesan. *Makes ½ cup.*

BASIL 'N' SUN-DRIED TOMATO DRESSING

Stir 4 tbsp chopped fresh basil and
   2 tbsp finely chopped oil-packed
   sun-dried tomatoes into
   1 cup light sour cream.
Drizzle over greens or use as a dip for
   vegetables.
Covered and refrigerated, dressing will keep
   up to 2 days. *Makes 1 cup.*

PESTO SAUCE

In a food processor, whirl 3 large garlic
   cloves, ¼ cup toasted pine nuts,
   ¼ tsp salt and ¼ tsp pepper.
Add 1½ cups fresh basil and purée.
With machine running, drizzle
   ¾ cup olive oil through feed tube.
Stir in 1 cup grated Parmesan.
Can be stored in a sealed jar in refrigerator
   for up to 1 week or freeze. *Makes 2 cups.*
(See page 142 for Ten Quick Ways With Pesto.)

BEANS ◆ Canned

Make way for beans. They're cheap, wholesome and health-smart.
When using canned beans, drain and rinse with cold water, unless otherwise noted.
See also CHICKPEAS.

NEW 3-BEAN SALAD

Trim ½ lb (250 g) each green and
yellow beans. If large, slice lengthwise.
Blanch in boiling water for 1 min.

Combine in a bowl with 19-oz can drained
black beans, 2 chopped seeded tomatoes,
½ cup canned or cooked kernel corn
and 3 sliced green onions.

Whisk grated peel of 1 lime with 2 tbsp lime
juice, 2 tbsp olive oil, 1 large crushed garlic
clove, ½ tsp salt and ¼ tsp cayenne.

Toss with salad. Sprinkle with chopped fresh
coriander. *Makes 12 cups.*

BLACK BEAN 'N' BASIL SALAD

Sauté 2 finely chopped red peppers,
1 small chopped onion and
2 tbsp chopped seeded jalapeño in
3 tbsp olive oil for 5 min.

Stir with 2 (14-oz) cans drained black beans,
¼ cup chopped fresh basil,
½ tsp dried thyme, ¼ tsp salt and
1 to 2 tbsp lime juice. *Makes 4 cups.*

PROTEIN PACKED SALAD

Mix 19-oz can drained kidney beans,
19-oz can drained Romano beans and
14-oz can drained pinto beans with
½ chopped small red onion, 1 chopped
red pepper, ¼ cup Italian dressing,
½ tsp cumin and ½ tsp ground coriander.
Makes 6 cups.

COMFORTING BEAN SOUP

In a saucepan, cook 1 chopped red pepper
and 1 chopped onion with 4 slices
chopped bacon over medium heat, stirring
often, 7 min.

Add 10-oz can chicken broth,
19-oz can undrained tomatoes,
19-oz can drained kidney or Romano beans
and 1 tsp dried thyme.

Simmer, stirring often, 10 min. *Makes 5 cups.*

8-MINUTE MICROWAVE BAKED BEANS

Place 2 slices chopped bacon and
1 chopped onion in a microwave-safe dish.

Microwave, covered, on high, 3 min.

Stir in ¼ cup ketchup, 2 tbsp brown sugar,
1 tbsp molasses, 1 tsp Dijon and
1 tsp Worcestershire.

Cover and microwave, on high, 3 min.,
until boiling.

Stir in 19-oz can drained white beans.

Microwave, on medium until hot and bubbly,
about 2 min. *Serves 2.*

PROVENÇAL BEAN SPREAD

Mash 14-oz can drained black beans until
chunky.

Stir in 1 chopped seeded tomato,
2 crushed garlic cloves, ¼ cup chopped
fresh coriander, ¼ tsp each salt,
dried oregano, dried basil and pepper.
Makes 2 cups.

HERBED BEAN SAUTÉ

Sauté 1 crushed garlic clove with
   1 chopped onion in 1 tsp butter, 5 min.
Add 19-oz can drained white
   or Romano beans.
Sprinkle with ½ tsp dried thyme and
   generous pinches of sage and cayenne
Stir gently over low heat just until warm.
Good with lamb or pork. *Serves 4.*

MEXICAN BEANS 'N' RICE

Chop 1 onion, 1 celery stalk and
   1 red pepper.
Sauté in 1 tsp olive oil with
   1 crushed garlic clove for 3 min.
Add 19-oz can undrained kidney beans,
   ¼ tsp dried oregano and
   ¼ tsp chili powder.
Stir gently until hot. Serve over rice. *Serves 4.*

GOOD 'N' EASY VEGETARIAN CHILI

In a large saucepan, stir 28-oz can
   undrained tomatoes with
   2 (19-oz) cans undrained kidney beans,
   1 crumbled vegetable bouillon cube,
   4 crushed garlic cloves,
   1 tbsp chili powder, 1 tsp cumin,
   ½ tsp dried oregano and
   pinches of sugar, salt and cayenne.
Simmer, stirring often, 15 to 20 min.
   Makes 7 cups.

NEW BEAN, TOMATO & OLIVE SALAD

Combine 19-oz can drained kidney beans
   with 2 coarsely chopped tomatoes,
   ⅓ cup thickly sliced stuffed green olives
   and 4 thinly sliced green onions.
Toss with ¼ cup Italian dressing.
Serve right away. *Makes 5 cups.*

NEW 3-BEAN SALAD

BEEF ◆ Burgers

Nothing defines relaxed eating better than burgers. So whenever you feel like a big juicy one, forget the fast-food joint and try these instead. All recipes make 4 burgers.

Ultimate BBQ Burger

Whisk I egg with 1/4 tsp salt and 1/4 tsp pepper.
Add I lb (500 g) ground beef.
Sprinkle with 1/4 cup dry bread crumbs.
Work together and shape into 4 patties.
Barbecue, broil or sauté until well done, 8 to 10 min. per side.

Canadian Cheddar Burger

Stir I cup finely grated cheddar and 1/4 cup chili sauce into Ultimate BBQ Burger mixture.

Italian Cheese Burger

Stir I cup grated Parmesan, 2 tsp Italian seasoning and 1/4 tsp hot red pepper flakes into Ultimate BBQ Burger mixture.

French Burger

Stir 1/3 cup sour cream, 1/4 cup snipped chives, 2 tbsp Dijon and 1/2 tsp dried tarragon into Ultimate BBQ Burger mixture.

Greek Feta Burger

Work I cup crumbled feta, 1 1/2 tsp dried oregano and 2 crushed garlic cloves into Ultimate BBQ Burger mixture.

Sassy Salsa Burger

Mix 1/4 cup hot salsa with I egg.
Add I lb (500 g) ground beef.
Shape into 4 patties and sauté or grill, 8 to 10 min. per side.

Double-Punch BBQ Burger

Whisk I egg with 1/4 cup barbecue sauce.
Add I lb (500 g) ground beef.
Sprinkle with 1/4 cup dry bread crumbs.
Shape into 4 patties. Barbecue, broil or sauté, 8 to 10 min. per side.

Whopping Cheese Burger

Whisk I egg with 2 tbsp ketchup, 1/4 tsp salt and 1/4 tsp pepper.
Add I lb (500 g) ground beef.
Sprinkle with 1/2 cup grated Asiago and 1/4 cup crushed seasoned croutons or dry bread crumbs.
Shape into 4 patties.
Barbecue 8 to 10 min. per side. Place slice of Asiago on each patty during last 2 min.

Chèvre Burger

Form about 4 tbsp creamy goat cheese into 4 balls. Shape about 1/4 lb (125 g) ground beef around each cheese round, making a large ball. Flatten into 4 thick patties.
Barbecue, broil or sauté, about 8 to 10 min. per side.

Oriental Sesame Burger

Whisk I egg with I tbsp soy sauce, 2 tsp regular mustard, I crushed garlic clove and pinches of salt, pepper and ginger.
Work in I lb (500 g) ground beef, 1/4 cup dry bread crumbs, 2 tbsp toasted sesame seeds and 2 sliced green onions.
Shape into 4 patties.
Barbecue, broil or sauté, 8 to 10 min. per side.

A
B
C
D
E
F
G
H
I
J
K
L
M
N
O
P
Q
R
S
T
U
V
W
X
Y
Z

Beef ◆ Burger Toppings

Top off a burger's seductive taste and soothing texture with a little sassy sauce or a spread with gusto. These toppings make enough for 4 to 6 burgers.

Onion & Garlic

Sauté 1 sliced onion with
   1 crushed garlic clove in
   1 tbsp butter over medium-high heat.
   Sprinkle with cayenne.
Stir often until soft, 5 min. Season with salt.
Spoon over beef and veal burgers.

Curried Dijon

Mix 2 tbsp Dijon and
   2 tbsp sour cream with
   1/4 tsp curry powder.
Spoon over beef, chicken and lamb burgers.

Perfect Pickle Relish

Finely chop 1 large dill pickle.
Stir with 2 tbsp mayonnaise,
   1 tbsp chopped green onion and
   1/4 tsp hot pepper sauce.
Spoon over fish, chicken and beef burgers.

Hot Tex-Mex

Stir 2 tbsp barbecue sauce with 2 tbsp salsa.
Spoon over beef and pork burgers.

Creamy Horseradish

Mix 2 tbsp horseradish with
   1/4 cup sour cream, 1 chopped green onion
   and pinch of pepper.
Spoon over beef or veal burgers.

Kid-Pleasing Bacon 'n' Cheese

Blend 1/4 cup cheese spread with
   1 tbsp bacon bits and 1 tbsp ketchup.
Spread on beef burgers.

Pesto Goat Cheese

Stir 1/4 cup creamy goat cheese with
   1 tbsp pesto sauce (see recipe page 23).
Spoon over beef, lamb or veal burgers.

Italian Express

Mix 1/4 cup pizza or spaghetti sauce with
   1 tbsp grated Parmesan,
   1/4 tsp each hot red pepper flakes,
   dried basil and dried oregano.
Spoon over beef burgers.

Honeyed Sauce

Blend 2 tbsp Dijon with
   2 tbsp sour cream and 1 tbsp liquid honey.
Spoon over beef, pork and veal burgers.

Spanish Sauce

Stir 1/2 cup chili or salsa sauce with
   1/2 cup sliced stuffed olives,
   1/4 cup finely chopped Spanish onion and
   1 crushed garlic clove.
Spoon over fish, chicken and beef burgers.

BEEF ◆ Ground

Take a pound or two of ground, add a dash of this and that and you've got good tempting chilies, casseroles and sauces. See also MEAT, Ground.

CURRIED BEEF 'N' BEANS

In a frying pan, combine
    1 lb (500 g) ground beef with 1 chopped
    red pepper, 1 chopped onion, 1 crushed
    garlic clove and $\frac{1}{2}$ tsp coriander, $\frac{1}{2}$ tsp
    cumin and $\frac{1}{2}$ tsp curry powder.
Cook, stirring often, 10 min.
Stir in 19-oz can drained Romano beans.
Serve over rice or in tortillas. *Serves 4.*

LAZY DAYS TOMATO & MACARONI DINNER

Cook 1 chopped onion in 1 tsp vegetable oil,
    5 min. Add 1 lb (500 g) ground beef.
Cook, stirring often, until meat is browned.
    Drain off fat.
Stir in 19-oz can undrained tomatoes,
    2 cups cooked macaroni, $\frac{1}{2}$ tsp paprika
    and $\frac{1}{4}$ tsp each dried oregano, chili
    powder, garlic powder, salt and pepper.
Bring to a boil. Cover and simmer, stirring
    often, 10 min.
Uncover and boil if not thick enough. *Serves 4.*

THICK 'N' TEMPTING CHILI

In a large saucepan, cook
    2 lbs (1 kg) ground beef with
    2 chopped onions and 3 crushed garlic
    cloves, 5 min. Drain off fat.
Stir in 19-oz can drained chopped tomatoes,
    19-oz can rinsed drained kidney beans,
    $7\frac{1}{2}$-oz can tomato sauce,
    1 chopped green pepper, 1 tbsp chili
    powder, 1 tsp cumin, $\frac{1}{2}$ tsp salt and
    dash of hot pepper sauce.
Bring to a boil, then simmer, uncovered and
    stirring often, 20 min. *Serves 6.*

MOIST MEATBALLS

Whisk 1 egg with $\frac{1}{4}$ cup barbecue sauce,
    1 tbsp mustard, $\frac{1}{2}$ tsp Worcestershire
    and pinches of salt and pepper.
Add 1 lb (500 g) ground beef, $\frac{1}{2}$ cup dry
    bread crumbs and 3 sliced green onions.
Mix, then form into $1\frac{1}{2}$-in.(4-cm) meatballs.
Sauté in a lightly oiled pan over medium
    heat, stirring often, until cooked through,
    about 8 to 12 min. *Serves 4.*

MICROWAVE BEEF STROGANOFF

In a pie plate, microwave 1 lb (500 g) ground
    beef and 1 chopped onion, uncovered,
    on high, 6 min. Stir partway through.
Remove mixture. Place 1 tbsp butter and
    2 cups sliced mushrooms in pie plate.
Microwave, uncovered, on high, 3 min.
Stir in 1 tbsp tomato sauce, 1 tsp paprika,
    1 tsp Dijon, $\frac{1}{4}$ tsp Worcestershire and
    pinches of salt and pepper.
When blended, stir in beef mixture.
Microwave, uncovered, on medium, 3 min.
Stir in $\frac{1}{4}$ cup sour cream and
    $\frac{1}{4}$ cup chopped parsley.
Serve on rice or noodles. *Serves 4.*

SPANISH DINNER

In a large saucepan, brown 1 lb (500 g)
    ground beef in 1 tbsp olive oil.
Add 2 cups kernel corn,
    28-oz can undrained tomatoes,
    $\frac{1}{4}$ cup sliced stuffed olives,
    1 cup instant rice and $\frac{3}{4}$ tsp dried thyme.
Cover tightly. Simmer, stirring often, 10 min.
    Serves 4.

New-Fashioned Spaghetti 'n' Meatballs

GREEN PEAS & BEEF À L'INDIENNE

In a frying pan, sauté 1 chopped onion,
  2 crushed garlic cloves,
  1 lb (500 g) ground beef, 1 tsp turmeric
  and ½ tsp each ground coriander,
  crushed red pepper and salt, stirring
  often, until brown, 10 min.
Stir in 19-oz can drained tomatoes and
  12-oz (350-g) pkg frozen peas.
Cook, uncovered, stirring often, 10 min.
  Serves 4.

MEAT LOAF FOR ONE

Whisk 1 egg.
Add ¼ lb (125 g) ground beef,
  2 tbsp dry bread crumbs,
  1 to 2 tbsp ketchup,
  ¼ tsp Worcestershire and
  pinches of salt and pepper.
Shape into an oval loaf, 5 in. (12.5 cm) long.
Place on a piece of foil in a shallow dish.
Bake at 350°F (180°C) for 45 min. *Serves 1.*

ZIPPY MEXICAN TACO CASSEROLE

Sauté 1 lb (500 g) ground beef in 1 tsp oil.
Add 14-oz can tomato sauce, 1 tsp cumin
  and ½ tsp chili powder. Simmer for 10 min.
Cover bottom of an 8-in. (2-L) casserole dish
  with ½ (5-oz/150-g) bag taco chips.
  Sprinkle with ½ cup grated mozzarella.
Cover with meat mixture. Scatter remaining
  chips over top. Sprinkle with ½ cup cheese.
Bake at 375°F (190°C) until cheese melts,
  about 5 min. Sprinkle with chopped
  tomatoes and avocados. *Serves 4.*

NEW-FASHIONED SPAGHETTI 'N' MEATBALLS

In a saucepan, bring 3 cups spaghetti sauce
  to a boil.
Form 1 lb (500 g) ground beef into small
  ¾-in. (2-cm) balls. Add to sauce.
  Cover and simmer, 10 min.
Add 2 chopped seeded peppers.
  Cover and simmer, 5 min.
Toss with ½ lb (250 g) cooked spaghetti.
  Sprinkle with Parmesan. *Serves 3.*

BEETS

The natural sweetness of beets, coupled with their unique, intense color, puts them in a root-vegetable class by themselves. And don't forget the greens, they're an excellent source of beta-carotene and vitamin C and they're delicious too.

PERFECTLY COOKED BEETS

Cut off greens, leaving 1 in. (2.5 cm) at stem end.

Place beets in a large pot of water. Boil gently, uncovered, until tender, 30 to 45 min.

Drain, rinse with cold water and peel.

Slice and toss with butter and grated orange peel.

INSTANT BORSCHT

Drain liquid from 2 (10-oz) cans beets into a saucepan.

Add 1½ cups vegetable cocktail juice and heat.

Shred beets and stir in. Cover and simmer, stirring often, about 5 min.

Sprinkle with chopped fresh dill. *Makes 3 cups.*

REAL COOL BORSCHT

In a food processor, whirl 10-oz can consommé with 1 cup sour cream, ¼ cup chopped fresh dill or 1 tsp dried dillweed, ¼ cup coarsely chopped onion, 1 tbsp lemon juice, 2 crushed garlic cloves and pinches of sugar and pepper.

Remove to bowl and add 12 grated medium-size cooked or canned beets.

Cover and refrigerate until cold.

Serve cold with a dollop of sour cream and a sprig of fresh dill. *Serves 6.*

EASY BEET SALAD

Whisk ½ cup sour cream or yogurt with 1 tsp sugar, ½ tsp horseradish and pinches of salt and pepper.

Drizzle over 19-oz can sliced beets or 2 cups cooked cold sliced beets on a bed of greens. Sprinkle with chopped chives. Great with fish. *Serves 4.*

BEET & APPLE SALAD

Whisk ¼ cup olive oil with 2 tbsp lemon juice, 2 tbsp chopped fresh dill, 1 tsp Dijon, ¼ tsp salt and ¼ tsp pepper.

Tear 1 small head romaine lettuce into bite-size pieces.

Dice 1 green-skinned apple and ½ lb (250 g) cooked beets.

Toss lettuce with half the dressing.

Toss apple with 1 tbsp dressing and scatter over lettuce.

Toss beets with remaining dressing and spoon in centre of salad. *Serves 4.*

CINNAMON-SCENTED BEETS

In a large frying pan, heat 2 cups julienned sliced cooked beets with juice from 2 oranges, grated peel of 1 orange, ¼ tsp cinnamon and 2 tsp butter.

Stir often until most of liquid is absorbed, about 5 min. *Serves 4.*

Harvard Beets

DILLED BEETS 'N' CREAM

In a frying pan, heat
   2 cups diced cooked beets with
   $\frac{1}{2}$ cup sour cream or table cream,
   2 to 3 tbsp chopped fresh dill or
   $\frac{1}{2}$ tsp dried dillweed, $\frac{1}{2}$ tsp horseradish
   and pinches of salt and pepper.
Stir often, until hot, about 3 min. *Serves 4.*

SAUTÉED GREENS

Wash beet greens well. Slice into
   $\frac{1}{2}$-in. (1-cm) strips.
Sauté, stirring often, in a large frying pan
   with no water added, until wilted.
Season with a sprinkle of sugar,
   drizzle of red wine vinegar and
   pinches of salt and pepper.

CREAMY DIJON BEETS

Sauté 2 cups sliced cooked beets in
   2 tsp melted butter until hot.
Stir $\frac{1}{2}$ cup sour cream with 1 tsp Dijon.
Stir into beets and heat through. *Serves 3.*

HARVARD BEETS

In a saucepan, stir $\frac{1}{4}$ cup brown sugar with
   1 tbsp cornstarch, $\frac{1}{4}$ tsp dry mustard,
   $\frac{1}{4}$ tsp salt and generous pinches of
   ginger and pepper.
Stir in 2 tbsp lemon juice or vinegar and
   $1\frac{1}{2}$ cups diced cooked or canned beets.
Stir over medium heat until thick, about
   3 min. Continue stirring often,
   5 more min. *Serves 4.*

BREAD

No need to labor and knead to fill your kitchen with the seductive aroma of baking bread.
Just follow our lead and add herbs, garlic and cheese to store-bought bread.

FAST GARLIC BREAD

Slice 1 small baguette in half lengthwise.
Stir ¼ cup room-temperature butter
  with ½ tsp garlic powder or
  1 tsp crushed garlic and
  pinch of pepper.
Spread over bread.
Broil until toasted, about 2 to 3 min.

FRESH TOMATO BRUSCHETTA

Slice crusty Italian bread into 8 rounds,
  about 1 in. (2.5 cm) thick.
Brush with olive oil.
Bake at 375°F (190°C) until golden,
  about 10 min.
Stir 3 chopped seeded tomatoes with
  1 crushed garlic clove and
  pinches of salt and pepper.
Spoon on toasted bread.
Sprinkle with grated Parmesan.
Bake until heated through, about 7 min.
  Makes 8 appetizers.

HOT PARMESAN BREAD

Slice 1 small baguette in half lengthwise.
Brush with olive oil. Sprinkle with
  ¼ cup grated Parmesan,
  ½ tsp dried basil and pinch of pepper.
Broil until golden, about 2 to 3 min.

BROILED BASIL BAGUETTE

Slice 1 small baguette in half lengthwise.
Spread both sides with butter.
Generously sprinkle with
  dried basil and pepper.
Broil until toasted, about 2 to 3 min.

HERBED HARVEST CROUTONS

Slice ½ loaf crusty bread into
  1-in. (2.5-cm) cubes.
Stir 2 tbsp olive oil with
  1 large crushed garlic clove.
Toss with cubes.
Stir ½ tsp dried basil with
  ½ tsp dried oregano,
  ¼ tsp salt and
  pinch of cayenne.
Sprinkle over cubes and toss.
  Spread on a baking sheet.
Bake at 375°F (190°C), stirring often until
  toasted, 20 min.
Toss with ¼ cup grated Parmesan. Sprinkle
  over salad. *Makes about 60 croutons.*

FRESH HERBED CRUSTY BREAD

Stir 3 tbsp room-temperature butter
  with 1 tbsp chopped chives,
  1 tbsp chopped parsley and
  pinches of salt and pepper.
Spread over 4 slices crusty baguette.
Broil until toasted, 2 to 3 min.

PESTO CROÛTES

Slice 10-in. (25-cm) baguette, lengthwise, into 3 long slices.

Broil cut-sides down until toasted.

Turn and spread each with ½ tbsp pesto. Sprinkle with grated Parmesan.

Broil until bubbling, 1½ to 3 min.

WHOLESOME FRUIT & NUT STUFFING

Remove crusts from 24-oz (750-g) loaf bread. Cut into ¼-in. (0.5-cm) cubes. Toast.

Stir 1½ tsp ground sage with 1½ tsp ground dried thyme, 1 tsp salt, ½ tsp marjoram and pinch of pepper. Toss with bread.

Sauté 2 chopped onions in ½ cup butter until soft.

Toss with cubes and 1 chopped peeled apple, 2 stalks chopped celery, ½ cup raisins and ⅓ cup chopped walnuts. *Makes 14 cups.*

MAPLE FRENCH-TOAST BAKE

Pack **6** thick crusty bread slices in a buttered 9x13-in. (3-L) baking dish.

Whisk **6** eggs with 2½ cups milk, ½ cup maple syrup, ½ tsp cinnamon and ¼ tsp salt. Pour over bread.

Bake, uncovered, at 400°F (200°C) until golden, about 20 to 30 min. *Serves 6.*

LITTLE TYKE'S MICROWAVE BREAD PUDDING

Sprinkle 1 slice toast with pinch of cinnamon. Cut into bite-size pieces.

In a round-bottomed microwave-safe bowl, beat 1 egg with ¾ cup milk, 1 tbsp sugar and ½ tsp vanilla. Stir in toast.

Microwave, covered, on medium until set, about 4½ min.

Let stand until lukewarm, at least 5 min.

MAPLE FRENCH-TOAST BAKE

Broccoli

*Broccoli is a dietary superstar. This flowering green is a great source of fibre,
low in fat and considered a cancer fighter. All recipes serve 4.*

Oriental Broccoli

In a large frying pan, sauté 2 tsp minced
garlic in 1 tsp sesame or vegetable oil, 2 min.
Add 2 tbsp water and 6 cups broccoli florets.
Stir often over medium-high heat, 3 min.
Add drained 10-oz can sliced water chestnuts.
Sprinkle with 2 tbsp teriyaki sauce and
stir until hot. *Serves 4.*

Light & Creamy Soup

Purée 3 to 4 cups well-cooked broccoli
pieces with 10-oz can condensed
chicken broth.
Heat and stir in ¼ to ½ cup light sour cream.
Serve hot or cold. *Makes 3 cups.*

Broccoli Roquefort Salad

Combine 2 cups small broccoli florets
with 3 coarsely chopped tomatoes and
¼ cup Roquefort or Peppercorn Ranch
dressing. Serve over shredded lettuce.

Chèvre Broccoli

Break 1 head broccoli into florets.
Cook in 1 in. (2.5 cm) boiling water until
tender-crisp, 2 min. Drain.
Dab with 2 tbsp creamy goat cheese and
generous pinch of pepper.
Stir over low heat until melted.

Citrus Butter Broccoli

Break 1 large head broccoli into florets.
Cook in 1 in. (2.5 cm) boiling water, 2 min.
Sprinkle with grated peel of 1 orange.
Cover and cook, 2 min. Drain and toss with
butter and pinches of salt and pepper.

Buttery Balsamic Broccoli

Break 1 head broccoli into florets.
Cook in 1 in. (2.5 cm) boiling water until
tender-crisp, 2 min.
Meanwhile, melt 1 tbsp butter and
whisk with 1 tbsp balsamic vinegar and
pinches of sugar and salt.
Toss with hot drained broccoli.

Cheese Gratin

Place 4 cups raw broccoli florets in an
8-in. (2-L) square baking dish.
Sprinkle with 2 tbsp water, then 2 tbsp dry
bread crumbs and ¾ cup grated cheddar.
Bake, covered, at 400°F (200°C), 10 min.
Uncover and bake until cheese is melted,
5 to 10 more min.

Shallots & Mushrooms

Sauté ¼ cup finely chopped shallots and
1 cup sliced mushrooms in 1 tbsp butter.
Toss with 4 cups cooked broccoli.
Serve as a side dish or toss with ½ lb (225 g)
cooked pasta and 2 tbsp olive oil.

Stir-Fried Zesty Broccoli

Heat juice from 1 orange, ½ tsp dillweed and
1 tbsp butter in a frying pan.
Add 1 large head broccoli, broken into
florets. Stir-fry until tender-crisp.

Broccoli Parmesan & Eggs

Scramble 4 eggs in a little butter.
Stir in ½ cup cooked broccoli florets and
2 to 4 tbsp grated Parmesan or Asiago.

BUTTERMILK

Buttermilk is wonderfully thick and rich-tasting, yet contains less fat and calories than 2% milk. Enjoy it in potatoes, soups and dressings.

COOL HONEYDEW SOUP

In a food processor, whirl 1 peeled seeded honeydew in 2 batches. Pour into a bowl.
Stir in ½ to ¾ cup buttermilk and juice from ½ lime.
Refrigerate until cold. *Makes about 4 cups.*

FRESH PEACH SOUP

Cover 6 very ripe peaches with boiling water for 30 sec. Drain, peel and remove pits. Coarsely chop.
Whirl in a food processor until smooth.
Stir in 1 cup buttermilk, ½ cup orange juice and pinches of ginger and cinnamon.
Refrigerate until cold. *Makes 3 cups.*

COOL CUCUMBER SOUP

In a food processor, purée 1 chopped unpeeled English cucumber until coarsely ground. Drain pulp and discard juice.
Stir pulp with 4 cups buttermilk, ½ cup sour cream, 1 tsp lemon juice, ½ tsp salt and pinch of white pepper. *Makes 6 cups.*

LIGHT BUTTERMILK MASHED POTATOES

Cook 4 large potatoes in salted water until tender. Drain and peel. Mash with potato masher. (Do not use food processor.)
Beat in ½ cup buttermilk and ¼ tsp salt and ¼ tsp white pepper.
Sprinkle with chopped chives. *Serves 4.*

SUMMER STRAWBERRY SHAKE

In a blender, whirl 1 cup buttermilk with 1 cup strawberries and liquid honey to taste. *Serves 2.*

LOW-CAL FALL FRUIT NOG

In a blender, whirl 1 peeled cored pear with ½ to ¾ cup buttermilk and dash of fresh lemon juice.
Sprinkle with grated nutmeg. *Serves 1.*

BANANA BUTTERMILK BLAST

In a blender, whirl 1 banana with ½ to ¾ cup buttermilk and dash of vanilla.
Sprinkle with grated nutmeg. *Serves 1.*

CREAMY SPINACH TOSS

Whisk ¼ cup buttermilk with ¼ cup light sour cream.
Stir in 2 tbsp chopped fresh dill and pinches of salt and pepper.
Tear 1 bunch spinach into large pieces. Combine with 2 chopped tomatoes and ¼ red onion, thinly sliced.
Drizzle with dressing. *Serves 4.*

BASIL BUTTERMILK DRESSING

Whisk ½ cup buttermilk with ½ cup sour cream.
Add 3 tbsp chopped fresh basil and pinches of salt, pepper and cayenne. *Makes 1 cup.*

LEMON BUTTERMILK PIE

Whisk 4 eggs with ¾ cup granulated sugar and 2 tbsp all-purpose flour.
Beat in 1½ cups buttermilk, ¼ cup melted butter, 3 tbsp lemon juice and 1 tsp vanilla.
Pour into a 9-in. (23-cm) unbaked deep piecrust. Sprinkle with cinnamon.
Bake on bottom rack at 375°F (190°C) until set, 30 to 35 min. *Serves 10.*

C is for Corn...

CHICKEN WITH DRIED FRUIT *(see recipe page 46) is a glistening entrée of dried apricots and apples simmered to perfection in fresh orange juice and zest – and it's ready in about 20 minutes.*

CABBAGE

*Cabbage, one of our oldest cultivated vegetables, is just beginning to get respect.
It's far from boring, though. Add it to sautés, stir-fries and salads and enjoy its subtle flavor.*

COLORFUL CABBAGE SALAD

Toss 2 cups shredded cabbage with
    1 cup grated carrots and
    ¼ cup creamy cucumber dressing.
Sprinkle with 2 slices crumbled cooked bacon.
    Serves 2 to 3.

CHILI COLESLAW

In a food processor, shred 1 head cabbage,
    4 carrots and 4 green onions.
In a large bowl, stir 1 cup creamy cucumber
    dressing with 1 tbsp sugar,
    1½ tsp chili powder and 1 tsp celery seed.
Stir with vegetables. *Makes 7 cups.*

JAZZY YOGURT COLESLAW

Stir ½ cup plain yogurt with
    1 tbsp white vinegar, ½ tsp celery seed,
    ½ tsp mustard and pinch of sugar.
Toss with 4 to 6 cups shredded cabbage.
    Serves 4.

RED CABBAGE & APPLES

In a wide frying pan, sauté 1 chopped onion
    in 1 tbsp butter.
Add ½ head shredded red cabbage,
    3 diced peeled apples, 1 tsp red wine vinegar
    and pinches of salt, pepper and allspice.
Cover and simmer, 10 min. *Serves 4.*

CABBAGE SAUTÉ

Sauté 2 tbsp chopped walnuts in 1 tbsp
    butter for 1 min. Remove to a dish.
Add 4 cups shredded cabbage to pan. Sauté
    until just tender. Toss with nuts. Sprinkle
    with salt and cayenne pepper. *Serves 2 to 3.*

ALLSPICE CABBAGE

Cook ½ head shredded cabbage and
    ½ sliced onion in 1 cup water over
    medium heat, 10 to 15 min. Stir often.
Stir 2 tbsp vinegar with 2 tbsp sugar,
    ½ tsp dried thyme and ¼ tsp allspice.
Stir into cooked drained vegetables. *Serves 4.*

BALSAMIC CABBAGE

Sauté 4 cups shredded cabbage in
    2 tsp olive oil until tender-crisp.
Stir in 1 to 2 tbsp balsamic vinegar and
    1 to 2 tbsp sugar. *Serves 2 to 3.*

LOW-FAT APPLE COLESLAW

Whisk ¼ cup cider vinegar with
    2 tbsp sugar, 1 tbsp vegetable oil,
    ¼ tsp salt and ¼ tsp pepper.
Stir in 4 cups shredded cabbage, 2 diced
    unpeeled apples and 2 sliced green onions.
    Makes 6 cups.

DANISH DILLED CABBAGE

Sauté ½ head shredded cabbage in
    2 tbsp butter until tender-crisp.
Stir in ½ cup sour cream, 1 tbsp chopped
    fresh dill or ½ tsp dried dillweed and
    salt and pepper to taste. *Serves 4.*

ORIENTAL CABBAGE

Stir-fry ½ head shredded cabbage in
    1 tbsp oil, 5 min.
Stir 3 tbsp soy sauce with 2 tbsp sherry,
    1 tbsp sugar and pinches of garlic powder
    and ginger. Add to cabbage.
Stir-fry until tender-crisp. *Serves 4.*

CARROTS

The carrot has come a long way from its origins as a bitter weed growing in Afghanistan. Today, it is recognized as a powerhouse veggie, rich in vitamins and that all-important beta-carotene.

SMOOTH CARROT SOUP

Simmer 2 cups sliced carrots in
   2 cups chicken bouillon, I cup milk and
   ¼ tsp ginger until very tender.
Purée in a food processor until smooth.
   Serves 4.

CHILLED CARROT-ORANGE SOUP

Sauté I finely chopped onion in
   I tbsp butter until soft, 3 min.
Add 5 thinly sliced carrots,
   2 cups chicken broth, ½ cup orange juice
   and pinches of salt and pepper.
Cook, covered, until very tender.
Purée in a food processor. Chill. Serve
   sprinkled with chopped fresh dill. *Serves 4.*

ROSEMARY CARROTS

Heat I tsp butter with I tsp olive oil and
   I tsp crumbled dried rosemary.
Add 2 cups julienned carrots.
Sauté, stirring often, until tender-crisp,
   5 min. *Serves 4.*

ORANGE SAUTÉ

Cook 2 cups grated carrots in
   ½ cup orange juice, I tbsp butter,
   I tbsp brown sugar and ¼ cup golden
   raisins, uncovered, until most of liquid
   evaporates. Stir often. *Serves 2.*

ONION TOSS

Cook 3 cups sliced carrots until
   tender-crisp, 5 min.
Drain and toss with I tbsp butter, 2 sliced
   green onions and ¼ tsp mace. *Serves 6.*

LEMON CARROTS

Cook 2 cups julienned carrots until
   tender-crisp, 5 min.
Drain and toss with 2 tsp butter, I tsp lemon
   juice and I tsp grated peel. *Serves 4.*

ITALIAN-HERB CARROTS

Cook 2 cups sliced carrots until tender-crisp.
Drain and toss with I tsp olive oil,
   ½ tsp dried basil and ¼ tsp dried oregano.
   Serves 3.

GRILLED CARROTS & HOT PEPPERS

Place 8 baby carrots on 2 pieces of foil.
Add ¼ chopped seeded hot pepper and
   I tsp butter to each packet.
Sprinkle with sugar, salt and pepper.
Seal packets tightly.
Grill 20 to 25 min., turning every 10 min.
   Serves 2.

TANGY CUMIN CARROTS

Heat 2 cups thinly sliced carrots with
   ½ cup orange juice, 2 tsp butter and
   ½ tsp cumin or pinch of dried dillweed.
Cover and simmer, stirring often, until
   carrots are tender-crisp, 8 to 10 min.
   Serves 4.

ROASTED GINGER CARROTS

Combine I lb (500 g) baby carrots,
   about 2 cups, ½ cup orange juice,
   2 tbsp grated fresh ginger and
   pinch of salt in a pie plate.
Roast, uncovered, at 375°F (190°C), 30 min.
   Stir often. *Serves 4.*

CAULIFLOWER

Even after cooking, a cup of cauliflower supplies more than our daily vitamin C requirement. High in fibre, yet low in calories, it's a must for your crudité tray and great in soups and salads.

SOOTHING CAULIFLOWER SOUP

Place 2 cups milk, 1 tbsp butter and
   2 chicken bouillon cubes in a saucepan.
   Add pinches of nutmeg and white pepper.
   Heat, stirring until bouillon dissolves.
Add 1 head cauliflower, broken into florets.
Cover, reduce heat, and cook until
   cauliflower is tender, about 10 min.
In a food processor, purée cauliflower with a
   little of milk mixture. Return to pan.
Add 3 sliced green onions and 2 cups grated
   Swiss cheese. Stir until cheese melts,
   about 2 min. *Serves 4.*

PICTURE-PERFECT SALAD

Whisk ¼ cup olive oil with 1 crushed garlic
   clove, 1 tbsp vinegar, 1 tbsp lemon juice,
   1 tsp sugar, ¼ tsp dried tarragon,
   ¼ tsp salt and ¼ tsp pepper.
Toss with 10-oz (300-g) pkg frozen or 4 cups
   cooked cooled cauliflower, 1 chopped red
   pepper, 1 chopped green onion and
   ¼ cup sliced black olives. *Serves 4.*

YOGURT-DRESSED CAULIFLOWER

Cook 1 head cauliflower, broken into florets,
   in 1 in. (2.5 cm) hot water, 5 min.
Meanwhile, warm ½ cup yogurt with
   ½ tsp paprika and ¼ tsp dried dillweed
   over low heat, about 2 min. Stir often.
Drain cauliflower and place in a serving dish.
   Pour sauce over top. *Serves 6.*

COLORFUL CURRIED CAULIFLOWER

In a large saucepan, melt 2 tsp butter.
Add 1 finely chopped onion, 2 finely chopped
   seeded jalapeños and 2 crushed garlic
   cloves. Sprinkle with 2 tsp curry powder
   and ¼ tsp cumin. Sauté 5 min.
Add 1 medium head cauliflower, broken into
   florets, and 4 coarsely chopped tomatoes.
Cook on medium-high, stirring often, 10 to
   15 min. Stir in ½ cup light sour cream.
Serve over rice. *Serves 4.*

CURRIED CAULIFLOWER & POTATOES

Sauté 1 chopped onion and 2 crushed garlic
   cloves in 1 tbsp butter, 5 min.
Sprinkle with 2 tbsp flour. Stir until absorbed.
Stir in 2 cups apple juice and stir over
   medium heat until thickened, about 2 min.
Add 1 head cauliflower, broken into florets,
   and 3 finely chopped peeled potatoes.
   Cover and simmer, stirring often, 15 min.
Stir in 2 chopped tomatoes, 1 cup frozen
   peas, 2 tbsp lemon juice and ½ tsp salt.
   Stir often until hot, 5 min. *Makes 7 cups.*

MIXED-VEGETABLE MEDLEY

In a frying pan, stir 2 cups small cauliflower
   florets and 2 cups frozen peas in
   2 tbsp butter, until cauliflower is
   tender-crisp, 5 min.
Add 1 julienned red pepper and sauté until
   hot. *Serves 6.*

MICROWAVE PARMESAN CAULIFLOWER

Slice thick end from 1 cauliflower.
Hollow out core.
Place whole cauliflower in a glass pie plate.
Spread outside of cauliflower with
1 to 2 tbsp butter. Cover with plastic wrap.
Microwave, on high, 4 to 6 min.
Sprinkle with ¼ cup grated Parmesan,
¼ cup chopped parsley and pinch of salt.
Let stand, covered, 3 min. *Serves 6.*

ZESTY CITRUS CAULIFLOWER

In a frying pan, heat
juice from 1 orange,
1 tbsp butter and
½ tsp cumin or curry powder.
Add 3 cups small cauliflower florets.
Stir until tender-crisp, 5 min. *Serves 6.*

MARINATED CAULIFLOWER & BROCCOLI

Whisk ⅔ cup vegetable oil with
⅓ cup white vinegar, 1 cup water,
½ tsp sugar, 1 tsp celery seed,
1 tsp chervil, ¼ tsp dry mustard and
pinch of pepper.
Add 1 head cauliflower and
1 bunch broccoli, both cooked and
broken into florets.
Refrigerate until chilled. *Serves 4.*

CHEESY CAULIFLOWER

Cut up 1 head cauliflower.
Sauté in 2 tbsp butter until
tender-crisp, 5 min.
Sprinkle with 2 sliced green onions and
¼ cup grated Parmesan. *Serves 6.*

COLORFUL CURRIED CAULIFLOWER

CHEESE

From cheddar to mozzarella, everybody loves cheese. Spike it with sherry for a high-protein dip or add tomato for a grown-up grilled sandwich.

CHEDDAR POPOVERS

Stir 1 cup all-purpose flour with $\frac{1}{4}$ tsp salt
   and $\frac{1}{8}$ tsp cayenne.
Beat 2 eggs with 1 cup milk and
   1 tbsp melted butter.
Add to dry ingredients. Beat until smooth.
Spoon 1 tbsp batter into 10 greased
   muffin cups.
Sprinkle each with 1 tbsp grated cheddar.
   Alternate batter and cheese in layers.
Bake at 450°F (230°C), 10 min. Reduce heat
   to 350°F (180°C) and bake, 15 to 20 min.
   Makes 10.

HERBED ANTIPASTO CHEESE

Stir 3 tbsp olive oil with 2 tbsp chopped
   parsley, 1 crushed garlic clove
   and pinch of pepper.
Stir in 2 cups cubed mozzarella.
Refrigerate, covered, up to 2 days.
   Use on an antipasto tray or toss in a salad.

NIPPY MICROWAVE CHEESE SAUCE

In a microwave-safe bowl, heat 2 tbsp butter,
   uncovered, on high until melted, 40 sec.
Whisk in 2 tbsp all-purpose flour until
   smooth, then $1\frac{1}{2}$ cups milk, $\frac{1}{2}$ tsp dry
   mustard and pinches of salt and pepper.
Microwave, uncovered, on high, $3\frac{1}{2}$ to 4 min.
   until creamy, stirring 3 times.
Stir in 1 cup grated old cheddar until melted.
Serve warm over broccoli. *Makes 2 cups.*

CREAMY MICROWAVE WINE SAUCE

Microwave 2 tbsp butter, uncovered, on
   high, 40 sec., until melted.
Whisk in 2 tbsp all-purpose flour until
   smooth, then $1\frac{1}{2}$ cups milk,
   2 tbsp white wine and $\frac{1}{4}$ tsp salt.
Stir in $\frac{1}{2}$ finely chopped onion.
Microwave, uncovered, on high, $3\frac{1}{2}$ to 4 min.,
   until creamy. Stir every min.
Then, stir in $\frac{1}{4}$ cup grated Parmesan.
Serve over beans or broccoli. *Makes 1⅓ cups.*

NEW GRILLED CHEESE SANDWICH

Rub both sides of 2 thick slices multigrain
   bread with 1 tsp olive oil mixed with
   1 crushed garlic clove.
Toast under broiler. Remove.
   Turn toasted-side down.
Top 1 slice with fresh basil leaves, then with
   1 cheese slice.
Top other slice with sliced tomato.
Broil until cheese melts. Place halves together.

SHERRY-CHEDDAR SPREAD

In a food processor, whirl
   1 lb (500 g) grated cheddar cheese with
   $\frac{1}{2}$ (8-oz/250-g) pkg cream cheese, cut into
   cubes, 1 crushed garlic clove and
   2 tbsp dry sherry.
When fairly smooth, spoon into crock or jar.
Cover and refrigerate. It will keep several
   weeks. Great on bagels. *Makes 2 cups.*

NEW GRILLED CHEESE SANDWICH

BLUE CHEESE & NUT SPREAD

Mash 4 oz (125 g) blue cheese with
  2 tbsp sour cream until fairly smooth.
Stir in 2 tbsp chopped walnuts. Spread on
  whole-grain crackers. *Makes ½ cup.*

MICROWAVE CHEDDAR 'N' ALE SOUP

Place ¼ cup butter in an 8-cup (2-L)
  microwave-safe dish. Cover and
  microwave, on high, 1½ min.
Whisk in ¼ cup all-purpose flour and
  ¼ tsp dry mustard. Cover and microwave,
  on high, 30 sec.
Whisk in ⅓ cup beer, 1 cup chicken bouillon
  and 1 cup milk. Cover and microwave, on
  high, 4 min., stirring partway through.
Add 2 cups grated cheddar. Cover and
  microwave, on high, 1 min. Stir and let sit
  for 3 min. *Makes 4 cups.*

CLASSY BLUE CHEESE DRESSING

In a blender, whirl ½ cup crumbled
  Roquefort or blue cheese with
  2 tbsp milk, 1 tbsp lemon juice or
  white vinegar, 1 sliced green onion
  and ¼ tsp pepper.
If necessary, thin by adding more milk, 1 tbsp
  at a time.
Toss with crisp greens or drizzle over sliced
  pears on lettuce. *Makes ⅓ cup.*

LEMONY PARMESAN DRESSING

In a jar, combine ¼ cup freshly grated
  Parmesan with ¼ cup olive oil,
  1 tbsp lemon juice,
  1 crushed garlic clove, 1 tsp dried basil,
  ¼ tsp dried oregano and ¼ tsp pepper.
Shake until blended. Good tossed with
  spinach and zucchini. *Makes ½ cup.*

CHICKEN ◆ Breasts, Bone-in

We're having a love affair with chicken: consumption has increased dramatically in the last 10 years. Here, we continue the passion.

FAST ITALIAN CHICKEN

Pour 14-oz can spaghetti sauce into a
    large frying pan.
Skin 4 chicken breasts and place, bone-side
    up, in pan. Cover and bring to a gentle boil.
Add 1/4 lb (125 g) sliced mushrooms,
    1 diced green pepper, 1/4 tsp Italian
    seasoning and 1/4 tsp hot red pepper flakes.
Cover, simmer, until chicken is springy to
    touch, about 35 to 45 min. Serve over pasta
    with grated Parmesan. *Serves 4.*

BAKED HERBED CHICKEN

In a baking dish, combine 2 tbsp lemon juice
    with 1 tsp vegetable oil, 1 crushed garlic
    clove, 1/2 tsp chervil, 1/2 tsp salt and pinch
    of pepper. Place 2 skinless chicken breasts,
    meat-side down, in mixture.
Bake, covered, at 375°F (190°C), 20 min.
    Turn chicken and bake 30 min.,
    uncovered, basting twice. *Serves 2.*

MANDARIN-GLAZED CHICKEN

In a small baking dish, stir juice from
    10-oz can mandarin oranges with
    1 tbsp soy sauce, 1 tbsp liquid honey and
    1 crushed garlic clove.
    Add 2 chicken breasts, skin-side down.
Bake, uncovered, at 375°F (190°C), 30 min.
    Turn chicken. Bake 20 min., basting often.
Add mandarins for last 5 min. of cooking.
    Serves 2.

CREAMY CHICKEN

In a large frying pan, lightly brown
    4 chicken breasts, about 5 min. per side.
Add 10-oz can condensed cream of
    mushroom soup and
    1 tsp Italian seasoning or curry powder.
    Stir until hot, about 3 min.
Add 1 chopped zucchini.
Simmer, covered, 35 to 45 min. Turn chicken
    at least once. Serve over rice. *Serves 4.*

SOUTHWEST CHICKEN

Place 6 to 8 skinless chicken breasts in a
    9x13-in. (3-L) pan.
Stir 1 cup hot salsa with 1/2 cup white wine
    and 3 tbsp olive oil. Pour over chicken.
Bake, uncovered, at 375°F (190°C), until chicken
    feels firm to the touch, about 45 min.
    Baste every 15 min. to keep moist. *Serves 6.*

TERIYAKI CHICKEN

Place 4 chicken breasts, skin-side up,
    in a small baking dish.
Brush with 1 tbsp melted butter stirred with
    1 1/2 tbsp dry mustard.
Bake, uncovered, at 350°F (180°C), 20 min.
    Drain fat from pan.
Stir 2 tbsp soy sauce with 2 tbsp liquid
    honey, 1/4 tsp ginger and 1/4 tsp garlic
    powder. Pour over chicken.
Bake, uncovered, basting often, 30 more min.
    Serves 4.

CHILEAN CHICKEN

Place 4 chicken breasts in a 10-in. (25-cm)
    pie plate.
Stir 7½-oz can tomato sauce with
    2 crushed garlic cloves, 1 tsp dried basil,
    ¼ tsp hot pepper sauce and ¼ cup grated
    Parmesan. Pour over chicken.
Bake, uncovered, 50 min., baste often. *Serves 4.*

HONEY-GINGER ORANGE CHICKEN

Melt 2 tbsp butter in a 9-in. (23-cm) baking
    dish. Stir in finely grated peel and juice of
    1 large orange, 2 tbsp liquid honey,
    ½ tsp ginger and generous pinches of
    nutmeg, garlic powder, salt and pepper.
Arrange 4 chicken breasts in sauce,
    skin-side down.
Bake, uncovered, at 350°F (180°C), 45 min.
    Turn chicken skin-side up. Continue
    baking, basting often, until golden, 10 min.
    Serves 4.

EASY BAKE LIME-GINGER CHICKEN

Place 4 chicken breasts, bone-side up,
    in a large baking dish.
Stir juice from 2 limes with
    grated peel of 1 lime, 2 tbsp liquid honey,
    1 crushed garlic clove, ¼ tsp ginger and
    ¼ tsp salt. Pour over chicken.
Bake, uncovered, at 375°F (190°C), 25 min.
    Turn bone-side down and baste. Bake until
    golden brown, about 25 to 30 more min.
    Baste often. *Serves 4.*

CALYPSO CHICKEN

Mix ½ tsp allspice with ½ tsp cinnamon,
    ½ tsp cumin, ¼ tsp salt and ¼ tsp pepper.
    Sprinkle over 4 chicken breasts.
Bake at 375°F (190°C), uncovered, until cooked
    through, 50 min. Baste at least once.
Serve with mango chutney and Curried
    Coconut Rice (see recipe page 156). *Serves 4.*

CALYPSO CHICKEN WITH CURRIED COCONUT RICE

CHICKEN ◆ Breasts, Skinless Boneless

Skinless, boneless chicken breasts are a favorite fast food. Whether sautéed or broiled, they're high in protein and low in calories. Recipes use 4 breasts and serve 2 to 4.

CHICKEN WITH DRIED FRUIT

In a large frying pan, sauté 1 chopped onion
    in 1 tsp butter, 5 min.
Add grated peel and juice from 1 orange,
    1 cup dried fruit such as apples and apricots,
    and $\frac{1}{2}$ cup chicken broth. Add chicken.
Cover and cook, turning once, 12 to 15 min.

ROSEMARY-GARLIC

Sauté 1 crushed garlic clove in 2 tbsp olive oil,
    2 min.
Add chicken. Sprinkle with $\frac{1}{2}$ tsp crushed
    dried rosemary. Sauté 4 min. per side.
Cover and cook, 4 to 6 min.

TARRAGON-MUSTARD

Sauté chicken in 1 tbsp butter, 4 min. per side.
Meanwhile, stir 2 tbsp grainy mustard with
    $\frac{1}{2}$ tsp liquid honey and
    $\frac{1}{4}$ tsp dried tarragon. Top each breast with
    a rounded tsp of mustard mixture.
Cover and cook, 4 to 6 more min.

SANTA FE GRILL

Stir $1\frac{1}{2}$ tbsp olive oil with $1\frac{1}{2}$ tsp cumin,
    $\frac{3}{4}$ tsp dried oregano and $\frac{1}{8}$ tsp cayenne.
Brush over both sides of chicken.
Barbecue or broil 6 to 8 min. per side.
    Squeeze lime juice over top.

PROVENÇAL

Sauté chicken in 1 tbsp butter, 4 min. per side.
Add $\frac{1}{2}$ cup tomato sauce,
    $\frac{1}{2}$ tsp sugar, 1 tbsp sliced black olives and
    $\frac{1}{4}$ tsp Italian seasoning.
Cover and simmer, 4 to 6 min.

CRUNCHY PECAN

Dip chicken into beaten egg. Press $\frac{1}{4}$ cup
    finely chopped pecans into chicken.
Sauté chicken in 1 tbsp butter, about 6 to 8
    min. per side.

FAST SZECHUAN

Stir 2 tbsp soy sauce with 2 tsp brown sugar,
    1 crushed garlic clove and
    dash of hot pepper sauce.
Slice chicken into 1-in. (2.5-cm) wide strips.
    Brush soy mixture over chicken.
    Place on skewers.
Grill, about 2 to 4 min. per side.

HERBED BALSAMIC

Sauté chicken in 2 tsp butter, 4 min. per side.
    Sprinkle with 2 tbsp balsamic or
    raspberry vinegar, $\frac{1}{2}$ tsp sugar and
    $\frac{1}{4}$ tsp dried tarragon.
Cover, reduce heat and simmer, 4 to 6 min.
    Turn partway through cooking.

ELEGANT SAUTÉ

Sauté chicken in 2 tsp butter, 4 min. per side.
Add $\frac{1}{4}$ cup cognac. Stir in 1 tsp Dijon,
    $\frac{1}{4}$ tsp dried dillweed and pinch of salt.
Cover, reduce heat and simmer, 4 to 6 min.,
    turning often. Serve with squeeze of lemon.

LIME-GINGER

Sauté chicken in 1 to 2 tbsp butter over
    medium heat, 3 min. per side.
Add 2 tbsp chopped ginger in syrup,
    2 tsp lime juice and pinch of white pepper.
    Sauté over low heat for 4 min. per side.

CHICKEN ◆ Cooked

Leftover cooked chicken is a perfect starter for a light supper or in salads, sandwiches and pasta.

TARRAGON CHICKEN SANDWICH

Stir 1½ cups finely chopped cooked chicken
   with ¼ cup chopped celery and
   1 sliced green onion.
Stir 2 tbsp sour cream with 2 tbsp mayonnaise,
   ½ tsp dried tarragon and pinches of salt
   and pepper. Stir into chicken mixture.
Good in pita or whole wheat rolls. *Serves 2.*

CREAMY CAESAR SANDWICH

Spread bread with creamy Caesar dressing.
Top with sliced cooked chicken, tomato,
   cooked bacon and grated Parmesan.
Top with slice of bread.

EASY CHICKEN CHOWDER

Heat 2.5-oz (77-g) pkg leek soup mix with
   4 cups water.
Add 2 cups fresh or frozen mixed vegetables,
   ½ tsp Dijon and ¼ tsp tarragon.
Heat, covered, until vegetables are cooked,
   5 min.
Stir in 2 cups cooked chicken pieces and
   1 cup sour cream. *Serves 4.*

HONEY-LIME SALAD

Blend ¼ cup sour cream with
   1 tsp liquid honey and
   grated peel of 1 lime.
Stir in 2 cups cooked chicken cubes and
   1 cup cubed honeydew melon. *Serves 2.*

SIMPLY SPICED SALAD

Blend ½ tsp cumin and pinch of cayenne into
   3 tbsp mayonnaise. Stir with 2 cups
   cooked chicken. *Serves 2.*

CURRIED CHUTNEY SALAD

Stir 1 tbsp mango chutney and ¼ tsp curry
   powder into ¼ cup mayonnaise.
Toss with 2 cups cooked chicken cubes.
   Serves 2.

EASY THAI CHICKEN SALAD

Toss 3 to 4 cups cooked corkscrew pasta
   with ½ cup peanut sauce,
   2 cups cubed cooked chicken and
   2 cups chopped cucumber.
Sprinkle with coriander. *Makes 5½ cups.*

CURRIED CHICKEN SALAD

Stir ¼ cup light sour cream with
   1 tbsp chutney and ¼ tsp curry powder.
Mix in 1 cup diced cooked chicken,
   ½ chopped unpeeled apple or pear,
   1 chopped celery stalk and 1 sliced green
   onion. Serve on greens. *Makes 2¼ cups.*

CHICKEN CAESAR SALAD

Stir pinch of poultry seasoning into your
   favorite creamy Caesar dressing.
Toss dressing with crisp pieces of romaine
   lettuce, strips of cooked chicken and
   chopped roasted red peppers.

OLD-FASHIONED CHICKEN PASTA

Heat 3 cups spaghetti sauce with
   2 cups cooked chicken,
   2 sliced celery stalks,
   2 sliced green onions and
   generous pinches of sage and savory.
Toss with 1 lb (450 g) cooked rotini or shell
   pasta. *Serves 3 to 4.*

CHICKEN ◆ Drumsticks

Finger-lickin' good is what most of us want from juicy drumsticks.
Here's how to achieve it with herbs, garlic, sesame, yogurt and more.

HERBED GARLIC CHICKEN

In a large frying pan, brown 4 drumsticks
    in 1 tsp butter.
Add 1 cup chicken broth, juice from 1 lemon,
    2 crushed garlic cloves, ½ tsp dried thyme
    and pinches of salt and pepper.
    Cover and simmer, 35 min. Turn once.
Remove chicken. Stir 2 tsp cornstarch with
    2 tbsp cold water. Stir into pan juices and
    cook, stirring often, until thick and clear,
    3 to 5 min. Pour over chicken. *Serves 4.*

ROSEMARY-LEMON DRUMSTICKS

In a 9x13-in. (3-L) baking dish, stir
    juice and peel from 2 lemons with
    1 tsp crumbled dried rosemary,
    4 crushed garlic cloves and ½ tsp pepper.
Add 6 drumsticks, skin-side down.
Roast, uncovered, at 375°F (190°C), 20 min.
    Turn. Roast, uncovered, basting often,
    35 more min. *Serves 4 to 6.*

SESAME-YOGURT CHICKEN

Coat 4 drumsticks with ½ cup yogurt
    stirred with ½ tsp liquid honey.
Then roll in 2 tbsp sesame seeds mixed with
    ½ cup dry bread crumbs, ¼ tsp curry
    powder and pinches of salt and pepper.
    Place on a rack in a shallow dish.
Bake, covered, at 375°F (190°C), 30 min.
    Uncover and bake, 20 min. *Serves 4.*

GOLDEN SESAME CHICKEN

Stir ½ cup dry bread crumbs with
    ¼ cup sesame seeds and pinches of salt
    and cayenne.
Whisk ¼ cup sesame oil with 2 tbsp liquid
    honey. Brush over 6 drumsticks. Coat with
    crumb mixture. Place on a baking sheet.
Bake, covered loosely, at 375°F (190°C), 15 min.
    Uncover and bake, 40 min. Turn once.
    Serves 4 to 6.

GINGER LEMON CHICKEN

Stir grated peel and juice from 2 lemons with
    ¼ cup chopped fresh ginger,
    2 crushed garlic cloves, 1 tbsp liquid honey
    and pinches of salt and pepper.
Place 4 drumsticks, skin-side down,
    in a baking dish.
    Spoon lemon mixture over each.
Roast, uncovered, at 350°F (180°C), 1 hour.
    Turn partway through. Baste often. *Serves 4.*

APPLE CHICKEN SMOTHERED WITH ONIONS

Brown 4 drumsticks in 2 tsp butter.
Stir in 2 chopped onions, 1 cup apple juice
    and generous pinches of cinnamon,
    allspice and pepper.
Cover and simmer, 35 to 40 min. Turn once.
    Remove chicken.
Boil sauce, uncovered, until thick, about 7
    min. Stir often. Pour over chicken. *Serves 4.*

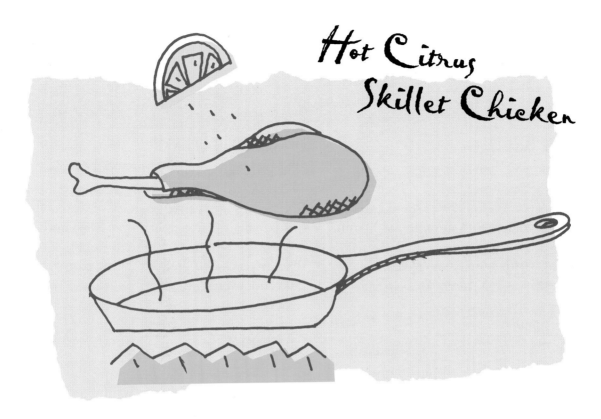

Hot Citrus Skillet Chicken

QUICK GARLIC CHICKEN

Coat 4 chicken drumsticks with
   1/3 cup creamy garlic salad dressing.
   Roll in 1/2 cup dry bread crumbs.
Bake at 375°F (190°C), 45 to 50 min. Turn
   after 30 min. *Serves 4.*

APRICOT SKILLET CHICKEN

Brown 4 chicken drumsticks in 2 tsp butter.
Add grated peel and juice from 1 orange,
   1/4 cup apricot jam and 1 tsp soy sauce.
Cover and simmer, 35 to 40 min. Turn often.
   Remove chicken.
Boil sauce, uncovered, until thick, about 7
   min. Stir often. Pour over chicken. *Serves 4.*

HOT CITRUS SKILLET CHICKEN

In a large frying pan, brown 6 drumsticks
   in 1 tbsp butter.
Add peel and juice from 1 orange,
   1/2 to 1 tsp hot red pepper flakes and
   pinches of ginger, salt and pepper.
Cover, simmer, 35 to 40 min.
   Turn often. *Serves 4 to 6.*

FRESH LEMON-TARRAGON CHICKEN

Stir juice from 1 lemon with 2 tbsp melted
   butter, 1 tsp dried tarragon and
   pinch of garlic powder.
Place 6 drumsticks, skin-side up, in a baking
   dish. Brush with mixture.
Roast, uncovered, at 375°F (190°C), 45 min.
   Baste often. *Serves 4 to 6.*

CHICKEN ◆ Thighs

Packages of chicken thighs are about your best chicken buy and they're as nutritious as legs or breasts.

NEW-STYLE B.L.T.

Sprinkle 4 skinless boneless thighs
   with coarse black pepper.
Sauté in 1 tbsp butter and 1 crushed garlic
   clove until golden both sides, about 20 min.
Squeeze ½ lemon over top.
Serve on rolls with crisp bacon slices,
   lettuce and tomato. *Serves 2.*

CREAMY CURRY

Sauté 4 skinless thighs in 1 tsp butter until
   browned on both sides, about 20 min.
Sprinkle with 1 chopped onion and
   1 tsp curry powder.
Add ¼ cup chicken bouillon. Cover.
Simmer over medium-low heat, 20 min.,
   turning once. Remove thighs.
Boil sauce, uncovered, until slightly reduced.
Remove from heat. Stir in ¼ cup light sour
   cream. Spoon over thighs. *Serves 2.*

SESAME-GINGER

Rub 6 skinless thighs with a few drops of
   sesame oil. Sauté in a nonstick frying pan
   over medium heat until golden on both
   sides, about 20 min.
Stir in 3 tbsp soy sauce, 2 tbsp grated
   fresh ginger, 2 tbsp sesame seeds and
   1 tbsp brown sugar.
Sauté, turning often, until thighs are glazed,
   from 10 to 20 min. *Serves 3.*

CAESAR CORN CRUNCH

Coat 8 skinless thighs with ½ cup light
   Caesar or Creamy Ranch dressing.
Roll in 2 cups crushed corn or tortilla chips
   stirred with 1 tsp Italian seasoning and
   pinch of pepper.
Place on rack in a shallow baking pan.
Bake, uncovered, at 375°F (190°C), 45 min.
   Serves 4.

SPICY BBQ

Place 8 thighs in a shallow baking pan.
Stir ½ cup barbecue sauce with
   1 tbsp soy sauce and ¼ to ½ tsp hot
   pepper sauce. Brush thighs with sauce.
Bake, uncovered, at 375°C (190°C), 20 min.
   Turn thighs, brush with sauce and
   continue baking, brushing often,
   25 more min. *Serves 4.*

PRESTO MICROWAVE PASTA SAUCE

Place 1 thinly sliced onion and
   1 thinly sliced green pepper in a
   microwave-safe casserole.
Microwave, on high, uncovered, stirring
   once, 3 min.
Stir in 2 cups spaghetti sauce and
   4 skinless thighs
Cover and microwave, on high, 15 min.
   Stir partway through and turn thighs.
Spoon over pasta and sprinkle with grated
   Parmesan. *Serves 2.*

RED WINE BBQ BAKE

Place **8** skinless chicken thighs in a
9 x 13-in. (3-L) baking dish.

Pour ½ cup barbecue sauce stirred with
½ cup red wine over top.

Bake, uncovered, at 350°F (180°C), basting
often, until bubbling and golden, about 40
to 50 min. *Serves 4.*

BALSAMIC-GARLIC THIGHS

Place **4** skinless chicken thighs in a 9-in.
(23-cm) pie plate.

Pour **3** tbsp balsamic vinegar over chicken.

Scatter **6** peeled whole garlic cloves around
chicken.

Bake, covered, at 350°F (180°C), 30 min.
Turn chicken. Bake, uncovered, basting
often, 20 to 30 more min.

Remove chicken. Mash garlic into vinegar
mixture and pour over chicken. *Serves 2.*

TANGY ITALIAN

Place **6** thighs, bone-side up, in an 8-in.
(2-L) square baking dish.

Drizzle with ¼ cup Italian dressing.

Bake, uncovered, at 375°F (190°C), 20 min.
Turn thighs and continue baking, 30 more
min. Baste occasionally with dressing.
Serves 3.

PIZZA PARMIGIANA

Place **8** skinless thighs in an oiled
9 x 13-in. (3-L) baking dish. Spread with
½ cup pizza or spaghetti sauce.

Bake, uncovered, in centre of 375°F
(190°C) oven, 25 min.

Cover thighs with slices of mozzarella.
Continue baking, 25 more min.

Serve thighs with pan juices spooned over
hot rice or pasta. *Serves 4.*

CAESAR CORN CRUNCH THIGHS

CHICKEN ◆ Wings

Spicy or subtle, who can resist saucy chicken wings, either oven-baked, barbecued or microwaved. Serve up a big platter dressed in a variety of sauces from Ginger Saigon to Fiery Rebel Jalapeño.

FABULOUS OVEN-BAKED WINGS

Remove wing tips from
   3 lbs (1.5 kg) chicken wings and discard.
   Cut wings in half at joint.
Brush wings with sauce (see recipes below).
Place rack on a foil-lined baking sheet.
Arrange chicken wings on rack.
Bake, uncovered, at 375°F (190°C), 25 min.
   Turn wings and brush with any remaining
   sauce. Continue baking until golden and
   crisp, about 25 to 30 more min.
   Makes 48 pieces.

BASTING SAUCES

SASSY SALSA

In a food processor, purée 1½ cups salsa with
   2 tbsp vegetable oil. Use any remaining
   sauce for dipping.

THAI PEANUT

Stir 1½ cups bottled peanut sauce with
   several dashes of hot pepper sauce.

HOT CAESAR

Stir ¾ cup creamy Caesar dressing with
   2 to 3 tsp hot pepper sauce.

HOT SESAME-GINGER

Stir 3 tbsp sesame oil with
   3 tbsp rice wine vinegar,
   1 tbsp chili-garlic sauce,
   1 tsp ginger and ½ tsp salt.

CRISPY MEXICAN WINGS

Crush 4-oz (120-g) bag tortilla chips.
Beat 2 eggs with ¼ cup water.
Dip wings in mixture, then roll in crumbs
   until lightly coated.
Arrange wings on a rack on a foil-lined
   baking sheet.
Follow recipe for Fabulous Oven-Baked
   Wings, but do not baste.

CRISPY CURRIED WINGS

Whisk ¼ cup peanut oil with
   3 tbsp curry powder, 2 tbsp cumin,
   1 tbsp freshly grated ginger,
   1 tsp paprika, ½ tsp salt, ½ tsp cayenne,
   ¼ tsp allspice and pinch of pepper.
Pour over 3 lbs (1.5 kg) wings. Toss.
Barbecue, turning often, 20 to 30 min.
   Remove.
Squeeze juice from 1 lemon over top.
   Makes 24.

GINGER SAIGON BARBECUED WINGS

Whisk ¾ cup soy sauce with
   ½ cup brown sugar, ½ cup vegetable oil,
   ¼ cup sesame oil, 2 tbsp grated fresh
   ginger, 2 tbsp dry mustard and
   4 crushed garlic cloves.
Pour over 3 lbs (1.5 kg) wings. Toss to coat.
Refrigerate overnight. Barbecue wings,
   turning often, 20 to 30 min.
   Makes 24.

A PARTY LINE-UP OF WINGS (FROM TOP): GINGER SAIGON BARBECUED, CRISPY MEXICAN AND ORIENTAL WINGS

FIERY REBEL JALAPEÑO WINGS

Whisk 14-oz can tomato sauce with
 4 crushed garlic cloves, ¼ cup chopped
 seeded jalapeños, 2 tsp chili powder,
 1½ tsp cumin, 1 tsp dried oregano,
 ½ tsp cayenne and pinch of salt.
Pour over 3 lbs (1.5 kg) wings. Toss to coat.
Barbecue, turning often, about 20 to 30 min.
 Makes 24.

HERBED GARLIC WINGS

Whisk ¾ cup olive oil with
 ⅓ cup lemon juice, 4 crushed garlic cloves,
 ¼ cup chopped parsley,
 1 tsp dried thyme, ¼ tsp salt and
 pinch of pepper.
Pour over 3 lbs (1.5 kg) wings. Toss to coat.
Barbecue, turning often, 20 to 30 min.
 Makes 24.

MICROWAVE ORIENTAL WINGS

Stir ¼ cup ketchup with
 ¼ cup soy sauce,
 ¼ cup apricot jam,
 ¼ tsp garlic powder and
 ¼ tsp cayenne.
Microwave, on high, 1 min.
Stir with 2 lbs (1 kg) wings.
Place in a single layer in a microwave-safe
 dish with meatiest sides toward outside.
 Cover with waxed paper.
Microwave, on high, 8 min. Turn and baste.
 Cook on high, 4 min. Let stand for 3 min.
 Makes 16.

CHICKPEAS

*The chickpea is a versatile little legume. Open a can and use it like
they do in Mediterranean countries, in sandwiches, salads and spreads.*

HEALTHY APPETIZER

Sauté 1 chopped onion in
2 tbsp butter with 2 crushed garlic cloves
and ½ tsp ginger, about 2 min.
Add liquid from 19-oz can chickpeas.
Boil until reduced to ¼ cup.
Stir in chickpeas and heat through.
Serve warm, sprinkled with parsley.
Delicious cold or hot. *Makes 2½ cups.*

TRADITIONAL HUMMUS

In a food processor, whirl
1 cup drained chickpeas with
¼ cup tahini paste, ¼ cup water,
1½ tbsp lemon juice,
3 crushed garlic cloves, ¼ tsp salt and
generous pinch of cayenne.
Use as a dip for pita or pepper strips.
Refrigerated it will keep for several days.
Makes 1⅔ cups.

CURRIED PEA SALAD

Stir ½ cup yogurt with
¼ cup chutney (such as mango) and
1 tsp curry powder.
Stir with 19-oz can drained chickpeas and
2 cups frozen peas.
Serve on a bed of shredded lettuce.
Makes 4 cups.

HEARTY HUMMUS SPREAD

In a food processor, purée 19-oz can drained
chickpeas with 3 tbsp lemon juice,
2 tbsp water, 1 tbsp sesame oil,
2 crushed garlic cloves, ½ tsp cumin,
dash of hot pepper sauce and
generous pinches of salt and pepper.
Makes 1¾ cups.

HUMMUS BURRITOS

In a food processor, whirl 19-oz can drained
chickpeas with ¼ cup water,
2 tbsp tahini paste, 2 tbsp lemon juice,
1 tbsp olive oil, 1 crushed garlic clove,
1 tsp cumin, ¼ tsp salt and
¼ tsp cayenne until smooth.
Spread over 8 tortillas. Top with shredded
lettuce, sliced green onions, cucumber and
dash of hot pepper sauce. Roll up.
Makes 8 burritos.

CHICKPEAS ON THE BARBIE

Whisk ¼ cup olive oil with
1 tbsp lemon juice, 2 tsp curry powder
and pinch of cayenne.
Stir in 2 crushed garlic cloves,
2 sliced green onions and
19-oz can drained chickpeas.
Seal in 2 to 3 large pieces of heavy foil.
Grill, turning often, about 15 min. Or bake in
a 400°F (200°C) oven for 15 min.
Serves 2.

Super Hearty Vegetarian Sandwich

SUPER HEARTY VEGETARIAN SANDWICH

In a food processor, whirl 19-oz can drained
  chickpeas with 1 tbsp butter,
  1 coarsely chopped onion,
  ¾ tsp cumin, ¼ tsp salt and
  generous pinch of chili powder.
Spread over 4 slices bread.
  Top with lettuce and tomato. *Serves 4.*

CHICKPEA, GARLIC & TOMATO TOSS

Whisk 3 tbsp olive oil with 4 tsp lemon juice,
  1 crushed garlic clove, 3 sliced green
  onions, ¼ tsp dried basil and
  pinches of salt and pepper.
Toss with 19-oz can drained chickpeas
  and 2 chopped tomatoes. *Serves 3.*

CHICKPEA CURRY TOSS

Combine 3 chopped seeded ripe tomatoes
  with 19-oz can drained chickpeas and
  2 chopped green onions.
Whisk 1 tbsp olive oil with 1 tsp curry
  powder. Toss with chickpeas.
  Makes 4 cups.

CHICKPEA & ROASTED RED PEPPER SALAD

Drain 19-oz can chickpeas, rinse with cold
  running water and drain again.
Stir in ½ (10-oz/340-g) jar chopped drained
  roasted red peppers
  or 1 roasted seeded red pepper,
  2 chopped seeded jalapeños.
Sprinkle with ¼ cup chopped fresh basil or
  ½ tsp dried basil. Stir until mixed.
Add 2 tsp lime juice and toss until evenly
  coated. *Makes 1½ cups.*

Chocolate

Whether it's a lick, a sip, a crunch or a melt-in-your-mouth experience, chocolate has enthralled us for centuries. Here are 10 divinely decadent ways to satisfy any craving.

World's Fastest Mousse

Beat ⅔ cup chocolate syrup with
    1 cup whipping cream and 1 tbsp coffee or
    orange liqueur until peaks form. *Serves 4.*

Glamorous Apricots

Dip bottom half of 12 dried apricots in
    ½ cup semisweet melted chocolate.
Place on a waxed-paper lined tray.
Refrigerate until firm, about 20 min.

Double-Chocolate Brownies

Stir 3 oz (85 g) chopped bittersweet
    chocolate into 20-oz (640-g) fudge-
    brownie mix. Prepare according to
    package directions. *Makes 18.*

Decadent Truffles

Melt 6 oz (170 g) bittersweet chocolate.
    Stir in ¼ cup icing sugar, ⅓ cup unsalted
    butter and 2 tbsp coffee liqueur.
Refrigerate until firm enough to shape into
    1-in. (2.5-cm) balls. Roll in cocoa. *Makes 26.*

Instant Hot Sauce

Chop 3 oz (85 g) bittersweet chocolate.
    Place in a saucepan with ¼ cup whipping
    cream. Stir over low heat until blended.
Pour over ice cream. *Makes ⅓ cup.*

Double Hot Chocolate

Prepare 4 cups of your favorite hot chocolate.
Stir in 2 oz (56 g) chopped bittersweet or
    semisweet chocolate.
    Stir over low heat until melted. *Serves 4.*

Nutty Pancakes

Prepare 1 cup pancake mix according
    to package directions.
Stir in ½ cup chocolate chips and
    ¼ chopped pecans before cooking.
    Serves 4.

Decorative Leaves

Dip a small brush in warm melted chocolate.
    Thinly coat underside of small fresh leaves.
Place leaves, chocolate-side up, on waxed
    paper. Refrigerate until set, about 15 min.
Hold leaf by stem and slowly and carefully
    peel off chocolate.

Chic Chocolate Mousse

Combine 4 squares (4 oz/112 g)
    unsweetened or bittersweet chocolate
    in a small saucepan with ¼ cup sherry.
    Stir over low heat until chocolate is
    melted. Stir until smooth.
Beat 4 egg yolks. Slowly beat in warm
    chocolate mixture.
With clean beaters, beat 4 egg whites until
    peaks will form. Gradually beat in
    ½ cup granulated sugar.
Fold in chocolate mixture. Spoon into dessert
    dishes. Refrigerate. *Serves 4 to 6.*

Coconut Clusters

Melt 6 oz (170 g) semisweet chocolate.
Stir in 1 cup chopped salted peanuts and
    ½ cup toasted coconut.
Drop by spoonfuls onto waxed-paper lined
    tray. Refrigerate until firm, about 20 min.
    Makes 24.

COOKIE MIXES

Here's a fast way to fill the cookie jar. Start with $\frac{1}{2}$ *(2-lb/900-g) package of cookie mix — oatmeal or chocolate chip — then spice it up with the following stir-ins. Each recipe yields 30 cookies.*

ALMOND & APRICOT

Stir $\frac{1}{2}$ cup coarsely chopped almonds, $\frac{1}{2}$ cup chopped dried apricots and $\frac{1}{4}$ to $\frac{1}{2}$ tsp almond extract into $\frac{1}{2}$ pkg oatmeal cookie mix. Prepare following package directions.

PEANUT BUTTER & BANANA CHIP

Stir $\frac{1}{2}$ cup coarsely chopped banana chips and $\frac{1}{2}$ cup peanut butter into $\frac{1}{2}$ pkg chocolate-chip cookie mix. Prepare following package directions.

APPLE 'N' SPICE

Stir 1 finely chopped peeled apple and $\frac{1}{2}$ tsp cinnamon into $\frac{1}{2}$ pkg oatmeal cookie mix. Prepare following package directions, using $\frac{1}{4}$ cup apple juice in place of water.

HEALTHY RAISIN

Stir $\frac{1}{2}$ cup yogurt-coated raisins, $\frac{1}{2}$ cup golden raisins and 1 tsp cinnamon into $\frac{1}{2}$ pkg oatmeal cookie mix. Prepare following package directions.

SOUTHERN CRUNCH

Stir 1 cup dried tropical-fruit mix into $\frac{1}{2}$ pkg oatmeal cookie mix. Prepare following package directions.

GINGER CRISP

Stir $\frac{3}{4}$ cup desiccated coconut and 1 to 2 tbsp finely chopped candied ginger into $\frac{1}{2}$ pkg chocolate-chip cookie mix. Prepare following package directions.

BUTTERSCOTCH-NUT

Stir $\frac{1}{2}$ cup butterscotch chips and $\frac{1}{2}$ cup coarsely chopped peanuts into $\frac{1}{2}$ pkg oatmeal cookie mix. Prepare following package directions.

CHOCOLATE-MINT

Stir $\frac{1}{2}$ cup mint chips into $\frac{1}{2}$ pkg chocolate-chip cookie mix. Prepare following package directions.

HAZELNUT-ORANGE

Stir 1 cup coarsely chopped hazelnuts, finely grated peel of 1 orange and $\frac{1}{4}$ to $\frac{1}{2}$ tsp freshly grated nutmeg into $\frac{1}{2}$ pkg oatmeal cookie mix. Prepare following package directions.

CHRISTMAS MINCEMEAT

Prepare $\frac{1}{2}$ pkg oatmeal cookie mix following directions. Roll into 1-in. (2.5-cm) balls and place on a baking sheet. Make a deep thumbprint in centre of each ball. Fill each with $\frac{1}{4}$ to $\frac{1}{2}$ tsp mincemeat or raspberry jam. Bake as directed.

CORN

After the cobs have finished for the season, canned and frozen corn kernels top our favorite vegetable list. Besides simply heating, there are a myriad of ways to add taste variations without a lot of work.

CREAMY CORN CHOWDER

Heat 10-oz can cream of celery soup
 with 1 can water.
Add 1 cup canned or cooked kernel corn,
 7-oz can drained salmon and
 2 sliced green onions.
Stir often until hot. *Serves 4.*

CHILI CORN SALAD

Stir 12-oz can drained kernel corn with
 1 finely chopped tomato,
 1 tbsp bottled vinaigrette and
 pinch of hot red pepper flakes.
 Makes 2 cups.

SWEET CORN TOSS

Slice kernels from 2 cooked corn cobs,
 about 1½ cups.
Mix with 1 chopped red pepper,
 2 sliced green onions and
 ¼ cup Italian dressing. *Makes 2 cups.*

3-ALARM CORN ON THE COB

Stir 3 tbsp chopped chives,
 ¼ tsp pepper, ¼ tsp chili powder,
 ¼ tsp white pepper and ¼ tsp cayenne
 into ½ cup room-temperature butter.
Can be refrigerated up to a week.
 Spread over hot corn on the cob.
 Makes enough for 8 cobs.

QUICK TARRAGON CORN ON THE COB

Stir ½ tsp dried tarragon and
 ¼ tsp pepper into ¼ cup butter.
Spread over hot corn on the cob.
 Makes enough for 4 cobs.

MICROWAVE FIERY CORN ON THE COB

Remove husks and silk from 4 ears of corn.
 Wrap each in plastic wrap.
Place in microwave in spoke pattern with
 small ends toward middle of microwave.
Microwave, on high, 5 min.
Stir ¼ cup butter with
 ⅛ tsp hot red pepper flakes.
Unwrap corn and spread with butter.
 Serves 4.

SOUTHWEST SIDE DISH

Sauté 1 chopped red pepper and
 1 chopped jalapeño in
 1 tbsp butter or vegetable oil.
Add 2 cups canned or cooked kernel corn
 and ½ tsp cumin.
Stir until hot. *Serves 4.*

CURRIED CORN

Heat 1 tsp butter in a frying pan.
Add 2 cups canned or cooked kernel corn,
 1 tsp curry powder and ⅛ tsp cayenne.
Stir constantly until hot. *Serves 4.*

Sweet Corn Toss

SKILLET SUMMER RATATOUILLE

In a large frying pan, sauté
  2 crushed garlic cloves and
  1 large chopped onion in
  1 tbsp olive oil.
Add 2 cups cooked, canned or
  frozen kernel corn,
  28-oz can drained tomatoes,
  2 sliced zucchini and
  1 tsp Italian seasoning.
Simmer, covered, 10 min, stirring often.
  Serves 6.

VEGGIE STIR-FRY

Stir-fry 1 chopped red pepper in
  2 tsp melted butter, 2 min.
Add 14-oz can drained baby corn,
  1 sliced zucchini and
  ½ tsp lemon pepper or
  ¼ tsp black pepper.
Stir-fry until hot, about 4 min. *Serves 4.*

COUSCOUS

Couscous is as much a staple in North African cuisine as pasta is in Italian.
Its popularity is rising here because it's wholesome and takes mere minutes to make.

LUSTY COUSCOUS SALAD

Stir 1 cup cooked couscous with
    1 chopped green pepper,
    1 chopped tomato,
    1 sliced green onion and
    ¼ cup Roquefort dressing.
Add squeeze of lemon juice and pinches of
    salt and pepper. Serve on lettuce leaves.
    Makes 2½ cups.

TABBOULEH SALAD

Stir 1 cup cooked couscous with
    1 chopped tomato, 1 sliced green onion
    and ¼ cup chopped parsley.
Whisk 1 tbsp olive oil with 1 tbsp lemon
    juice and pinches of salt, pepper and
    allspice. Stir into salad. Serve cold.
    Makes 2 cups.

ORANGE & RAISIN COUSCOUS

Bring 1½ cups chicken bouillon,
    ½ cup chopped oranges or clementines
    and ¼ tsp grated orange peel to a boil
    in a saucepan.
Stir in 1 cup dry couscous and ¼ cup raisins.
Cover, remove from heat. Let stand for 5 min.
    Fluff with a fork and stir in 2 tbsp currants
    or raisins. *Makes 3½ cups.*

MIDDLE EASTERN HOT CEREAL

Bring 1 cup milk, 1 cup water and
    1 tsp butter to a boil.
Stir in 1 cup couscous and
    generous pinches of cinnamon and salt.
Cover, remove from heat. Let stand for 5 min.
Sprinkle with brown sugar. *Serves 2 to 4.*

COUSCOUS STUFFED TOMATOES

Slice 4 tomatoes in half. Leaving shell intact,
    scoop out pulp and coarsely chop.
Mix pulp with ½ cup cooked couscous,
    ½ cup diced cucumber,
    3 sliced green onions,
    2 tbsp chopped fresh or ½ tsp dried basil
    and Italian dressing to moisten.
Spoon into tomato halves.
    Serves 4 to 8.

COUSCOUS WITH BROCCOLI

Stir 1 tbsp olive oil, 1 cup chopped broccoli,
    ¼ tsp celery salt, generous pinch of
    cayenne and 1 large crushed garlic clove
    into 1¼ cups boiling water.
Boil for 1 min. Stir in ¾ cup couscous. Cover.
    Let sit for 5 min.
    Makes 3 cups.

A
B
C
D
E
F
G
H
I
J
K
L
M
N
O
P
Q
R
S
T
U
V
W
X
Y
Z

SAUSAGE & PEPPERS

Cut 2 Italian sausages into ½-in. (1-cm)
    pieces. Cook in a large frying pan.
Add 1 chopped red pepper and
    ¾ cup water.
When boiling, stir in ½ cup couscous.
Cover and remove from heat. Let stand for
    5 min. *Serves 2.*

ORANGE HERBED COUSCOUS

In a saucepan, bring ½ cup orange juice,
    1 tbsp grated orange peel and
    1¾ cups chicken broth to a boil.
Stir in 1 tbsp butter, 1½ cups couscous,
    ¼ tsp dried thyme and ¼ tsp salt.
Cover, remove from heat. Let stand for 5 min.
    Makes 3½ cups.

GRAINS & GREENS

Bring 1 cup water, 1 tbsp butter and
    generous pinches of celery salt and pepper
    to a boil.
Add 2 cups broccoli and boil, 2 min.
Stir in ½ cup couscous.
Cover, remove from heat. Let stand for
    5 min. Toss and serve. *Serves 3.*

COUSCOUS TUNA SUPPER

Prepare ½ cup couscous according to
    package directions, substituting
    1 tbsp olive oil for butter.
After standing time, stir in
    1½ tbsp lemon juice and
    1 crushed garlic clove.
Then stir in 2 sliced green onions and
    7½-oz can drained tuna. *Makes 2 cups.*

COUSCOUS STUFFED TOMATOES

CRANBERRIES

Cranberries are a colorful fixture of the festive season. Whether you use them fresh, canned or jellied, there are many easy ways to add their terrific tartness to your year-round table.

FROSTED CRANBERRIES

Dip fresh cranberries in beaten egg white, then toss in sugar until coated.
Place on a baking sheet and refrigerate.
Use as a trim around roasted turkey.

FRESH CRANBERRY CHUTNEY

In a food processor, whirl 2 cups fresh cranberries with 1 peeled orange, 1 chopped peeled apple and 1 tbsp grated fresh ginger. Pour into a saucepan.
Add ⅔ cup brown sugar, ¼ tsp cinnamon, ¼ tsp salt and pinch of allspice.
Bring to a boil, stirring often. Then simmer, uncovered, stirring often, until thick, 5 to 7 min. Wonderful with pork or turkey. *Makes 1¾ cups.*

FRESH CRANBERRY RELISH

In a food processor, whirl pulp of 1 orange with 1 cup fresh cranberries and 2 to 3 tbsp sugar. *Makes ½ cup.*

FRESH CRANBERRY-PEAR SALSA

Stir 1 coarsely chopped peeled orange with ½ cup chopped fresh cranberries, 1 chopped peeled pear, ½ cup chopped parsley and 1 tsp sugar. Serve with roast turkey or pork. *Makes 1¼ cups.*

RAISIN-ORANGE SAUCE

Stir 14-oz can whole cranberry sauce with ¼ cup golden raisins and 1 tbsp finely grated orange peel.
Excellent with smoked turkey or cold roast pork. *Makes 2 cups.*

CRANBERRY DIPPING SAUCE

Place 1 cup cranberry sauce, ½ cup red currant jelly, 2 tbsp lemon juice, 2 tbsp port and 1 tbsp Dijon in a saucepan.
Whisk over medium heat until fairly smooth and hot. Great dip for chicken fingers, chicken wings or egg rolls.
Makes 1¼ cups.

GINGER-BERRY SAUCE

Stir 14-oz can whole cranberry sauce with ¼ cup stemmed ginger in syrup, finely chopped. Good with turkey or duck.
Makes 2 cups.

CRANAPPLE SAUCE

Stir 14-oz can whole cranberry sauce with ½ cup applesauce. Wonderful with roast pork or sausage. *Makes 2 cups.*

CHRISTMAS SPREAD

In a food processor, whirl ¼ cup fresh cranberries with 1 tbsp orange juice.
Add 4-oz (125-g) pkg creamy goat cheese and whirl until combined. Add sugar, if needed. Spread on thinly sliced baguette or use as a vegetable dip. *Makes ⅔ cup.*

ROSEMARY-RUM CHRISTMAS PUNCH

In a large saucepan, heat 16 cups (4 L) apple cider with 1 cup whole cranberries, 1 sliced lemon, 1 sliced orange, 2 cinnamon sticks, 4 whole cloves and 1 tsp dried rosemary. When boiling, stir in 1 cup rum and ¼ cup sugar.
Serve warm. *Makes 40 (½-cup) servings.*

CREAM CHEESE

Whether it's a casual or formal gathering, you usually want to put out nibbles. Cream cheese is the perfect way to start. The following dips and spreads will impress any guests.

CURRIED CRAB

Stir ½ (8-oz/250-g) pkg whipped or spreadable cream cheese with ½ cup sour cream or mayonnaise, 5-oz (142-g) can drained crab and generous pinches of curry powder. Serve with celery sticks or bread wedges. *Makes 1½ cups.*

LEMON-PEPPER CHEESE

In a food processor, whirl ½ (8-oz/250-g) pkg cream cheese with finely grated peel of 1 lemon, ¼ tsp pepper and pinch of cayenne. Spread on smoked salmon or roast beef sandwiches. *Makes ½ cup.*

CHIC CAVIAR

In a food processor, whirl ½ (8-oz /250-g) pkg cream cheese with ¼ cup sour cream, 2 hard-boiled eggs, 2 sliced green onions and 2 oz (50 g) red caviar. Good with vegetable sticks and florets. *Makes 1 cup.*

EASY VEGETABLE SPREAD

In a food processor, whirl 8-oz (250-g) pkg cream cheese, cubed, with 2 tbsp dry vegetable-soup mix, 2 tbsp mayonnaise and dash of hot pepper sauce.
Serve at room temperature. Good as a spread or dip. *Makes 1 cup.*

CURRIED CHUTNEY SPREAD

In a food processor, whirl 8-oz (250-g) pkg cream cheese, cubed, with ¼ cup mango chutney and ½ tsp curry powder.
Good as a filling for celery or spread for pita wedges. *Makes 1 cup.*

DIJON SANDWICH SPREAD

Blend ¼ cup cream cheese with 2 tbsp Dijon. Spread on tomato, beef or turkey sandwiches. *Makes ⅓ cup.*

MERRY MEDITERRANEAN SPREAD

Stir ½ (8-oz/250-g) pkg spreadable light cream cheese with ¼ cup crumbled feta, 2 tbsp finely chopped black olives, 2 tbsp chopped fresh basil, 1 finely sliced green onion and 1½ tsp lemon juice.
Use as a spread or vegetable dip. *Makes ¾ cup.*

ISLAND GINGER SPREAD

Blend ½ (8-oz/250-g) pkg cream cheese with ¼ cup drained crushed pineapple and 1½ tsp chopped crystallized ginger.
Good with sesame crackers. *Makes ½ cup.*

FIERY CREAM CHEESE DIP

In a food processor, whirl 8-oz (250-g) pkg cream cheese with 2 crushed garlic cloves, 1 red pepper and 1 seeded jalapeño until coarsely chopped.
Stir in 2 to 4 tbsp chopped fresh coriander. Dip should be chunky. Good with tortilla chips or vegetables. *Makes 2 cups.*

NEW ONION DIP

Simmer 1 cup chopped shallots, 2 crushed garlic cloves, ¼ cup white wine and 1 tbsp olive oil, 10 min. Stir often.
Place 8-oz (250-g) pkg light cream cheese in a bowl. Stir in warm shallot mixture with ½ tsp dried tarragon, ¼ tsp salt and pinch of pepper. *Makes 1½ cups.*

E is for Eggplant...

DEVILED SCRAMBLED EGGS (see recipe page 69) take less than 10 minutes to make, yet deliver all the old-fashioned creamy taste of fussed-over hard-boiled stuffed eggs. We found that using light sour cream, at about one-tenth the calories of mayonnaise, gave us the tangy deviled taste without all that fat.

EGGPLANTS

Eggplants used to be grown only for their seductive good looks.
Today they are adored by everyone because of their meaty textured interior. Grill them for
vegetarian "steaks" or purée them into dips.

GARLIC DIP

Prick 1 large whole eggplant several times
  with a fork. Place on a paper towel in a
  microwave. Cook on high, 3 min., until
  very soft. Scoop out pulp.
In a food processor, purée pulp with
  1 garlic glove, 2 tbsp olive oil,
  1 tbsp lemon juice and generous pinches
  of salt, pepper and sugar. *Makes 2 cups.*

CREAMY EGGPLANT DIP

Broil 1 large whole eggplant, turning often,
  until soft, about 10 to 12 min. Let sit,
  uncovered, until cool enough to handle,
  about 7 min. Peel off skin and remove seeds.
Whirl pulp in a food processor with
  1 garlic clove.
Add ½ cup light sour cream, ¼ tsp cumin,
  ¼ tsp salt and pinch of pepper and whirl.
Great as a vegetable dip. *Makes 2½ cups.*

TOMATO & FETA EGGPLANT STEAK

Slice 1 unpeeled eggplant, lengthwise, into
  ½-in. (1-cm) slices. Sprinkle both sides
  with salt. Place in an ungreased baking dish.
 Sprinkle with ½ tsp sugar,
  ½ tsp dried basil, ¼ tsp dried oregano and
  ¼ tsp garlic powder.
Top with sliced tomatoes. Sprinkle with
  1 cup crumbled feta.
Bake, uncovered, at 375°F (190°C), until
  eggplant is tender, 30 to 35 min. *Serves 2.*

FETTUCCINE WITH FETA & EGGPLANT

Sauté 2 cups chopped peeled eggplant in
  1 tbsp olive oil over medium heat, 10 min.
Stir in 1½ cups spaghetti sauce,
  ½ tsp dried basil and pinch of sugar.
Heat and toss with cooked fettuccine.
  Crumble feta over top and toss.
  Makes 4 cups.

GRILLED VEGETARIAN SANDWICHES

Thinly slice 2 Japanese eggplants lengthwise.
Whisk ¼ cup olive oil with
  ¼ cup red wine vinegar,
  2 crushed garlic cloves and ½ tsp salt.
Add ½ cup chopped fresh basil.
Brush over eggplant slices and grill for 5 min.
  per side, basting often, until browned.
Slice 2 pieces focaccia bread horizontally.
Grill for 2 min. per side.
Overlap eggplant slices on focaccia bottoms.
  Top with sliced Asiago cheese, tomatoes
  and whole basil leaves. Add focaccia tops.

FIERY EGGPLANT FETTUCCINE

In a saucepan, heat 3 cups spaghetti sauce
  with ⅓ cup red wine and 1 tsp sugar.
  Stir in 2 diced small Japanese eggplants.
Cover, reduce heat and simmer, stirring
  often, until eggplant is tender, 30 min.
Toss with cooked pasta and sprinkle with
  grated Parmesan or Asiago. *Serves 4 to 6.*

A
B
C
D
E
F
G
H
I
J
K
L
M
N
O
P
Q
R
S
T
U
V
W
X
Y
Z

*TOMATO & FETA
EGGPLANT STEAK*

ITALIAN SLICES

Arrange 2 (½-in/1-cm) thick slices of
  eggplant in an oiled microwave-safe dish.
  Overlap slices if necessary.
Stir ½ cup tomato sauce with ¼ tsp Italian
  seasoning. Pour over eggplant. Sprinkle
  with ¼ cup grated Parmesan.
Microwave, covered, on high, 5 min., or until
  soft. Good with chicken. *Serves 2.*

MICROWAVE EGGPLANT MEDLEY

Stir 1 chopped peeled eggplant with
  2 tbsp olive oil, 1 chopped onion,
  1 sliced green pepper,
  2 crushed garlic cloves, 1 tsp dried basil,
  ¼ tsp hot red pepper flakes and
  generous pinches of salt and pepper.
Microwave, covered, on high, 6 min.
  Stir partway through.
Stir in 1 chopped tomato and
  1 cup tiny mozzarella cubes.
Microwave, covered, on high, 2 min. Stir.
  Let stand, covered, 5 min. Good with
  grilled chicken and fish. *Serves 3.*

AMAZING MICROWAVE RATATOUILLE

Stir 1 cubed peeled eggplant with
  2 tbsp olive oil, 1 chopped onion and
  2 crushed garlic cloves.
Microwave, covered, on high, 4 min.
  Stir partway through.
Stir in 3 chopped tomatoes, 1 chopped
  zucchini, 1 diced green pepper,
  1 tbsp drained capers, 1 tsp dried basil,
  ¼ tsp salt and pinch of pepper. Cover.
Microwave, on high, until bubbling, 6 min.
  Stir partway through.
Good with fish or burgers. *Makes 7 cups.*

BROILED HERBED EGGPLANT

Slice 1 unpeeled eggplant, lengthwise, into
  ½-in. (1-cm) thick slices.
Blend ¼ cup olive oil with ½ tsp dried
  oregano, ¼ tsp dried basil, ¼ tsp salt and
  pinches of garlic powder and pepper.
  Brush over slices.
Broil or barbecue, turning and basting often
  until tender, about 10 min. Great with
  grilled steaks. *Serves 3 to 4.*

EGGS

Eggs work perfectly beyond breakfast for lunch, brunch or dinner.
At the heart of the matter – a complete protein that can be ready in as little as 3 minutes.

FRENCH TOAST

Beat 4 eggs with 2 tsp sugar, ½ tsp salt and
   pinch of nutmeg.
Whisk in 1½ cups milk and ¼ tsp vanilla.
Dip 8 slices bread into egg mixture, then fry
   in butter over medium heat until browned
   on both sides. *Makes 8 slices.*

SMOKED SALMON EGG SALAD

Combine 4 coarsely chopped hard-boiled
   eggs with ¼ cup chopped smoked salmon,
   ¼ cup light sour cream,
   1 tbsp chopped drained capers,
   1 tbsp chopped chives and pinch of pepper.
Serve on baguette. *Makes 1¾ cups.*

DILLED EGG

Blend 3 tbsp mayonnaise with 1 tsp Dijon
   and 1 tbsp finely chopped fresh dill or
   ½ tsp dried dillweed. Stir in 4 chopped
   hard-boiled eggs. *Makes 1 cup.*

MICROWAVE POACHED EGGS

Heat 1 tbsp water or 1 tsp butter in custard
   cup. Add 1 egg. Sprinkle with salt,
   white pepper and grated Parmesan.
Cover and microwave, on medium, 45 to 75 sec.
   Let stand, covered, 1 min.

DEVILED EGGS

Slice 6 hard-boiled eggs in half. Mash yolks
   with ¼ cup mayonnaise, ½ tsp vinegar,
   generous pinches of dry mustard, salt,
   pepper and dash of Worcestershire.
Stir in thinly sliced green onion. Mound into
   egg whites. Sprinkle with paprika. *Makes 12.*

HONEY-MUSTARD DEVILED EGGS

Slice 6 hard-boiled eggs in half. Mash yolks
   with 2 tbsp mayonnaise, 1 tsp Dijon and
   ½ tsp honey. Spoon into whites. *Makes 12.*

GINGER-CUMIN DEVILED EGGS

Slice 6 hard-boiled eggs in half. Mash yolks
   with ¼ cup mayonnaise, ½ tsp grated
   fresh ginger and pinch of cumin.
Spoon into whites. *Makes 12.*

BLENDER CRÊPES

Whirl 1 cup all-purpose flour, 1¾ cups milk,
   3 eggs, 2 tbsp melted butter and
   ¼ tsp salt in a blender.
Pour 2 tbsp onto a hot greased 6-in. (15-cm)
   frying pan. Tip to coat bottom.
Cook over medium heat until edges dry,
   1 min. Turn and brown other side.
Repeat with remaining batter. *Makes 24.*

SUPERB HOLLANDAISE SAUCE

In top of a double boiler, whisk 3 egg yolks
   with juice from half a lemon or lime,
   dash of hot pepper sauce and ¼ tsp salt.
Cut ½ cup cold unsalted butter into 16 pieces.
Place mixture over simmering, not boiling,
   water. Whisk constantly, beating in butter,
   one piece at a time. Superb over poached
   eggs or fish. *Makes 1 cup.*

EGG CHUTNEY SPREAD

Mash 3 finely chopped hard-boiled eggs with
   2 tbsp mayonnaise, 1 tbsp mango chutney
   and ¼ tsp curry powder.
Spread on rye or stuff in pitas. *Makes ¾ cup.*

Eggs ◆ Scrambled

Scrambled eggs make a fine light dinner or brunch. Each recipe serves 2 and requires 4 eggs whisked with 2 tbsp of water, salt and pepper to taste. Scramble in 1 tsp of melted butter in a nonstick pan.

Salsa & Green Pepper

Sauté ¼ cup finely chopped green pepper in 1 tbsp butter, 2 min.

Add eggs and scramble. Just before serving, stir in 2 tbsp salsa.

Bacon & Cheddar

Cut 2 strips of bacon into 1-in. (2.5-cm) pieces. Cook until crisp. Remove from pan. Drain off all but 2 tsp fat.

Add eggs and scramble.

Sprinkle with bacon, ⅓ cup diced tomatoes and ¼ cup grated cheddar.

Zucchini & Pesto

Sauté ⅓ cup diced zucchini in 1 tsp butter over medium heat, 2 min. Stir in 1 to 2 tbsp pesto. Remove from pan.

Scramble eggs. Stir in zucchini mixture.

Chèvre & Watercress

Mix 2 tbsp soft goat cheese with 2 tbsp sour cream.

Stir in 2 tbsp coarsely chopped watercress.

Scramble eggs. Add spoonfuls of chèvre mixture. Stir until distributed.

Herbed Eggs

Scramble eggs. Stir in ½ tsp fresh snipped chives, ½ tsp parsley and ½ dried basil. Oregano, dill or tarragon is also good.

Scrambled Eggs & Olives

Whisk eggs with 1 tsp Dijon. Scramble.

Stir in ¼ cup sliced stuffed green olives.

Spoon onto crusty buttered bread. Top with tomato slices.

Herb & Garlic

Add 2 oz (60 g) herb-and-garlic cream cheese or finely cubed Boursin to eggs.

Stir over low heat until done as you like.

Southern Comfort

Stir eggs over low heat until they start to set.

Add ½ cubed avocado. Sprinkle with ½ tsp cumin, ¼ tsp chili powder, ¼ tsp salt and ¼ tsp pepper.

Stir over low heat until done as you like.

Deviled Scrambled Eggs

Beat eggs with 2 tbsp light sour cream, ½ tsp Dijon, 1 sliced green onion and generous pinches of salt and pepper.

Stir over medium-high heat, until creamy, about 2½ to 3 min.

Creamy Smoked Salmon

Scramble eggs.

When almost done, dot with 3 tbsp cream cheese.

Sprinkle with 2 tbsp chopped smoked salmon, 1 tbsp chopped fresh dill and generous pinch of pepper.

Stir into eggs until cream cheese starts to melt.

F is for Fish...

MEDITERRANEAN FISH STEAKS
(see recipe page 74) are flavorfully baked
in seasoned tomatoes spiked with heady
black olives and a sprinkle of cayenne.

FISH FILLETS

Fish fillets can always be counted on for a fast meal. Adding a robust flavor booster is the trick that quickly turns them into a satisfying delicious dinner. See also SOLE.

POTATO COUNTRY CHOWDER

Heat 10-oz can cream of potato soup with
   1½ cups milk and ½ tsp dried thyme.
   Stir often.
Add 2 chopped green onions,
   1 chopped red pepper and
   1 lb (500 g) chopped cod fillets.
Cover and simmer, 10 min., stirring often,
   until fish flakes easily. *Serves 4.*

OVEN-BAKED FRENCH FILLETS

Place 1 lb (500 g) fish fillets in a large oven
   dish. Loosely cover with foil.
Bake at 450°F (230°C) for 5 min., or 10 min.
   if fish is frozen. Drain off liquid.
Spread with ½ cup light sour cream stirred
   with 2 tsp Dijon and ½ tsp dried tarragon.
   Sprinkle with 3 tbsp grated Parmesan.
Bake, uncovered, until golden, 5 min.
   Serves 3.

TOMATO HERBED CHOWDER

Heat 28-oz can undrained tomatoes with
   2 chopped onions, 1 tsp dried basil,
   ¼ tsp dried thyme and
   pinches of garlic powder, salt and pepper.
Add 1 lb (500 g) frozen fish fillets, cut into
   8 pieces. Bring to a boil.
Cover and simmer, 20 min. Stir often. *Serves 3.*

MICROWAVE FILLETS WITH DIJON SAUCE

Place 1 lb (500 g) turbot or sole fillets
   in a microwave-safe dish, overlapping
   thin edges.
Microwave, covered, on high, 5 min.
Stir ⅓ cup sour cream with 2 tsp Dijon,
   1 tsp dried dillweed and pinches of salt
   and pepper. Drain liquid from fish.
Spoon sour cream mixture over fish.
Microwave, uncovered, on medium, 1 min.
   Let stand, covered, 2 min. *Serves 3.*

ORANGE-BASIL FISH

In a large frying pan, heat 2 tsp butter.
Add 1 lb (500 g) mild-flavored fish fillets,
   juice and peel from 2 oranges,
   ½ tsp dried basil and
   pinches of salt and pepper.
Sauté for 3 min. per side. *Serves 3.*

CURRIED FISH 'N' RICE DINNER

In a large saucepan, stir 2 cups chicken
   bouillon with 1 cup milk and
   1 tbsp curry powder. Bring to a boil.
Stir in 1 cup uncooked rice, 1 chopped onion
   and 1 lb (500 g) frozen fish, cut
   into 8 pieces.
Cover and simmer, 30 min. Stir often.
   Serves 3.

OVEN-BAKED SALSA FILLETS

Arrange 10-oz (280-g) pkg thawed fish fillets
in a 9-in. (23-cm) pie plate.
Spread with ½ cup salsa.
Generously sprinkle with
2 tbsp grated Parmesan.
Bake, uncovered, at 425°F (220°C) until
bubbling, 8 to 12 min. *Serves 3.*

FLORIDA FISH BAKE

Place 4 fish fillets, fresh or frozen,
on separate pieces of foil.
Top each with 1 tsp butter,
1 tbsp orange juice concentrate and
1 chopped green onion.
Wrap and seal.
Bake at 450°F (230°C), 10 to 15 min. for fresh
fish or 20 to 25 min. for frozen fish.
Serves 4.

PESTO FISH BAKE

Place fish fillets on a baking sheet.
Spread with pesto.
Sprinkle with grated Parmesan.
Bake at 450°F (230°C) until fish flakes
easily, about 5 to 8 min.

FAST MEDITERRANEAN MICROWAVE

Lightly brush both sides of 1 lb (500 g) fish
fillets with olive oil. Arrange in a shallow
microwave-safe dish, overlapping thin edges.
Top with 2 sliced tomatoes,
¼ cup sliced black olives, 1 tbsp capers,
1 tbsp chopped parsley
and pinches of salt and pepper.
Drizzle with 2 tbsp white wine.
Microwave, covered, on high, 4 to 5 min.
Let stand, covered, 2 min. *Serves 3.*

FAST MEDITERRANEAN MICROWAVE

FISH STEAKS

Fish steaks are the fastest "steak" you can cook. Use halibut, tuna, salmon or your favorite fish steak. Recipes are for 4 steaks (unless otherwise noted), 1-in. (2.5-cm) thick. See also SALMON STEAKS.

TARRAGON BUTTER

Broil or barbecue fish for 4 min. Turn.
Spread with 2 tbsp butter blended
 with 1 crushed garlic clove,
 ½ tsp dried tarragon and pinch of pepper.
Broil or barbecue 4 to 5 more min.

CREAMY FRENCH

Broil fish for 3 min. Turn.
Spread with ¼ cup mayonnaise blended
 with 1 tbsp grainy Dijon and
 1 tbsp chopped parsley. Broil 6 more min.

ANCHOVY-PARSLEY

Sauté fish in 2 tbsp butter stirred with
 1 tbsp anchovy paste over medium heat,
 4 to 5 min. per side.
Sprinkle with finely chopped fresh parsley.

FIERY ORIENTAL

Stir 1½ tbsp sesame oil with
 1 tsp soy sauce and ¼ tsp cayenne.
 Brush on both sides of fish.
Broil or barbecue for 4 to 5 min. per side.

GINGER-LIME

Sauté fish in 1 tbsp vegetable oil or butter
 over medium heat, 4 min. Turn.
Drizzle with 3 tbsp lime juice blended
 with 1 tbsp finely chopped candied ginger.
Sauté 4 to 6 more min.

PESTO BUTTER

Sauté fish in 1 tbsp butter, 4 to 5 min. per side.
Blend 2 tbsp pesto with 1 tbsp butter.
 Spoon over hot fish.

KID-PLEASING STEAKS

Place steaks in a lightly greased baking dish.
 Spread each steak with
 1 tbsp mild salsa or spaghetti sauce.
Sprinkle with 1 tbsp grated Parmesan
 or mozzarella.
Bake, uncovered, at 450°F (230°C),
 12 to 14 min.

MEDITERRANEAN FISH STEAKS

Stir 19-oz can drained Italian-style
 tomatoes with 1 tbsp olive oil,
 1 chopped celery stalk, 3 sliced green
 onions, ½ cup black olives and
 ¼ tsp cayenne.
Pour over fish steaks in a baking pan just
 large enough to hold them.
Cover and bake, at 425°F (220°C), until fish
 flakes, 30 to 40 min. Baste often.

TERIYAKI STEAKS

In a pie plate, stir 2 tbsp teriyaki sauce with
 2 tbsp orange juice concentrate and
 ¼ tsp pepper. Place 3 steaks in sauce.
Cover, microwave, on medium, 7 to 8 min.
 Turn steaks partway through. Let stand,
 covered, 5 min. *Serves 3.*

LIGHT 'N' CREAMY CHUTNEY

Sauté fish in 1 tbsp butter over medium heat,
 4 to 5 min. per side.
Blend ½ cup plain yogurt with
 2 tbsp mango chutney and
 pinch of pepper. Spoon over fish.

FISH STICKS

Fish sticks rank right up there with pizza as a child's favorite dinner.
We baked all our gussied-up versions of frozen fillets at 400°F (200°C) for 13 to 15 minutes.

CHEDDAR

Place fish sticks on a baking sheet and
  sprinkle with finely grated cheddar or top
  with a strip of your favorite sliced cheese.
Add pinches of hot red pepper flakes,
  if you like.

SURPRISE THAI

Spread each fish stick with thick peanut sauce.
Place on a baking sheet and sprinkle with
  chopped fresh coriander or dried parsley.

ORIENTAL

Drizzle a few drops of soy sauce
  over fish sticks.
Place on a baking sheet and add pinches of
  ginger, garlic powder and sesame seeds.

DIJON-SWISS

Thinly spread Dijon on fish sticks.
Place on a baking sheet and sprinkle with
  finely grated Swiss cheese.

PIZZA PLEASER

Place fish sticks on a baking sheet.
Spoon about 1 tbsp spaghetti sauce or hot
  salsa on each.
Sprinkle with finely grated mozzarella
  or Monterey Jack.

BARBECUE & BACON

Drizzle fish sticks with barbecue sauce.
Place on a baking sheet.
Sprinkle with crumbled cooked bacon or
  bacon bits.

HOT CAJUN

Sprinkle fish sticks with generous pinches
  of garlic powder, white pepper,
  black pepper and cayenne.
Serve with sour cream to soothe the palate.

INDIAN

Sprinkle fish sticks with curry powder.
Serve with mango chutney or yogurt.

CUCUMBER & DILL

Roll fish sticks in creamy cucumber dressing.
Place on a baking sheet and generously
  sprinkle with dried dillweed.

CAESAR PARMESAN

Roll fish sticks in
  creamy-style Caesar dressing.
Place on a baking sheet.
Sprinkle with grated Parmesan and
  pinch of pepper.

G is for Garlic...

PEPPERED WILD RICE, (see recipe page 81) a confetti of diced sweet peppers and nutty-flavored wild rice, is a most welcome companion to roast chicken, turkey or duck.

GRAINS

*Fast-fixing grains are adding healthy texture to everyday dinners.
Thanks to new quick-cooking wild rice, bulgur and quinoa, it's faster to do a toss or salad of one of
these nutrient-rich grains than to boil pasta. See also* COUSCOUS, OATS *and* RICE.

FRUIT & NUT BULGUR

Toast $\frac{1}{2}$ cup slivered almonds.
Whisk $\frac{1}{3}$ cup vegetable oil with
    grated peel from 1 lemon and 1 orange,
    2 tbsp lemon juice and $\frac{1}{4}$ tsp cinnamon.
Toss with 1 cup cooked bulgur, 2 sliced green
    onions and 2 chopped nectarines.
Sprinkle with toasted nuts. *Serves 4 to 6.*

CREAMY MILLET PORRIDGE

Bring 1$\frac{1}{4}$ cups water, $\frac{1}{4}$ cup milk, 1 tbsp
    brown sugar and $\frac{1}{4}$ tsp salt to a boil.
Add $\frac{1}{2}$ cup millet.
Simmer, covered, 35 to 40 min. or until soft
    and liquid is absorbed.
    Stir often, especially as it thickens.
Serve with milk and maple syrup. *Serves 1.*

QUINOA PILAF

Sauté 1 tbsp minced garlic and 1 chopped
    onion in 1 tbsp butter or oil for 5 min.
Add 1 cup well-rinsed quinoa, 1 tsp cumin,
    $\frac{1}{4}$ tsp salt and $\frac{1}{4}$ tsp cayenne.
Stir for 2 min. Add 2 cups chicken or
    vegetable bouillon and bring to a boil.
Simmer, covered, until almost all liquid is
    absorbed, about 15 to 18 min. Stir
    occasionally. Let stand, covered, 5 min.
Fluff with a fork. Sprinkle with parsley.
    Serve with a green vegetable and chicken.
    Or stir in Parmesan for a vegetarian entrée.
    Serves 2.

BULGUR PILAF

In a large saucepan, melt $\frac{1}{4}$ cup butter.
Add 2 cups bulgur and stir for 3 min.
Stir in 1 chopped onion, 2 cups beef or
    vegetable bouillon, 2 cups water and
    2 tbsp lemon juice. Bring to a boil.
Reduce heat and cook, covered, stirring
    often, until liquid is absorbed, about
    10 min. Add pinch of pepper. *Serves 4.*

LEMONY KASHA

In a large frying pan, heat 2 tbsp butter.
Add 2 crushed garlic cloves and
    1 chopped onion. Sauté 5 min.
Add 1 cup whole kasha, 2 cups water
    and $\frac{1}{2}$ tsp salt. Bring to a boil.
Cover, simmer until kasha is tender, about
    10 min.
Whisk $\frac{1}{4}$ cup olive oil with 2 tbsp lemon
    juice and toss with kasha. *Serves 4.*

WILD RICE WITH HORSERADISH

Melt 2 tbsp butter in a large saucepan.
When bubbling, add 1 cup wild rice,
    1 cup brown rice, 3$\frac{1}{2}$ cups water,
    1 tbsp horseradish and $\frac{1}{2}$ tsp salt.
Cover and bring to a boil. Reduce heat to low.
    Simmer until rice is tender, about 40 min.
Stir in $\frac{1}{4}$ cup chopped parsley.
    Makes 4 cups.

PEPPERED WILD RICE

Sauté 1 chopped red pepper and
1 chopped yellow pepper in
1 tbsp butter over medium heat.
When cooked, but still firm, stir in
2 cups hot cooked wild rice,
2 thinly sliced green onions and ¼ tsp salt.
Makes 3 cups.

TABBOULEH WITH FRESH MINT

Cover 1 cup bulgur with boiling water.
Let soak 10 min. Drain well.
Stir 2 tbsp olive oil with juice from 1 small
lemon, 1 tsp sugar and ½ to 1 tsp salt.
Stir into bulgur with 3 seeded chopped firm
tomatoes and ½ cup coarsely chopped
mint, ¼ cup chopped parsley and
3 thinly sliced green onions.
Serve right away or refrigerate, covered, up to
1 day. *Makes 4 cups.*

CUMIN-SPICED CRUNCHY SALAD

Place 1 thinly sliced large carrot
and place in a large mixing bowl.
Add 1 cup coarse bulgur and cover
generously with water.
Let stand until bulgur is tender, about
20 min. Then drain well.
Whisk 2 tbsp bottled or homemade
vinaigrette salad dressing with
½ tsp cumin.
Stir into bulgur mixture with
¼ to ½ cup raisins or almonds.
Serve at room temperature sprinkled with
chopped fresh coriander or parsley.
Makes 3 cups.

CURRIED WILD RICE

Stir ½ cup light sour cream with
½ tsp curry powder or cumin.
Then stir in 2 cups cooked wild rice,
½ cup thinly sliced celery,
1 chopped seeded tomato,
¼ cup chopped fresh coriander and
2 sliced green onions.
Serve right away or refrigerate. *Makes 3 cups.*

Peppered Wild Rice

GREEN BEANS

Green beans have such a smooth taste they can accompany almost any dish.
For a little glamour, check out our ways to dress them for a starring role at the table.

GREEN BEANS WITH CUMIN VINAIGRETTE

Boil 1 lb (500 g) trimmed green beans,
uncovered, until tender-crisp, about
3 min. Place in a salad bowl with
1 sliced red pepper and 1 sliced onion.
Whisk ¼ cup vegetable oil with
2 tbsp tarragon vinegar or white vinegar,
1 crushed garlic clove, 1 tsp Dijon,
1 tsp cumin and pinch of pepper.
Toss with vegetables. *Serves 4.*

ORIENTAL WARM BEAN & PEA SALAD

Boil 1 lb (500 g) trimmed green beans,
uncovered, 2 min.
Add 2 cups shelled sweet peas.
Cook until tender-crisp, about 1 min.
Whisk 1 tbsp vegetable oil with
1 tbsp sesame oil, 1 tbsp soy sauce,
½ tsp grated fresh ginger and pinches of
salt and pepper. Drain beans and peas.
Toss with dressing. Garnish with
1 chopped red pepper. *Serves 6.*

TARRAGON GREEN BEANS

Boil 1 lb (500 g) trimmed green beans,
uncovered, until tender-crisp, about 3 min.
Whisk ¼ cup vegetable oil with
2 tbsp tarragon vinegar or white vinegar,
1 crushed garlic clove, ½ tsp dried basil,
¼ tsp dried tarragon and pinches of salt,
pepper and sugar.
Toss with beans and 2 chopped tomatoes.
Serves 4.

LEMONY GREEN BEANS

Boil ½ lb (250 g) green beans, until tender-
crisp, 3 to 5 min. Drain.
Stir in 1 tbsp butter, 1 tsp lemon juice and
1 to 2 tbsp chopped Italian parsley or
fresh coriander. *Serves 2 to 3.*

SLIVERED ALMONDS & BEANS

Sauté ⅓ cup slivered almonds in
2 tbsp butter.
Add 3 cups cooked green beans. Stir until
coated. *Serves 4 to 6.*

HOT ALMOND CRUNCH

Sauté 3 sliced garlic cloves and
½ cup sliced almonds in 2 tbsp olive oil
until golden.
Add 3 cups cooked green beans and 1 tbsp
Worcestershire. Stir until hot. *Serves 4 to 6.*

MICROWAVE MUSHROOMS & DILLED BEANS

Place 1 cup sliced mushrooms with
2 tbsp butter and 2 tbsp chopped
fresh dill in an 8-cup (2-L) microwave-safe
casserole dish.
Microwave, covered, on high, 1 min.
Stir in 10-oz (300-g) pkg frozen green
beans and pinches of salt and pepper.
Cover and microwave, on high, 4 min., until
tender-crisp. Stir partway through.
Sprinkle with 2 tbsp toasted sliced almonds.
Serves 4.

GARLIC PARMESAN TOSS

Sauté 1 crushed garlic clove in ½ tbsp butter.
Add 2 cups cooked green beans.
    Stir-fry until hot.
Toss with ¼ tsp dried basil, pinch of oregano
    and 3 tbsp grated Parmesan. *Serves 3.*

MICROWAVE HERB SAUCE FOR BEANS

Stir ½ cup sour cream with
    ¼ cup mayonnaise, 2 tbsp chopped
    parsley, 2 tbsp chopped fresh dill,
    1 sliced green onion and pinches of salt
    and pepper in a microwave-safe bowl.
Microwave, uncovered, on medium, 30 sec.
    Stir. Microwave for 40 more sec.
Serve over green beans. *Makes 1 cup.*

MICROWAVE NEW POTATO-BEAN NIÇOISE

Place 2 cups sliced green beans with
    4 thinly sliced unpeeled red-skinned
    potatoes and ¼ cup water in a 12-cup
    (3-L) microwave-safe casserole dish.
Microwave, covered, on high, 6 to 8 min.
    Stir partway through.
Meanwhile, whisk 3 tbsp olive oil with
    1 tbsp red wine vinegar,
    2 chopped anchovy fillets and
    pinches of salt and pepper.
Drain cooked vegetables. Toss with oil
    mixture and ¼ cup sliced black olives.
    Serves 4.

MICROWAVE HERB SAUCE ON GREEN BEANS

H is for Hot Dog...

SPICY HAM JAMBALAYA, *(see recipe*
page 87) a delightful mingling of cooked
ham, rice and spices, delivers full
Southern flavor in just 30 minutes.

HAM ◆ Cooked

Maximize dinner leftovers by adding bits of ham to spicy rice for a fast jambalaya or tuck into eggs for a Spanish Scramble.

INSTANT CURRY SAUCE

Heat 10-oz can cream of celery soup with
½ cup water and 1 tsp curry powder.
Add 2 cups chopped ham and 1 cup peas.
Simmer, covered, 5 min. Pour over cooked
pasta or rice. *Serves 2.*

PERFECT PÂTÉ

In a food processor, purée 1 cup cubed ham
with ¼ cup butter, ½ tsp Dijon and
pinch of cayenne.
Serve on crackers. *Makes 1 cup.*

CREAMY CRUNCHY SALAD

Blend ⅓ cup light mayonnaise with
½ tsp curry powder.
Stir in 1 cup diced ham, 1 chopped celery
stalk, 1 finely chopped carrot and
2 sliced green onions.
Serve on lettuce or spoon into pitas.
Makes 1½ cups.

EASY FRIED RICE 'N' HAM

Heat 2 tsp vegetable oil and 1 crushed garlic
clove in a frying pan over medium heat.
Add 2 cups cooked rice and
1 to 2 tbsp soy sauce. Stir often for 2 min.
Stir in 1 cup chopped ham,
1 cup frozen mixed vegetables and
½ tsp cayenne.
Sauté until hot, about 4 min. *Makes 4 cups.*

SPANISH SCRAMBLE

Heat 1 tbsp olive oil with 1 crushed garlic
clove in a large frying pan.
Stir in 1 chopped onion, 1 diced green
pepper and 1 chopped cooked potato.
Stir over medium heat until potato is golden.
Whisk 6 eggs with 3 tbsp water, ¼ tsp salt
and ¼ tsp pepper. Add to pan along with 1
cup chopped ham. Stir until almost set.
Sprinkle with 2 tbsp grated Parmesan and
pinch of paprika.
Broil in oven until golden. *Serves 3.*

TWICE-BAKED POTATOES

Slice 4 baked potatoes in half. Scoop out,
leaving ¼-in. (0.5-cm) shell.
Mash potatoes and stir in 1 cup chopped
ham, ½ cup light sour cream, 2 sliced
green onions, ½ tsp salt and ¼ tsp pepper.
Fill shells. Drizzle with 1 tbsp melted butter
and sprinkle with grated Parmesan.
Microwave, on high, until hot, about 5 min.
Broil until tops are golden. *Makes 8 halves.*

SPUDS & HAM HASH

Heat 1 tbsp butter in a frying pan.
Add 1 chopped onion,
2 finely chopped cooked potatoes,
½ tsp salt and ¼ tsp pepper.
Stir over medium heat until browned.
Add 1 cup chopped ham and 1 cup milk.
Stir until potatoes are soft. *Serves 3.*

A B C D E F G H I J K L M N O P Q R S T U V W X Y Z

SPICY HAM JAMBALAYA

Sauté 1 chopped onion with
   2 crushed garlic cloves,
   1 cup chopped red or green pepper,
   1 cup chopped celery and
   2 tsp dried thyme in 2 tbsp vegetable oil
   until onion is soft, about 5 min.
Stir in 1½ cups uncooked rice,
   3 cups chicken bouillon,
   1 tsp hot pepper sauce,
   2 whole bay leaves,
   2 chopped, peeled and seeded tomatoes
   and 2 cups cubed smoked ham.
Bring to a boil. Simmer, covered, 25 min or
   until liquid is absorbed. *Serves 4 to 6.*

THIN & CRISPY PIZZA

Slice 1 onion and 1 green pepper.
Sauté with 1 crushed garlic clove in
   1 tbsp olive oil until peppers are soft.
Stir in 1 cup chopped ham.
Spread on 4 (6-in./15-cm) tortillas.
   Sprinkle with 1½ cups grated fontina
   cheese and pinch of cayenne.
Bake at 450°F (230°C), 8 to 10 min.
   Makes 4 pizzas.

LINGUINE WITH HAM & PEAS

Sauté 1 crushed garlic clove in 1 tsp butter.
Stir in 1 cup chopped ham
   and 1 cup frozen peas.
When hot, stir in 1 cup light sour cream
   and 2 sliced green onions.
Toss with ½ lb (225 g) cooked linguine.
   Add grated Parmesan. *Serves 4.*

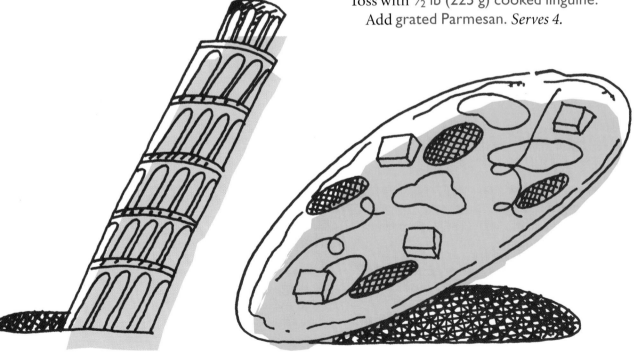

Thin & Crispy Pizza

HAM STEAKS

Ham is traditional Easter fare, but why not ham it up any time of the year. Here's some easy routes with precooked ham steaks from quickly glazed to curried-fruit coated.

COUNTRY HAM STEAKS

Melt 1 tbsp butter in a large frying pan.
Add 4 ham steaks. Cook over medium heat
   until lightly browned on both sides.
Stir ¼ cup Dijon with ¼ cup sour cream,
   2 tsp grated orange peel and ¼ tsp dried
   rosemary. Dollop on ham. *Serves 4.*

MUSTARD-GLAZED STEAKS

Place 2 ham steaks in a shallow dish.
Stir ½ cup brown sugar with ¾ tsp dry
   mustard, 1 tbsp flour and 1 tbsp vinegar.
Spread over steaks.
Bake at 425°F (220°C), basting often with
   glaze until hot, 15 to 20 min. *Serves 2.*

BAKED HAM WITH CURRIED FRUIT

Place 2 ham steaks , ¾ in. (2 cm) thick, on a
   pie plate. Spread with 2 tbsp liquid honey
   stirred with 2 tbsp Dijon.
Bake, uncovered, at 350°F (180°C), 40 min.,
   basting occasionally.
Meanwhile, stir 14-oz can drained pineapple
   chunks with 14-oz can drained fruit
   cocktail in a small baking dish.
Blend 3 tbsp room-temperature butter with
   ¼ cup brown sugar and
   ½ tsp curry powder. Dot over fruit.
Cover and bake with ham, at 350°F (180°C),
   30 min. Stir occasionally. Spoon over ham.
   Serves 2.

HAM WITH APPLE GLAZE

Whisk ¼ cup apple jelly with
   ¼ tsp curry powder.
Brush over 4 ham steaks, ½ in. (1 cm) thick.
Broil for 3 min. Turn and brush again. Broil
   until heated through, 2 to 3 more min.
Serve with remaining glaze spooned over top.
   Serves 4.

MICROWAVE HAM WITH CRANBERRIES

Slash outside edges of 2 ham steaks and place
   in a microwave-safe dish.
Top each with 2 orange slices.
   Scatter ¼ cup cranberries over top.
   Sprinkle with 1 tbsp brown sugar.
   Pour ⅓ cup orange juice around ham.
Microwave, covered, on high, 1 min. Then
   covered, on medium, 2 min. Spoon orange
   juice over ham. Cover and microwave, on
   medium, 2 more min. *Serves 2.*

HAM WITH FRUIT SAUCE

Heat 4 ham steaks, ½ in. (1 cm) thick,
   in ½ tbsp butter.
Meanwhile, pour juice from 10-oz can fruit
   cocktail into a saucepan. Remove 2 tbsp
   juice and stir with 1 tbsp cornstarch,
   1½ tbsp Dijon and pinch of ginger.
Add to juice in pan. Stir constantly over
   medium heat, until thick. Add drained
   fruit. Stir often until hot. Spoon over ham.
   Serves 4.

Ham Steaks with Creamy Mustard Sauce

Whisk ¼ cup sour cream with
2 tsp regular mustard and
¼ tsp dried dillweed.
Broil 4 ham steaks, ½ in. (1 cm) thick, 3 min.
Turn steaks and lavishly cover with
mustard sauce. Continue broiling until
heated through, 2 to 3 more min. *Serves 4.*

Dijon-Glazed Ham

Place 2 large ham steaks on 2 large pieces
of foil.
Stir 2 tbsp orange marmalade with
1 tbsp Dijon and 1 tsp brown sugar.
Spread over ham. Seal foil, tent fashion.
Bake at 425°F (220°C), until hot, 10 to 15 min.
Open foil. Broil ham until bubbly, 3 to 5 min.
Wonderful with broccoli. *Serves 4.*

Southwest Microwave Ham

Slash outside edges of 2 ham steaks
and place in a microwave-safe dish.
Stir 1 cup drained canned tomatoes with
3 tbsp salsa. Crush tomatoes slightly.
Pour over ham.
Microwave, covered, on high, 1 min. Then
covered, on medium, 4 min., spooning
tomato mixture over ham partway through.
Sprinkle with ½ cup grated mozzarella. *Serves 2.*

Maple-Glazed Steaks

Stir 2 tbsp rye whiskey or rum with
2 tbsp maple syrup.
Brush over 4 ham steaks.
Broil or grill, turning once and brushing
often with maple mixture, until lightly
browned. *Serves 4.*

Maple-Glazed Steaks

Hot Dogs

Soft, mild and easy to eat, hot dogs have a natural appeal for kids of any age.
Beyond wrapping them in buns, there's a variety of ways to brighten them for dinner.

Easy Mac 'n' Cheese

Heat 3 cups milk just until piping hot.
Stir in 1 tbsp regular mustard and
   1 tbsp butter.
Add 1½ cups uncooked macaroni and
   4 sliced wieners.
Simmer, covered, over low heat, stirring
   often, until macaroni is tender, about
   20 min.
Stir in 2 cups grated cheddar until melted.
   Serves 4.

Hot Macaroni Salad

Cook 2 cups macaroni with 4 sliced wieners
   in boiling water, 10 min. Drain.
Immediately stir in ½ cup mayonnaise,
   ½ cup sour cream or yogurt and
   ¼ cup pickle relish. *Makes 5 cups.*

Sweet 'n' Sour Dinner

In a frying pan, stir 2 tbsp sugar with
   3 tbsp cornstarch. Gradually stir in
   juice from 14-oz can pineapple chunks.
Place over medium heat. Stir often for 3 min.
Add pineapple, 6 sliced wieners,
   1 chopped green pepper,
   2 tbsp vinegar and 2 tbsp soy sauce.
Stir often until thickened, about 5 min.
Great on rice. *Serves 4.*

Soothing Turkey Pilaf

In a saucepan over medium heat, stir
   10-oz can cream of chicken soup with
   1¾ cups water and ½ tsp poultry
   seasoning. Bring to a boil, whisking often.
Stir in 6 chopped turkey wieners,
   1 cup uncooked rice and
   2 sliced celery stalks. Cover, reduce heat
   and simmer, 25 min. *Serves 4.*

Skillet Spanish Rice

In a large frying pan, bring 28-oz can
   undrained tomatoes to a boil.
Stir in 4 sliced wieners,
   1 cup uncooked rice,
   1 chopped zucchini,
   ½ tsp salt or garlic salt and
   ½ tsp dried thyme.
Cover and simmer for 25 min. *Serves 2 to 4.*

Microwave New-Style Quiche

Spread out 4 sliced wieners in a 9-in.
   (23-cm) pie plate. Top with
   1½ cups grated mozzarella or cheddar.
Whisk 6 eggs with ¼ cup milk,
   1 tsp mustard and ½ tsp Italian seasoning.
   Pour over cheese.
Microwave, uncovered, on medium, 11 min.,
   stirring after 3 and 6 min.
   Cover and let stand for 3 min.
Or bake in 400°F (200°C) oven, 30 min.
   Serves 4 to 6.

Sweet 'n' Sour Dinner

HOT BARBECUED RICE

In a saucepan, bring 1½ cups water,
  ½ cup barbecue sauce, 1 chopped onion
  and ½ tsp salt to a boil.
Add 1 cup uncooked rice, 4 sliced wieners
  and 1 chopped green pepper.
Cover and simmer for 20 to 25 min. Stir in
  ¼ cup grated Parmesan. *Makes 5 cups.*

SUPPER SPAGHETTI TOSS

Combine 4 thinly sliced wieners,
  1 cup spaghetti sauce and 1 cup frozen
  mixed vegetables or peas in a saucepan.
Cover and cook over medium heat, stirring
  often, until hot, about 5 to 8 min.
Or heat in microwave, covered, on high,
  5 min., stirring partway through.
Toss with cooked spaghetti. *Makes 2 cups.*

SPEEDY DINNER PIZZA

Lightly spread a store-bought pizza crust
  with pizza sauce. Cover with thinly sliced
  wieners and grated mozzarella.
Bake on a baking sheet at 450°F (230°C),
  12 to 15 min. *Serves 4.*

MICROWAVE FAJITA DOGS

Stir 1 sliced onion with ⅓ cup salsa in a
  microwave-safe dish.
Microwave, covered, on high, 2 min.
Stir in 4 thinly sliced wieners,
  1 green pepper, cut into strips, and
  ½ tsp chili powder.
Microwave, covered, on high, 4 min., stirring
  partway through.
Spoon on tortilla. Top with sour cream and
  wrap. *Serves 4.*

J is for Jam . . .

Hot peppers and salsa are mixed right into the beef
in this SPICY JALAPEÑO BURGER *(see recipe page 94).*
Beneath a topping of alfalfa sprouts, avocado and
gooey cheese, a juicy, fiery burger awaits.

JALAPEÑOS

Some like it hot! Bring a taste of Mexico to your dishes with fresh jalapeños or a can of hot green chilies to spice up everything from soups to scones.

FABULOUS CHILI DIP

In a food processor, whirl 8-oz (250-g) pkg cream cheese with 2 tbsp juice drained from 19-oz can tomatoes and 1 crushed garlic clove.

Remove to a bowl.

Stir in 19-oz can chopped drained tomatoes and 4-oz can drained chopped green chilies. *Makes 2 cups.*

JALAPEÑO CHICKEN SOUP

Heat 1 finely chopped seeded jalapeño with 10-oz can cream of chicken soup and 1 cup water.

Heat, stirring often, until hot.

Top with crushed tortilla chips.
Serves 2.

MEXICAN SALSA

Heat 19-oz can chopped drained tomatoes with 7½-oz can tomato sauce,
1 chopped onion,
4-oz can drained chopped green chilies,
1 crushed garlic clove,
1 tsp cumin,
½ tsp dried oregano and
pinches of salt and pepper until boiling.

Reduce heat to medium and cook, uncovered and stirring often until thick, about 10 min.

Great with ribs or chicken for dipping.
Makes 3 cups.

SPICY JALAPEÑO BURGER

Whisk 1 egg with ¼ tsp salt and ¼ tsp pepper. Add 1 lb (500 g) ground beef.

Blend 1 to 2 tbsp finely chopped seeded jalapeño with
¼ cup hot salsa and
1½ tsp cumin.

Add to beef mixture.

Sprinkle with ¼ cup dry bread crumbs. Work together and form into 4 patties.

Barbecue, grill or sauté until well done, 8 to 10 min. per side.

Top burgers with a slice of Monterey Jack cheese, salsa, sliced avocado and sprouts. *Makes 4.*

JALAPEÑO CORN BREAD

Beat 1 cup room-temperature butter with ½ cup granulated sugar and 2 eggs.

Beat in 3 cups milk.

Stir 2 cups all-purpose flour with
2 cups cornmeal,
2 tbsp baking powder and
1 tsp salt.

Make a well in centre and pour in milk mixture.

Add 3 tbsp chopped seeded jalapeños. Stir just until mixed. Turn into a greased 9x13-in. (3-L) baking pan.

Bake at 350°F (180°C) until bread springs back when touched, 35 to 40 min.
Makes 12 squares.

A B C D E F G H I J K L M N O P Q R S T U V W X Y Z

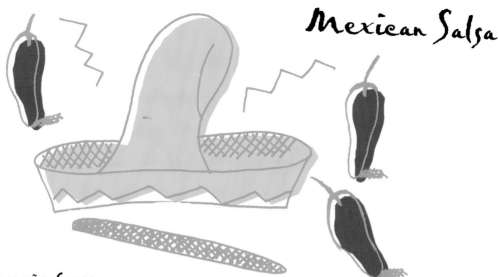

Mexican Salsa

APPLE-JALAPEÑO SALSA

Stir 2 chopped unpeeled apples with
    1 chopped seeded jalapeño or
    2 tbsp diced canned green chilies,
    1 sliced green onion,
    $\frac{1}{4}$ cup chopped fresh coriander,
    juice from 2 limes,
    $\frac{1}{2}$ tsp sugar and $\frac{1}{4}$ tsp salt.
Great with barbecued chicken. *Makes 3 cups.*

HOT PEPPER & CORIANDER SALSA

Combine 6 finely chopped seeded jalapeños
    with 5 finely chopped seeded tomatoes.
Stir 2 tbsp olive oil with 1 tbsp white vinegar,
    $\frac{1}{4}$ tsp salt and pinch of pepper.
Stir into vegetables with
    $\frac{1}{2}$ cup chopped fresh coriander.
Great on steaks or burgers. *Makes 2 cups.*

TACO SAUCE

Heat 2 cups crushed tomatoes with
    2 tbsp chopped seeded jalapeños,
    1 tsp cumin, $\frac{1}{2}$ tsp dried oregano
    and $\frac{1}{8}$ tsp garlic powder.
Spoon over spicy burgers, tacos or tortillas.
    Makes 2 cups.

JALAPEÑO VINAIGRETTE

Seed 1 small jalapeño and coarsely chop.
Combine in a blender with
    $\frac{1}{4}$ cup vegetable oil,
    2 tbsp lemon or lime juice,
    1 crushed garlic clove,
    $\frac{1}{4}$ tsp each salt, pepper and sugar.
Toss with romaine and grated cheddar or
    Asiago cheese. *Makes $\frac{1}{3}$ cup.*

CHEDDAR & JALAPEÑO SCONES

Stir 2 cups biscuit baking mix with
    1 cup grated old cheddar cheese,
    2 chopped seeded jalapeños and
    $\frac{1}{4}$ cup kernel corn.
Stir in $\frac{1}{2}$ cup milk.
Turn onto a floured surface.
    Flatten slightly, then fold in half twice.
Pat or roll dough into a 5½-in. (14-cm)
    circle. Cut into 12 wedges.
Bake on a greased baking pan at 425°F
    (220°C) until golden, 12 to 14 min.
    Makes 12 wedges.

Jams & Jellies

*From apricot to raspberry, what better way to preserve the fresh sweetness
of fruit than in jam. Here, a jar goes a long way beyond a spread for toast. Try our sauce
mixes on ribs, tortillas and chicken.*

Ginger Pancake Sauce

Melt ¼ cup ginger, orange or grapefruit
marmalade in a small saucepan over
low heat or in the microwave.
Stir in 1 cup yogurt.
Drizzle over warm gingerbread squares,
pancakes or French toast. *Makes 1 cup.*

French Toast Blueberry Topping

Combine ⅓ cup blueberry jam with
1 tbsp lemon juice, finely grated peel
of 1 lemon and pinch of nutmeg
in a small saucepan.
Stir over medium heat until warm.
Terrific topping for French toast.
Makes ⅓ cup.

Breakfast Tortilla-on-the-Go

Lightly spread 1 tortilla with
cream cheese or peanut butter,
then top with your favorite jam.
Roll up jelly-roll fashion. Great for eating on
the subway or in the car.

Pretty Chèvre Canapés

Buy a package of croustade cups
(tiny crisp pastry cups).
Just before serving, fill with creamy goat
cheese or whipped cream cheese,
then top with hot pepper jelly,
cranberry jelly or apricot jam.

Sweet & Sour Sophisticated Rib Sauce

Sauté 1 chopped onion and
1 chopped green pepper in
1 tbsp olive oil, 5 min.
Stir in ¾ cup apricot jam, ¼ cup ketchup,
1 tbsp vinegar and 1 tsp ginger.
Stir often until jam is melted, 3 min.
Generously baste over ribs for the last
15 min. of barbecuing or baking.
Makes 1¼ cups.

Apricot-Lemon Chicken Baste

Heat 2 tbsp apricot jam with
2 tbsp vegetable oil,
1 tbsp lemon juice and
pinches of salt and cayenne.
Stir until evenly blended.
Use to baste drumsticks. *Makes ¼ cup.*

Marmalade Ham Glaze

Heat ½ cup orange marmalade with
2 tbsp brown sugar, 2 tsp Dijon
and ¾ tsp ginger until blended.
Use as a baste for ham, pork tenderloin or
pork roast. *Makes ⅔ cup.*

SWEET & SOUR MEATBALLS

Bake **24** meatballs, homemade
or store-bought, at 350°F (180°C),
until brown, about 18 to 25 min.
Turn once.
In a large saucepan, stir
½ cup grape jelly with ½ cup ketchup
over low heat until jelly melts.
Add browned meatballs. Stir to coat.
Serve over cooked rice or with toothpicks as
appetizers. *Serves 6.*

GRIDIRON MEATBALLS

Mix 1½ lb (750 g) each ground beef
and veal with **1** cup chopped onion,
1 cup dry bread crumbs, **2** eggs,
2 tsp salt and ½ tsp pepper.
Shape into **30** (2-in./5-cm) meatballs.
Place on rack set in a shallow pan.
Bake at 375°F (190°C), until browned,
20 to 30 min., turning several times.
In a large saucepan, heat
10-oz bottle chili sauce with
9-oz jar grape jelly and
1 tbsp lemon juice, stirring often.
Add meatballs and bring to a boil.
Cover, reduce heat and simmer, 30 min.
Stir often. Serve over rice or spoon into
pita bread. *Makes 30 meatballs.*

RASPBERRY-COCONUT SQUARES

In a food processor, whirl
2 cups all-purpose flour with
1 tsp baking powder.
Add ½ cup room-temperature butter. Pulse
until fine crumbs form.
Add **2** beaten eggs and whirl until
dough forms.
Firmly press into a 9x13-in. (3-L) baking dish.
Spread with **1** cup seedless raspberry jam.
Beat **2** eggs with **1** cup granulated sugar.
Stir in ⅓ cup melted butter,
2 tsp vanilla, then
4 cups shredded coconut.
Spread over jam-coated base.
Bake at 350°F (180°C), until golden, 35 to 40
min. Cool on a rack. Cut into squares.
Makes 48.

Raspberry Coconut Squares

L is for Lemons…

Cool cucumber and luscious ripe tomatoes contrast with wholesome lentils in this trendy MIDDLE EASTERN SALAD (see recipe page 104). Fresh herbs and feta add unexpected freshness and creaminess.

LAMB CHOPS

Tiny lamb chops make a superb, yet fast, dinner.
Adorn them lightly, so nothing distracts from their natural taste.

PAN-SEARED LAMB CHOPS

Heat 2 tsp olive oil in a large frying pan over medium heat. Add 8 lamb chops.

Sauté until lightly browned, 3 to 5 min. per side. Transfer to a platter. Pour off fat.

Stir in 1 crushed garlic clove, 2 tbsp white wine, 1 tbsp Dijon and generous pinch of oregano. Stir constantly until hot. Spoon over chops. *Serves 4.*

MEDITERRANEAN LAMB SAUTÉ

Heat 1 tsp olive oil in a large frying pan over medium heat. Add 4 lamb chops.

Sauté until lightly browned, 3 to 5 min. per side. Transfer to a platter. Pour off fat.

Add 1 crushed garlic clove, 2 tbsp lemon juice, 6 halved cherry tomatoes, 1/4 cup black olives, 1/2 tsp dried oregano and 1/2 tsp dried rosemary. Stir until hot. Spoon over chops. Sprinkle with 1/4 cup crumbled feta. *Serves 2.*

HERB-CRUSTED LAMB CHOPS

Whisk 1 egg. In another dish, stir 1/3 cup dry bread crumbs with grated peel of 1 lemon, 1 tsp dried rosemary, 1 tsp dried thyme and pinch of pepper.

Individually dip 4 lamb chops in egg, then coat with crumb mixture. Place on waxed paper. Then cook chops in 1 tbsp olive oil in a large frying pan over medium heat, 3 min. per side for medium-rare. *Serves 2.*

10-MINUTE FRENCH LAMB CHOPS

Stir peel and juice from 1 lemon with 2 tbsp olive oil, 2 crushed garlic cloves, 1 tsp dried tarragon and pinches of salt and pepper. Brush over 4 lamb chops.

Broil or barbecue for 5 min.

Turn, brush generously and broil or barbecue for 4 more min.

Great with asparagus or broccoli. *Serves 2.*

LAMB CHOPS IN DEVILED SAUCE

Brown 4 lamb chops in 1 tsp vegetable oil. Remove from pan.

Add 1 crushed garlic clove and sauté 2 min.

Stir in 7 1/2-oz can tomato sauce, 2 tbsp brown sugar, 1 1/2 tsp Worcestershire, 1 1/2 tsp hot mustard, 1/4 tsp dried thyme, 1/4 tsp salt and dash of hot pepper sauce.

Bring to a boil. Place chops in sauce. Cover and cook for 5 min. Turn once. *Serves 2.*

LAMB CHOPS IN MUSTARD BUTTER

Place 4 oiled lamb chops on a greased broiler pan. Sprinkle with 1/4 tsp crushed rosemary and pinch of pepper.

Broil for 4 min. per side.

Stir 3 tbsp butter with 2 tbsp Dijon, grated peel of 1 orange and 1/2 tsp crushed rosemary.

When chops are finished cooking, place 1 tbsp butter mixture on top of each. *Serves 2.*

HONEY-ORANGE CHOPS

Brown 4 lamb chops in 1 tsp olive oil.
Add juice from 1 orange,
  1 tbsp liquid honey,
  ¼ tsp ginger and ¼ tsp curry powder.
  Stir until mixed.
Cook, uncovered, 2 to 3 min. per side.
  Serves 2.

GRILLED TARRAGON CHOPS

Place 8 lamb chops in a dish just large
  enough to hold them.
Whisk ⅓ cup vegetable oil with
  3 crushed garlic cloves,
  1 tsp dried tarragon and 1 tsp cumin.
Pour over chops. Cover and refrigerate for
  4 hours. Turn after 2 hours.
Barbecue or broil 5 min. per side, brushing
  often with marinade. *Serves 4.*

SPRING LAMB WITH RED WINE

Brown 4 lamb chops in 1 tsp olive oil.
Then add ½ cup red wine and
  2 tbsp chopped shallots.
Sprinkle with ½ tsp crushed rosemary and
  pinches of thyme, salt and cayenne.
Cook, uncovered, 2 min. per side. *Serves 2.*

LEMON-MINT CHOPS

Place 4 lamb chops on a greased broiler pan
  or barbecue.
Whisk 2 tbsp lemon juice with
  2 tbsp olive oil, 1 crushed garlic clove,
  ¼ tsp crushed dried mint and
  pinches of salt and pepper.
Brush over chops.
Barbecue or broil for 5 min. Turn, brush with
  marinade, broil for 4 min. *Serves 2.*

PAN-SEARED LAMB CHOPS

LEMONS

Lemons refresh many a dish. Their tart juice and peel brightens up everything from puddings to sauces to ice tea.

EVERLASTING LEMONADE

Dissolve 1 cup granulated sugar in
   ½ cup boiling water.
Stir in grated peel of 2 lemons and
   1¼ cups lemon juice (about 6 lemons).
Refrigerate.
For 1 glass, stir ⅓ cup lemonade syrup with
   ⅔ cup cold water.
For a pitcher, stir 2 cups syrup with 4 cups
   cold water.
   Makes 2 cups syrup.

ICED TEA PUNCH

Steep 8 tea bags in 4 cups boiling water,
   5 min. Remove bags.
Stir in ½ cup granulated sugar,
   grated peel and juice from 3 oranges
   and juice from 2 lemons.
Refrigerate until cold. *Makes 5½ cups.*

ICED TEA BASE

Steep 8 tea bags in 1½ cups boiling water,
   4 min. Remove bags.
Stir in 1 cup granulated sugar,
   1 tbsp grated lemon peel and
   1 cup lemon juice (about 5 lemons).
Store in refrigerator.
For 1 glass, stir ⅓ cup tea base with
   ¾ cup cold water.
For a pitcher, stir 2 cups tea base with
   5 cups cold water.
   Makes 3 cups base.

LEMON-PEPPER BUTTER

In a small saucepan, heat ¼ cup butter with
   2 tbsp lemon juice, ¼ tsp Worcestershire
   and generous pinches garlic powder and
   pepper until warm.
Spoon over fish steaks before grilling.
   Makes ⅓ cup.

GREEN VEGGIE DRESS-UP

Stir ½ cup grated Parmesan with
   grated peel of 1 lemon, 2 tbsp lemon juice,
   ¼ cup room-temperature butter,
   ¼ tsp salt and pinch of pepper.
Toss with piping hot green beans or peas.
   Makes ½ cup.

HOMEMADE HOT LEMON SAUCE

In a saucepan, stir ½ cup granulated sugar
   with 2 tbsp cornstarch.
Stir in 1 cup water, juice and peel from
   2 lemons and ¼ cup butter.
Bring to a boil, stirring often. Reduce heat
   and stir often until thickened, 5 to 7 min.
Drizzle over warm gingerbread or Christmas
   pudding. *Makes 1½ cups.*

CREAMY FRESH LEMON DRESSING

Whisk ⅓ cup lemon juice with 1 tbsp Dijon,
   3 tbsp mayonnaise, 2 crushed garlic cloves,
   ¼ tsp salt and ¼ tsp pepper.
Gradually whisk in ¾ cup olive oil.
   Makes 1¼ cups.

LEMONY ICE CREAM

Stir grated peel and juice from 1 lemon into
   2 cups soft vanilla ice cream.
Return to freezer until firm. *Serves 4.*

WARM LEMON PUDDING

In a food processor, whirl
   ⅔ cup granulated sugar with
   2 tbsp all-purpose flour,
   3 eggs, 1 cup milk,
   grated peel and juice from 1 large lemon
   and 1 tbsp room-temperature butter.
Pour into a 9-in. (23-cm) ungreased pie plate.
Bake at 325°F (160°C) until set, 25 to 30 min.
   Serves 6.

LEMON VINAIGRETTE DRESSING

Whisk ⅓ cup olive or vegetable oil with
   finely grated peel of half a lemon,
   2 tbsp lemon juice,
   ½ tsp dried oregano,
   ½ tsp sugar or liquid honey,
   1 large crushed garlic clove,
   ¼ tsp salt and ¼ tsp pepper.
Great tossed with mixed greens, a Greek
   salad, asparagus or green beans.
   Makes ½ cup.

EVERLASTING LEMONADE

Lentils

Lentils, quick-cooking legumes that don't need soaking, are high in fibre and nearly fat-free. Add them to soups, salads and stews for a protein-rich meal.

Red Lentil Dahl

Heat 1 tbsp olive oil.

Add 2 small chopped onions and 1 crushed garlic clove.

Sprinkle with ½ tsp curry powder or 1 tsp cumin. Sauté for 5 min.

Stir in ¾ cup red lentils (don't need rinsing), 2 cups chicken or vegetable bouillon and ½ tsp salt.

Bring to a boil and simmer, uncovered, 10 min. Stir often.

Spoon over hot rice or serve with vegetable curries. *Makes 2 cups.*

Bustling Burritos

Heat 1 tbsp vegetable oil with 1 chopped onion and 2 crushed garlic cloves and sauté for 3 min.

Sprinkle with 1½ tsp chili powder and ½ tsp cayenne.

Add ½ cup water. Boil gently, stirring often, until water is evaporated, about 5 to 8 min.

Meanwhile, mash 19-oz can rinsed drained lentils. Add to onion mixture and stir frequently until hot.

Stir in 1½ cups grated cheddar. Stir until melted.

Spoon in warm tortillas. Top with shredded lettuce, chopped tomatoes and green onions and roll up. *Makes 2½ cups.*

Lentil Italian Tomato Soup

Sauté 1 chopped onion and 1 crushed garlic clove in 1 tbsp olive oil until softened.

Stir in 1 cup red lentils, 2 cups chicken or vegetable broth or bouillon, 2 cups water and 19-oz can undrained Italian-flavored stewed tomatoes.

Bring to a boil, then cover and simmer, 10 min. Stir occasionally.

Serve with a dollop of sour cream and warm whole wheat pitas. *Makes 7 cups.*

Lamb-Lentil Burgers

Combine 1 lb (500 g) lean ground lamb with 19-oz can unrinsed well-drained lentils, ½ cup fine dry bread crumbs, 1 tbsp finely chopped garlic, ½ tsp salt, ¼ tsp pepper and 2 beaten eggs.

Shape into 6 patties. Sauté in 2 to 3 tbsp olive oil until browned, about 8 min. per side for medium-well. *Serves 6.*

Middle Eastern Salad

Whisk 2 tbsp olive oil with 2 tbsp red wine vinegar, 2 tsp Dijon and ½ tsp salt.

Stir in 19-oz can rinsed drained lentils, 2 chopped seeded tomatoes, ½ chopped English cucumber, 1 chopped onion, 1 crushed garlic clove and 2 tbsp chopped fresh dill or coriander.

Serve with feta or goat cheese crumbled over top. *Makes 3½ cups.*

A B C D E F G H I J K L M N O P Q R S T U V W X Y Z

FRESH TOMATO CURRY

Melt 1 tbsp butter. Add 1 chopped onion and
  2 crushed garlic cloves.
  Sauté over medium heat for 2 min.
Sprinkle with 2 tsp curry powder and add
  $\frac{1}{2}$ cup water.
Boil gently, stirring often, until most of
  the liquid evaporates, from 5 to 8 min.
Stir in 4 chopped large tomatoes and
  19-oz can rinsed drained lentils.
  Heat through. Taste and stir in $\frac{1}{2}$ tsp salt
  and $\frac{1}{2}$ tsp sugar, if needed.
For a creamy curry, stir in $\frac{1}{2}$ cup sour cream.
Sprinkle with chopped fresh coriander and
  serve over hot rice or scoop up in warm
  chapatis. *Makes 4 cups.*

SWIFT DINNER SALAD

Generously cover 2 cups
  green or brown lentils with water and
  bring to a boil. Boil gently, covered,
  from 30 to 35 min., then drain.
Stir in $\frac{1}{2}$ cup garlicky Italian dressing,
  4 chopped seeded tomatoes,
  2 chopped green peppers,
  $\frac{1}{2}$ tsp salt and $\frac{1}{2}$ tsp sugar.
Stir until coated. Serve warm or cold.
  Makes 8 cups.

NEW-STYLE MICROWAVE STEW

In a large microwave-safe dish, combine
  $\frac{1}{2}$ cup lentils, 1 chopped onion,
  1 chopped celery stalk, 1 chopped carrot,
  1 crushed garlic clove,
  19-oz can tomatoes with juice,
  4 cups chicken broth and $\frac{1}{4}$ tsp pepper.
Cover and microwave, on high, until boiling,
  15 to 20 min. Stir in $\frac{1}{4}$ cup long-grain rice.
Microwave, covered, on medium until
  lentils are tender, 35 min.
Stir in 3 sliced green onions. *Makes 6 cups.*

CURRIED LENTIL SOUP

In a large pot, melt 1 tbsp butter.
Stir in 1 chopped onion, 2 chopped carrots,
  2 chopped celery stalks, 2 crushed garlic
  cloves and 1 tbsp curry powder.
  Sauté, stirring often, 4 min.
Stir in 5 cups chicken broth and
  $1\frac{1}{4}$ cups red lentils.
Bring to a boil, stirring often. Reduce heat,
  cover and simmer until lentils soften,
  30 min. *Makes 7 cups.*

FRENCH LENTIL SALAD

Rinse 19-oz can lentils with cold water
  and drain well.
Whisk 2 tbsp olive oil with
  2 tbsp red wine vinegar, $\frac{1}{2}$ tsp Dijon,
  2 crushed garlic cloves, $\frac{1}{4}$ tsp dried thyme,
  $\frac{1}{4}$ tsp salt and $\frac{1}{4}$ tsp pepper.
Stir in lentils, $\frac{1}{2}$ cup chopped red onion,
  12-oz can drained kernel corn and
  1 chopped celery stalk.
Serve with whole-grain bread. *Makes 3 cups.*

Swift Dinner Salad

M is for Mushrooms...

Start with a package of macaroni and cheese and make this amazing VEGGIE BONUS (see recipe page 109) in 15 minutes. Besides crunch and good looks, red peppers add lots of vitamin C and beta-carotene. Include other vegetables and nutritionally balance this vegetarian dinner.

Meat ◆ Ground

Ground meat has always represented great value. Do think beyond beef, though, and try ground veal, lamb, pork or chicken in everything from burgers to chilies to meatballs. See also BEEF, GROUND.

1-2-3 Quick Chili

In a large saucepan, brown 1 lb (500 g)
   ground veal or beef in 2 tsp oil. Drain off fat.
Stir in 1 crushed garlic clove,
   2 tbsp chili powder, 1 tsp cumin,
   1 tsp dried oregano, 19-oz can drained
   kidney beans and 28-oz can undrained
   tomatoes. Cover and bring to a boil.
Reduce heat and simmer, 10 min. Stir often.
   Serves 4.

Low-Cal Microwave Spaghetti Dinner

Make a slit in a large spaghetti squash.
Microwave, on high, 15 min.
Meanwhile, sauté 1 lb (500 g) ground chicken
   until no pink remains.
Add 2 cups spaghetti sauce, 1 tsp Italian
   seasoning and ½ tsp hot red pepper
   flakes. Cover and simmer, stirring often.
Slice cooked squash in half. Remove seeds.
   Scrape squash from shell with a fork.
   Top with sauce. *Serves 3 to 4.*

Apple-Pork Burgers

Whisk 1 egg with 1½ tsp Dijon,
   ¼ tsp salt and pinch of pepper.
Stir in ⅔ cup thick applesauce and
   ½ cup dry bread crumbs.
Work in 1 lb (500 g) ground pork.
   Form into 4 to 6 patties.
Barbecue, broil or sauté, about 8 to 10 min.
   per side. *Makes 4 to 6.*

Russian Burgers

Whisk 1 egg with ¼ cup sour cream,
   1 finely chopped onion, 2 tbsp chopped
   fresh dill or ½ tsp dried dillweed,
   1 tbsp caraway seeds and
   pinches of salt and pepper.
Add 1 lb (500 g) ground beef and ½ lb
   (250 g) ground pork. Form into 6 patties.
Barbecue, broil or sauté, 8 to 10 min. per
   side. *Makes 6.*

Curried Burgers

Whisk 1 egg with ⅓ cup yogurt,
   2 tbsp chutney, 1 tsp Dijon, 1 tsp curry
   powder, ½ tsp salt and pinch of cayenne.
Stir in ½ cup dry bread crumbs.
Work in 1 lb (500 g) ground lamb, beef, pork
   or chicken. Form into 4 to 6 patties.
Barbecue, broil or sauté, about 8 to 10 min.
   per side. *Makes 4 to 6.*

Zesty California Burgers

Whisk 1 egg with 1 crushed garlic clove,
   finely grated peel of 1 orange,
   ½ cup sour cream, ½ tsp salt and
   pinch of pepper.
Stir in 3 sliced green onions and ⅓ cup
   dry bread crumbs.
Work in 1 lb (500 g) ground chicken,
   turkey or pork. Form into 4 to 6 patties.
Barbecue, broil or sauté, about 8 to 10 min.
   per side. *Makes 4 to 6.*

FAST CHICKEN TOSS

HEARTY DINNER PIZZA

Cook ½ lb (250 g) ground chicken and
2 crushed garlic cloves in 2 tsp olive oil.
Add 7½-oz can tomato sauce, 1 sliced green
onion, 1 julienned green pepper,
½ tsp dried oregano and ½ tsp dried basil.
Spread over 12-in. (30-cm) pizza crust.
Sprinkle with 2 cups grated mozzarella.
Bake at 475°F (240°C), 15 to 20 min. *Serves 4.*

SAVORY MEATBALLS

Whisk 1 egg with 2 tbsp milk. Work in
½ lb (250 g) each of ground veal and
ground pork, ¼ cup dry bread crumbs,
2 tsp paprika, 2 tsp marjoram,
¼ tsp salt and pinch of pepper.
Form into 1½-in. (3.5-cm) meatballs.
Place around outer rim of a 10-in. (25-cm)
microwave-safe dish.
Microwave, covered, on high, 8 to 10 min.
Turn partway through. *Serves 4.*

FAST CHICKEN TOSS

In a large saucepan, simmer
1 lb (500 g) ground chicken and
¼ cup chopped onion in ¼ cup water,
stirring often until chicken is no longer pink.
Add 2 cups spaghetti sauce, preferably with
mushrooms, 2 sliced celery stalks,
½ tsp Italian seasoning or ½ tsp dried
tarragon and ¼ tsp cayenne.
Cover, simmer, stirring often, 5 min.
Toss with noodles. *Serves 3 to 4.*

LIGHT 'N' EASY SPAGHETTI SAUCE

Sauté 1 lb (500 g) ground chicken or turkey
and 2 chopped onions in 1 tbsp olive oil
until no pink remains.
Add 14-oz can tomato sauce,
½ cup white wine, 1 tsp dried basil and
½ tsp dried sage or dried oregano.
Simmer, uncovered, stirring often,
8 to 10 min. *Makes 4 cups.*

Mushrooms

Whether you stuff, sauté or simmer them in soup, mushrooms are appealing and low-cal.
A 1½-cup serving supplies 25% of an adult's niacin needs, yet only 25 calories and no fat.

Mushroom & Ginger Soup

Bring 2 cups chicken bouillon,
   1 tbsp finely chopped fresh ginger,
   2 chopped green onions and
   ⅛ tsp hot red pepper flakes to a boil.
Simmer, covered, 5 min.
Add 2 cups sliced fresh mushrooms and
   simmer, covered, 5 min. *Serves 2.*

Marinated Mushrooms

Place 1 lb (500 g) small mushrooms,
   1 diced red pepper and
   2 sliced green onions in a bowl.
In another bowl, whisk ⅓ cup olive oil with
   2 tbsp red wine vinegar,
   2 crushed garlic cloves,
   ½ tsp dried oregano, ½ tsp dried basil and
   pinches of cayenne and salt.
Pour over mushrooms. Leave at room
   temperature, uncovered, at least 30 min.,
   or refrigerate, covered, up to 2 days. *Serves 4.*

Oriental Mushrooms & Green Beans

In a large frying pan, heat 1 tbsp light
   sesame oil or peanut oil.
Add 1 cup sliced mushrooms and sauté,
   2 min.
Add 3 cups cooked green beans,
   1 tbsp soy sauce and
   2 tbsp toasted sesame seeds.
   Stir until hot. *Serves 6.*

Grilled Pesto Mushrooms

Spoon ½ tbsp pesto each into
   12 mushroom caps on a broiler pan.
Top each with a small piece of cheddar.
Broil until hot, about 2 min. *Makes 12.*

Mushroom & Garlic Pasta

Cook 1 lb (450 g) penne following
   package directions.
Heat ⅓ cup olive oil in a frying pan over
   low heat.
Add 3 crushed garlic cloves and sauté, 3 min.
   Turn heat to medium.
Add 3 cups sliced mushrooms.
   Stir-fry for 3 min.
Toss with drained pasta and pinches of salt
   and pepper. Sprinkle with grated Parmesan.
   Serves 4.

Fresh Mushroom Rice

Bring 2 cups chicken bouillon to a boil in a
   saucepan.
Add 1 cup long-grain rice and ¼ tsp salt.
Cover and reduce heat to low. Cook 20 to 25
   min., until bouillon is absorbed.
Meanwhile, sauté 2 sliced green onions and
   6 finely chopped large mushrooms in
   2 tsp butter over medium heat, 5 min.
Toss with hot cooked rice and a sprinkle of
   grated Parmesan. *Serves 4.*

PROSCIUTTO & MUSHROOM SCRAMBLED EGGS

Sauté ⅓ cup sliced mushrooms in
  1 tsp butter in a frying pan over medium-
  high heat, 2 min. Remove from pan.
Scramble 4 eggs in 1 tsp butter in pan.
Stir in mushrooms, 2 tbsp julienned
  prosciutto and pinch of pepper. *Serves 2.*

MUSHROOM APPETIZERS

Remove stems from mushrooms and discard.
Brush mushroom caps with melted butter.
  Place stem-side up on a baking sheet
  lined with foil.
Fill each cap with grated cheese,
  then sprinkle with
  finely chopped small pepperoni and
  red peppers.
Top with thin slices of green onion.
Broil until cheese is melted.

TARRAGON-MUSHROOM SAUCE

Sauté 1 chopped onion and
  1 cup sliced mushrooms in
  2 tbsp butter until onions are soft.
Stir in 1 tsp cornstarch dissolved in
  ½ cup chicken bouillon and
  ¼ tsp dried tarragon. Stir over medium
  heat until thickened, about 4 min.
Wonderful over chicken. *Makes 1 cup.*

SHERRIED STROGANOFF SAUCE

Sauté 1 cup sliced mushrooms and
  1 crushed garlic clove in 1 tbsp butter
  over medium heat, 2 min.
Stir in 3 tbsp sherry and ¼ cup regular
  or light sour cream.
Toss with ½ lb (250 g) tortellini or other
  pasta. *Serves 2.*

Oriental Mushrooms & Green Beans

Mussels

Mussels are not only one of our least expensive seafoods, they're rich in protein, low in fat and cholesterol – perfect for a relaxing dinner or easy entertaining. Discard any mussels that do not open when cooked.

Appetizer Mussels

Purée ½ cup drained pimentos with
  dash of hot pepper sauce.
Steam 1 lb (500 g) mussels just until open.
Remove and discard top shells.
  Place bottoms holding mussels on a platter.
Spoon 1 tsp pimento sauce on top of each
  mussel. Sprinkle with chopped fresh basil
  or parsley. *Makes 24 appetizers.*

Mussels with Shallots & Wine

In a large saucepan, combine 1½ cups white
  wine with 3 tbsp chopped shallots,
  ¼ cup chopped fresh basil and generous
  pinch of cayenne. Boil gently, uncovered,
  5 min. Cook over medium heat until sauce
  is reduced to ½ cup, about 4 min.
Stir in 2 tbsp unsalted butter.
Add 4 lbs (2 kg) mussels. Cover, cook
  over medium heat, stirring once,
  until mussels open, 8 to 10 min. *Serves 3.*

Herbed Italian Mussels

In a large saucepan, combine
  19-oz can undrained Italian-stewed
  tomatoes with ½ cup white wine,
  ½ tsp hot red pepper flakes and
  ½ cup chopped parsley.
Boil, uncovered, stirring often, until thick.
  Add 3 lbs (1.5 kg) mussels. Cover. Cook
  over medium heat, stirring once, until
  mussels open, 8 to 10 min. *Serves 2.*

Mussels with Fresh Tomatoes

In a large saucepan, combine
  ½ cup white wine, 1 tbsp chopped garlic,
  3 chopped tomatoes, 3 sliced green
  onions and 2 chopped seeded jalapeños.
Boil gently, uncovered, 5 min.
Add 4 lbs (2 kg) mussels. Cover, cook over
  medium heat, stirring once, until mussels
  open, 8 min. Sprinkle with parsley. *Serves 3.*

Mussels & Rice

In a large saucepan, combine
  28-oz can undrained diced tomatoes with
  1 cup white wine, ½ cup instant rice,
  1 tsp dried basil and 1 tsp salt.
Cover and bring to a boil. Reduce heat to
  medium low. Cook, stirring often, until
  rice is tender, 5 to 10 min.
Add 3 lbs (1.5 kg) mussels. Cover, cook over
  medium heat, stirring several times, until
  mussels open, 8 to 10 min. *Serves 3.*

Portuguese Mussels

In a large saucepan, combine 1 chopped
  Spanish onion, 1 tbsp chopped garlic,
  2 smoked sausages, cut into julienne strips,
  and 1 cup white wine.
Boil gently, covered, 10 min. Stir often.
Stir in 3 cups sliced Swiss chard and
  4 lbs (2 kg) mussels. Cover, cook over
  medium heat, stirring several times, until
  mussels open, 8 to 10 min. *Serves 3.*

MICROWAVE MUSSELS

Arrange 1 lb (500 g) mussels around
    outside of a microwave-safe dish that is
    at least 12 in. (30 cm) wide.
Cover and microwave, on high, until mussels
    open, about 3 to 4 min. *Serves 1.*

SAFFRON MUSSELS

In a large wide saucepan, sauté
    ½ cup finely chopped shallots in
    1 tbsp butter for 5 min. Add ½ cup white
    wine and ½ tsp ground saffron.
Boil gently, stirring often, 5 min.
Then add 6 sliced green onions and
    4 lbs (2 kg) mussels. Cover, cook over
    medium heat, stirring once, until
    mussels open, 8 to 10 min.
Add a squeeze of lemon juice if you like.
    Serves 3.

FRENCH-HERBED MUSSELS

In a large wide saucepan, combine
    1 large chopped red onion with 1 cup
    white wine, 3 tbsp minced garlic, 2 tbsp
    balsamic vinegar and 1 tsp dried tarragon.
Boil gently, uncovered, 5 min. Add
    4 lbs (2 kg) mussels. Cover, cook over
    medium heat, stirring once, until mussels
    open, 8 to 10 min. *Serves 3.*

CURRIED ISLAND MUSSELS

In a large pan, boil 14-oz can coconut milk,
    1 chopped onion and 1 tbsp curry powder,
    uncovered, stirring often, until thick, 5 min.
Stir in 4 chopped seeded tomatoes and
    4 lbs (2 kg) mussels. Cover, cook over
    medium heat, stirring once, until mussels
    open, 8 to 10 min. Wonderful over rice.
    Serves 3.

MUSSELS WITH FRESH TOMATOES

N is for Nuts...

PRESTO CRAB SOUP (see recipe page 120) is a
3-ingredient wonder. We simply added high-protein
imitation crab pieces and slivers of fresh spinach to a
package of Oriental-style noodle soup and wound
up with this glamorous-looking supper soup.

Nuts

Add a hot 'n' fiery or sugar 'n' spice coating to nuts or toss with hot veggies – they're up to any festive occasion. Store nuts in an airtight container in the refrigerator or freezer.

Sugar Snap Peas & Cashews

Microwave 1 cup cashews, uncovered, on
    high, 3 min., until slightly toasted.
    Stir occasionally. Remove cashews.
Add 1 tsp butter to pan, then
    1 lb (500 g) sugar snap peas or snow peas.
Microwave, covered, on high, 2 to 3 min.,
    until peas are tender.
Stir twice during cooking. Toss with cashews.
    Add pinches of salt and pepper. *Serves 4.*

Cashew Butter

Melt 1 tbsp butter in a small frying pan.
Add ¼ cup coarsely chopped cashews,
    1 tsp lemon juice and generous pinches of
    dried basil and pepper. Stir over medium
    heat until nuts are lightly browned, 4 min.
Scatter over hot cooked asparagus or green
    beans. *Serves 2.*

Fiery Pecans

Blend 3 tbsp melted butter with
    1 tbsp Worcestershire,
    1 crushed garlic clove, 1 tsp salt,
    ¾ tsp cinnamon and ¼ tsp cayenne.
Add 1 lb (500 g) unsalted pecans or whole
    almonds and toss well. Spread out on an
    ungreased baking sheet.
Toast at 350°F (180°C) until lightly browned,
    10 min. Stir partway through. Cool
    completely. *Makes 6 cups.*

Spiced Mixed Nuts

Toss 10-oz can mixed nuts with
    1 tbsp olive oil.
Sprinkle with mixture of
    1 tsp chili powder, 1 tsp cumin,
    ½ tsp garlic powder and ¼ tsp cayenne.
    Spread out on an ungreased baking sheet.
Toast at 350°F (180°C), 10 min. Stir once.
    Makes 2 cups.

Sugar 'n' Spice Nuts

Beat 1 egg white until foamy.
Stir in 2 cups unsalted nuts, such as cashews,
    pecans or almonds, until coated.
Stir ¼ cup sugar with ½ tsp cinnamon,
    ½ tsp cayenne and ¼ tsp salt.
Toss with nuts until coated. Spread out on a
    greased baking sheet.
Bake at 325°F (160°C), stirring often, until
    golden, 20 to 25 min. Cool completely.
    Makes 2 cups.

Chili-Lime Peanuts

Stir peel and juice from 1 lime with
    2 cups roasted salted peanuts.
While stirring, sprinkle with 1 tsp chili
    powder, 1 tsp cumin and ¼ tsp cayenne.
Spread out on an ungreased baking sheet.
Bake at 325°F (160°C), stirring once, until
    nuts are dry, about 15 min. Nuts will
    become crispy when cool. *Makes 2 cups.*

A B C D E F G H I J K L M **N** O P Q R S T U V W X Y Z

TOASTED SPICED NUTS

Spread 2 cups unblanched almonds on an
ungreased baking sheet.
Drizzle with 1 tbsp olive oil and toss to coat.
Bake at 350°F (180°C), 5 min.
Sprinkle with mixture of ½ tsp cumin,
½ tsp curry powder, ½ tsp cinnamon,
¼ tsp ginger, ¼ tsp cayenne and ¼ tsp salt.
Toss and toast another 5 min. *Makes 2 cups.*

HOT SPICY PEANUTS

Stir ¼ tsp curry powder, ¼ tsp garlic
powder, ¼ tsp ground coriander and
pinch of cayenne into 2 tsp melted butter.
Toss with 1 cup roasted salted peanuts.
Spread out on an ungreased baking sheet.
Bake at 350°F (180°C), 8 min. Stir often.
Makes 1 cup.

FLAMBÉED BRANDIED NUTS

Stir 2 tbsp butter and ¼ cup brown sugar in
a small frying pan until sugar dissolves.
Add ½ cup pecans, cashews or mixed nuts.
Stir until bubbly. Remove from heat.
Immediately add 2 to 4 tbsp brandy or rum
and flambé. Then spoon over French
vanilla or coffee ice cream.

BOMBAY-SPICED CASHEWS

Stir 1 tbsp butter with 1 crushed garlic clove,
2 tsp curry powder, 1 tsp Worcestershire,
½ tsp chili powder and ¼ tsp cayenne in a
large frying pan over medium heat.
When bubbly, add 2 cups roasted salted
cashews and stir often until hot and
coated, 3 to 4 min.
Spread on paper towels to cool. *Makes 2 cups.*

SUGAR 'N' SPICE NUTS

O is for Oats...

Flavor-boosting is only part of the double return you get from
marinating lean pork chops in a zesty ORANGE-PEPPERCORN
MARINADE (see recipe page 133). Orange juice and wine are
the tenderizers, shallots and peppercorns enhance the taste.
And the chops are melt-in-your mouth tender.

Oats ◆ Rolled

Turn high-fibre, iron-rich rolled oats into wholesome snacks and energy-boosting comforting cereals. Always store rolled oats in the freezer.

CLASSIC OATMEAL

Bring 3 cups water and ½ tsp salt to a boil.
Stir in 1⅓ cups quick-cooking oats.
Simmer, uncovered, 3 to 4 min.
 Stir occasionally. Remove from heat.
 Cover. Let sit for 2 min. *Makes 2⅓ cups.*

CHUNKY PEANUT

Cook 1 cup rolled oats according to package
 directions. During last minute of cooking,
 stir in 2 tbsp chunky peanut butter and
 1 tsp brown sugar.
Top with coarsely chopped banana chips.
 Serves 2.

FIBRE PLUS

Cook 1 cup rolled oats according to package
 directions. During last minute of cooking,
 stir in 2 tbsp bran, 1 tbsp brown sugar and
 ½ cup chopped unpeeled apple. *Serves 2.*

CRUNCHY NUT

Cook 1 cup rolled oats according to package
 directions. Then stir in ¼ cup slivered
 almonds, ¼ cup coarsely chopped
 hazelnuts and 1 tbsp liquid honey. *Serves 2.*

SPICY PEACH

Cook 1 cup rolled oats according to package
 directions. During last minute of cooking,
 stir in ½ cup chopped canned peaches,
 2 tsp brown sugar
 and pinch of cinnamon. *Serves 2.*

BASIC MICROWAVE OATMEAL RECIPE

Scoop ½ cup rolled oats into a 4-cup (1-L)
 round-bottomed bowl or measuring cup.
 Add 1 cup water and pinch of salt.
Microwave, uncovered, on high, 1 min. Stir.
 Microwave 1 to 1½ more min. Sprinkle
 with brown sugar. Add milk if you like.
 Serves 1.

FRUIT 'N' OAT MUFFINS

Using a fork, stir 1 cup all-purpose flour
 with 3 tsp baking powder,
 ½ tsp salt, ½ tsp cinnamon and
 pinch of nutmeg.
Stir in ¾ cup rolled oats,
 ½ cup brown sugar and
 ¼ cup chopped dried apricots.
Beat 1 cup milk with ¼ cup vegetable oil
 and 1 egg. Pour into oat mixture.
 Stir until mixed, but still lumpy.
Fill 12 greased muffin cups ⅔ full.
Bake at 400°F (200°C), 18 min.
 Makes 12 muffins.

MICROWAVE OATMEAL WEDGES

Stir 2 cups rolled oats with
 ⅓ cup brown sugar,
 ½ cup chocolate chips and ½ tsp salt.
In another bowl, whisk 1 egg with
 ¼ cup corn syrup, ¼ cup melted butter
 and 1 tsp vanilla. Stir into oat mixture.
Turn into a 9-in. (23-cm) pie plate and firmly
 pat into an even layer.
Microwave, uncovered, on high, 6 min.
 Cool before cutting. *Makes 16 wedges.*

*MICROWAVE
OATMEAL WEDGES*

CINNAMON-OATMEAL COOKIES

Stir 1 cup all-purpose flour with
½ tsp baking soda, ½ tsp salt and
½ tsp cinnamon until blended.
In a large bowl, beat ¾ cup room-
temperature butter with a spoon until
creamy. Beat in ⅓ cup brown sugar
and ⅓ cup granulated sugar.
Then beat in 1 egg, finely grated peel
of 1 orange and 1 tsp vanilla.
Stir in flour mixture and 2 cups rolled oats
(not instant). Spoon heaping tablespoons
onto a greased baking sheet.
Bake at 325°F (160°C), until edges are
golden, about 13 to 15 min. *Makes 3 dozen.*

OATMEAL CHEWS

Melt ⅓ cup butter over medium heat.
Stir in ¾ cup brown sugar and 1 tsp vanilla
until sugar dissolves. Remove from heat.
Stir in 1½ cups rolled oats and
½ cup chocolate chips (optional).
Spread out on a baking sheet to form a
9-in. (23-cm) square.
Bake, uncovered, at 350°F (180°C), until
golden, 10 to 12 min. Cut while warm.
Makes 24 chews.

Olives

Whether you prefer brine-cured black or spicy green, olives are seductive.
Let their heady aroma and rich fruity taste enrich your sauces and spreads.

Spanish Mustard Spread

Stir ¼ cup chopped stuffed green olives
    with 1 chopped green onion,
    2 tbsp Dijon and 1 tbsp mayonnaise.
Great on sausages or hot dogs.
    Makes ⅓ cup.

Marinated Olives

Whisk ½ cup olive oil with 2 tbsp balsamic
    or red wine vinegar, ½ tsp dried rosemary
    and ⅛ tsp hot red pepper flakes.
Stir in a few thinly sliced red onion rings and
    2 cups small black olives.
Refrigerate, covered, stirring occasionally, for
    a few hours to blend flavors. *Makes 2 cups.*

Mediterranean Olive Spread

In a food processor, whirl ½ cup stuffed
    green olives, ½ cup pitted black olives,
    2 tbsp drained capers and
    2 coarsely chopped garlic cloves.
While whirling, slowly pour ¼ cup olive oil
    through feed tube until coarsely ground.
Good on canapés, pizza and pasta.
    Store in a sealed jar in refrigerator.
    Keeps for up to 1 week. *Makes 1 cup.*

Spanish Grilled Cheese Sandwich

Cover buttered toast with
    sliced stuffed green olives and
    sprinkling of garlic powder.
Top with cheddar slice and grill. *Serves 1.*

Fish Steaks with Olives

Heat 1 to 2 tbsp butter over medium heat.
Add 4 fish steaks, such as halibut, and
    sauté, 4 min. Turn.
Sprinkle with ¼ tsp dried basil,
    ¼ tsp dried oregano, 2 tbsp lemon juice
    and 2 tbsp slivered black olives.
Sauté for 4 more min. *Serves 4.*

Great Greek Chicken

Sauté 2 crushed garlic cloves in
    1 tbsp olive oil over low heat for 2 min.
Add 4 skinless boneless chicken breasts
    and brown over medium heat,
    2 min. per side.
Add 5 chopped plum tomatoes or
    5 chopped canned tomatoes,
    12 small black olives and
    1½ tsp dried oregano.
Simmer, covered, 8 to 12 min. Stir often,
    turning chicken once. *Serves 4.*

Puttanesca Sauce

Sauté 1 crushed garlic clove in
    1 tbsp olive oil, 2 min. Mash in 1 anchovy.
Add ¼ cup finely chopped black olives,
    2 tbsp rinsed capers and
    19-oz can drained plum tomatoes.
Break up tomatoes and simmer sauce,
    uncovered, stirring often, until thick
    enough to coat pasta. Toss with hot pasta.
    Makes 2½ cups.

PUTTANESCA SAUCE ON TORTELLINI

OLIVE TORTELLINI

Heat ¼ cup olive oil with
1 large crushed garlic clove and
½ cup coarsely chopped stuffed olives.
Toss with 2 cups cooked cheese tortellini.
Sprinkle with grated Parmesan.
Serves 1 to 2.

SPANISH SAUCE

Sauté 2 crushed garlic cloves and
⅓ cup chopped stuffed green olives in
3 tbsp olive oil, 5 min., stirring often.
Toss with 2 cups cooked pasta. *Serves 1 to 2.*

OLIVE PASTA SAUCE

Cook ½ (1-lb/450-g) pkg spaghetti
according to package directions.
Bring 28-oz can undrained tomatoes,
2 crushed garlic cloves,
½ tsp dried thyme and
½ tsp sugar to a boil.
Meanwhile, slice ½ cup stuffed green and
½ cup pitted black olives.
Stir into sauce. Continue boiling, uncovered,
stirring often, 5 min.
Toss with drained pasta.
Sprinkle with grated Parmesan. *Serves 2.*

Onions

Onions are more than underpinnings for great sauces and side dishes. Next time a bag of onions is all you spy in the larder, try our Hot Curried Onions or Onions Provençal.

Easy Glazed Onions

Peel 8 small white onions.
  Cut a cross on the bottom of each.
In a large frying pan, melt ¼ cup butter.
Add 1 chicken bouillon cube,
  1 cup water and 2 tbsp sugar. Stir until
  bouillon is dissolved. Add onions.
Cook, covered, stirring occasionally, until
  fork-tender, about 15 min.
Uncover and stir frequently until onions are
  glazed, about 5 min. *Serves 4.*

Onions Provençal

In a large saucepan, bring 4 chopped
  Bermuda onions, 1 cup water,
  ¼ cup butter, ¼ cup tomato paste,
  ½ tsp salt and pinch of dried basil to a
  boil. Cover and simmer, 15 min.
  Stir occasionally.
Uncover and simmer until soft, 15 min. Stir
  often. Great with roast beef or scrambled
  eggs. *Makes 3½ cups.*

Herbed Barbecued Onions

Cut 3 cooking onions into ½-in. (1-cm)
  thick rounds. Lightly spread with
  1 tbsp room-temperature butter.
Sprinkle with pinches of dried oregano, basil
  and tarragon. Wrap 2 rounds each in foil.
Grill, turning every 5 min., until onions are
  hot, about 15 min.
Great with steak. *Serves 4.*

Curried Onions & Potatoes

In a 10-cup (2.5-L) casserole dish, stir
  2 tbsp melted butter with
  2 tbsp hot water, 1 tbsp curry powder
  and pinches of garlic powder and pepper.
Stir in 6 small halved onions and
  6 small quartered potatoes.
Cover, bake at 350°F (180°C), 45 min.
  Stir occasionally.
Stir in 1 cup sour cream.
Great with fish or chicken. *Serves 4.*

Hot Curried Onions

Slice 6 onions. Separate into rings.
Sauté in 2 tbsp butter sprinkled with
  1 tsp curry powder and
  ½ tsp dried thyme for 3 min.
When onions are soft, stir in ½ cup beer and
  ½ tsp Worcestershire. Boil gently,
  uncovered, until golden, 8 min. Stir often.
Serve warm with steak or burgers.
  Makes 2 cups.

Grilled Onions

Slice red or Spanish onions about ½-in.
  (1-cm) thick. Generously brush with oil.
Barbecue for 7 to 8 min. per side, with lid
  closed. Turn with a large spatula.
Great over burgers, stuffed in an omelette or
  stirred into a potato salad.

CALIFORNIAN SALAD

Whisk ⅓ cup vegetable oil with
   ¼ cup orange juice,
   1 tsp liquid honey,
   ½ tsp Dijon and
   pinches of salt and pepper.
Stir in ½ chopped red onion.
Line 4 salad plates with romaine lettuce.
   Top with 2 sliced peeled oranges and
   1 sliced avocado.
Sprinkle with 2 sliced green onions.
   Drizzle with dressing.
   Serves 4.

MICROWAVE FLOWERS

Slice a red or Spanish onion in half.
Microwave 2 halves, uncovered, on full
   power, 3 to 4 min. Sprinkle with chopped
   fresh herbs. Great with grilled meat.
   Serves 2.

SHALLOT BUTTER

Boil 2 tbsp chopped shallots in
   ¼ cup white wine until most of wine is
   evaporated. Add 1 tsp brandy and let
   evaporate, about ½ min.
Add ¼ cup butter and stir until melted.
Stir in 1 tbsp chopped parsley and refrigerate
   until firm.
Place a piece over hot fish steaks or burgers.
   Makes ¼ cup.

DEVILED BUTTER

In a food processor, whirl
   ½ cup room-temperature butter
   with ½ chopped onion,
   2 tbsp Worcestershire, ¾ tsp dry mustard
   and ¾ tsp hot pepper sauce.
Refrigerate until firm. Wonderful over
   burgers, grilled fish, steak or hot dogs.
   Makes ⅔ cup.

Microwave Flowers

Orange Juice

Orange juice, freshly squeezed or in a can of concentrate, makes a lot more than morning juice. A tablespoon or two packs a wallop of taste in everything from salad dressings to fiery barbecue sauce.

Orange Drumstick Baste

Whisk ¼ cup frozen orange juice concentrate with 2 tbsp olive oil, ½ tsp dried thyme and ½ tsp dried basil.

Great as a baste for chicken. *Makes ⅓ cup.*

Instant Oriental Rib Baste

Whisk ¼ cup frozen orange juice concentrate with ¼ cup soy sauce and ¼ cup vegetable oil.

Add 2 crushed garlic cloves and ¼ tsp cayenne.

Baste over chicken or ribs. *Makes ¾ cup.*

Rosemary-Orange Glaze

Stir ⅓ cup frozen orange juice concentrate with 2 tbsp vegetable oil, ¼ tsp crushed rosemary and generous pinches of salt and pepper.

Baste pork tenderloin or chicken during roasting or grilling. *Makes ½ cup.*

Fiery Orange-Chicken Sauce

Whisk 1 tsp cornstarch with ½ cup water in a saucepan.

Add grated peel and juice from 1 orange, 1 tbsp soy sauce and generous pinches of ginger and hot red pepper flakes.

Stir over medium heat until thickened. Serve over chicken. *Makes ½ cup.*

Orange Ham Glaze

Stir 6-oz (170-mL) can frozen orange juice concentrate with ½ cup brown sugar and 1 tbsp mustard. *Makes 1¼ cups.*

Sesame-Orange Sauce

Melt ¼ cup butter in a small saucepan.

Add grated peel from ½ orange, 3 tbsp orange juice, 1 tbsp toasted sesame seeds, 1 sliced green onion, ½ tsp soy sauce and ¼ tsp dried chervil or tarragon.

Heat and serve over cooked green beans, carrots or cauliflower. *Makes ½ cup.*

Tangy Citrus Barbecue Sauce

Sauté 2 chopped onions and 4 crushed garlic cloves in ¼ cup vegetable oil for 5 min.

Stir in 1 tbsp Dijon and 1 tsp each thyme, ginger, cumin, pepper and hot red pepper flakes.

Then add 1 cup orange juice, 1 cup ketchup, ¼ cup lemon juice, 2 tbsp Worcestershire, 2 tbsp soy sauce and 1 tbsp sugar.

Cook, uncovered, stirring often, until thickened, about 20 min.

Keep refrigerated. Spread generously over grilled chicken, burgers or ribs. *Makes 2 cups.*

Spiced Orange Tea

SPICED ORANGE TEA

Tie 2 cinnamon sticks, 5 whole cloves and
 3 whole allspice in cheesecloth.
Add to 8 cups water and bring to a boil.
Remove from heat. Add 4 tea bags.
 Steep, covered, 5 min. Remove bags.
Return to burner. Stir in 6-oz (170-mL) can
 frozen orange juice concentrate and
 ¾ cup light brown sugar.
Cover and simmer, 20 min.
 Remove spice bag.
Stir in ¼ cup orange-flavored liqueur.
Serve in mugs, with orange slices and grated
 nutmeg. *Makes 9 cups.*

HONEY-ORANGE DRESSING

Whisk ⅓ cup vegetable oil with
 2 tbsp white vinegar,
 ¼ cup frozen orange juice concentrate,
 3 tbsp liquid honey, ¼ tsp dry mustard
 and ¼ tsp salt.
Good drizzled over cubed honeydew melon
 with strawberries or other fruit.
 Makes 1 cup.

ORANGE-PEPPERCORN MARINADE

Whisk finely grated peel of 1 orange with
 ¼ cup orange juice,
 ¼ cup white wine,
 ¼ cup olive oil,
 4 chopped shallots and
 ½ tsp cracked black peppercorns.
Pour over 4 pork chops in a dish just large
 enough to hold them.
Cover and refrigerate at least 1½ hours.
Then barbecue about 10 min. per side.
 Baste often. *Serves 2 to 4.*

JAPANESE VINAIGRETTE

Whisk ⅓ cup vegetable oil with
 3 tbsp orange juice, ½ tsp soy sauce,
 ½ tsp sesame seeds and
 pinches of sugar and salt.
Good tossed with spinach. *Makes ½ cup.*

P is for Pears...

Cinnamon-scented banana purée adds a
taste of the tropics to BANANA BOOST PANCAKES
(see recipe page 136).

PANCAKE MIX

Here are 10 ways to jazz up your morning pancake batter instantaneously.
Begin with 1 cup of pancake mix and follow package directions. Each makes 6 to 8 pancakes.

FRESH APPLE

Stir in 1 finely chopped peeled apple.
Serve with sour cream or maple syrup.

BANANA BOOST

Stir in 1 well-mashed banana and
 $\frac{1}{4}$ tsp cinnamon.
Drizzle maple syrup over pancakes.

CHOCOLATE PLEASER

Stir in 1 tbsp cocoa, 1 tbsp sugar
 and 1 tsp vanilla.
Top pancakes with vanilla ice cream.

RAISIN & BRAN

Stir in 1 cup All-Bran cereal and
 $\frac{1}{4}$ cup golden raisins.
 Thin with milk if necessary.
Top pancakes with dollops of yogurt.

YOGURT-BLUEBERRY

Replace ½ cup milk called for in the package
 recipe with 1 cup plain yogurt.
Stir in $\frac{1}{4}$ cup fresh or frozen blueberries.
Sprinkle pancakes with brown sugar.

BACON PLUS

Replace shortening called for in the
 package recipe with bacon fat.
Stir in $\frac{1}{2}$ cup crumbled cooked bacon.
Spread pancakes with strawberry jam.

CHOCO-NUT

Stir in $\frac{1}{2}$ cup chocolate chips and
 $\frac{1}{4}$ cup chopped nuts.
Serve with fruit yogurt.

FIERY CORNMEAL

Use $\frac{1}{2}$ cup pancake mix and
 $\frac{1}{2}$ cup cornmeal in place of 1 cup pancake
 mix called for in the package recipe.
Stir in $\frac{1}{4}$ tsp salt and $\frac{1}{4}$ tsp hot red pepper
 flakes.
Serve with sausages.

SAUCY APPLE

Stir in 1 cup applesauce and $\frac{1}{4}$ tsp nutmeg.
Serve with sausages.

CHEDDAR QUICKIE

Stir in $\frac{1}{2}$ cup grated cheddar.
Serve with bacon and fried apple rings.

Peaches

Peaches are passion food. Capitalize on their all-too-short season and enjoy their natural sweetness in shakes, broils, chutneys and sautés.

Orange-Mint Salad

Stir ½ cup light mayonnaise with
   ¼ cup orange juice and
   2 tbsp chopped fresh or ½ tsp dried mint.
Stir in 4 sliced peaches. Serve on lettuce.
   Serves 4.

Walnut-Orange Salad

Combine 2 diced peeled peaches with
   4 cups bite-size lettuce pieces and
   ¼ cup chopped walnuts.
Toss with ¼ cup mayonnaise whisked with
   ¼ cup orange juice. *Serves 4.*

Spicy Sauté

Sauté 2 sliced peeled peaches and generous
   pinches of ginger, curry powder and sugar
   in 1 tbsp butter, until soft, about 7 min.
Great with chicken. *Serves 2.*

Warm Chèvre Peaches

Mix 2 tbsp crumbled goat cheese with
   1 tsp chopped chives, a grinding of
   black pepper and pinch of cayenne.
Pack into 4 peach halves.
   Broil until hot, about 2 min.
Serve with chicken or lamb. *Serves 4.*

Saged Chicken 'n' Peaches

Heat 1 tbsp butter in a frying pan.
Add 4 skinless boneless chicken breasts.
   Sprinkle with sage and sauté over medium
   heat, 5 min. per side.
Add 2 chopped peeled peaches and
   2 sliced green onions. Simmer until hot.
   Serves 4.

Sugar Peach Broil

Place peeled peach halves on a baking sheet.
   Fill centres with sour cream.
   Sprinkle with brown sugar.
Broil 4 in. (10 cm) from oven element for 8 min.

Microwave Baked Almond Peaches

Slice 4 peeled peaches in half. Discard pits.
Stir 2 tbsp brown sugar with
   2 tbsp chopped almonds and
   ¼ tsp cinnamon.
Spoon into centres. Top each filling with
   ½ tsp butter. Place on a pie plate.
Microwave, covered, on high, 2½ min.
   Rearrange peaches partway. *Serves 4.*

Decadent Rum Cream

Melt ¼ cup butter in a large frying pan.
Stir in ¼ cup brown sugar until dissolved.
Add ¼ cup rum, 1 tsp vanilla and 4 sliced
   peaches. Stir over medium heat until
   coated and hot, about 3 min.
Spoon over ice cream. *Serves 4.*

Spiced Peach Shake

In a food processor, whirl 1 cup yogurt
   with 1 tsp sugar, ⅛ tsp cinnamon and
   ½ (14-oz) can drained peach halves or
   2 very ripe peaches until smooth.
   Makes 1⅓ cups.

Fresh Fruit Chutney

Stir ¼ cup chutney with
   ½ cup finely chopped fresh peaches and
   ¼ tsp curry powder.
Great with pork or lamb. *Makes ¾ cup.*

PEARS

Pears are gorgeous savored with a little cheese, nuts or greens. Chop them into chutneys or coat richly with chocolate. Use any variety of pear that's ripe for these speedy recipes.

WARM PEARS & GORGONZOLA

Slice 2 pears in half and core.
 Top with slice of Gorgonzola cheese.
Bake at 400°F (200°C) until cheese melts, about 10 min. Slice and serve as an appetizer. Sprinkle with chopped toasted hazelnuts if you like. *Serves 4.*

CHÈVRE-PEAR SALAD

Thinly slice 2 pears.
 Arrange on shredded greens.
 Drizzle with a little lemon juice.
Sprinkle with ¼ cup toasted walnuts and ½ cup crumbled chèvre. *Serves 4.*

ITALIAN BAKED PEARS

Cut 2 pears in half and core. Stir finely grated peel of 1 lemon with ½ cup ricotta, 1 tsp vanilla and 2 tbsp sugar. Fill pears.
Bake at 350°F (180°C) until hot, 15 to 20 min. *Serves 4.*

MICROWAVE GINGER PEARS

Coarsely chop 2 pears.
 Stir with ¼ cup white wine, 2 tsp sugar and ¼ tsp ginger. Dot with 1 tbsp butter.
Microwave, covered, on high, 2 min. Serve topped with yogurt. *Serves 2.*

MICROWAVE PEARS & RUM

Slice 2 pears in half and core.
 Stir 1 tbsp brown sugar with
 1 tbsp room-temperature butter and
 1 tbsp rum. Spoon into cavity of pear.
Microwave, covered, on high, about 4 min, until warm. *Serves 4.*

CLASSY CHOCOLATE PEARS

Slice 3 pears and fan on 4 dessert dishes.
Combine 4 oz (112 g) bittersweet chocolate and ⅓ cup whipping cream in a saucepan. Stir over low heat until melted.
Stir in 1 tsp almond-flavored liqueur.
Spoon over pears. *Serves 4.*

PRONTO PEAR CRISP

Spread 4 coarsely chopped peeled pears in an 8-in. (20-cm) buttered pan.
Stir ½ cup room-temperature butter with ½ cup brown sugar. Work in ½ cup rolled oats and ¼ cup all-purpose flour.
Sprinkle over pears. Bake at 375°F (190°C) until golden, 20 to 25 min. *Serves 4.*

PEAR SMOOTHIE

Whirl 2 quartered peeled pears in a blender with 1 cup orange juice and pinch of cinnamon. When smooth, whirl in ¾ cup yogurt. *Makes 3 cups.*

PEAR-CUMIN CHUTNEY

Simmer 2 diced peeled pears with 1 chopped onion, ¼ cup chopped red pepper, ¼ cup granulated sugar, ¼ cup cider vinegar and generous pinches of hot red pepper flakes and cumin, uncovered, 10 min. Stir often.
Great with pork tenderloin. *Makes 1 cup.*

PEAR & SPINACH SALAD

Toss 10-oz (300-g) spinach, about 7 cups, with 2 chopped unpeeled pears and ¼ to ⅓ cup Lemon Vinaigrette (see page 103). *Serves 4.*

Peas

Peas top the veggie hit parade – especially with kids – so here's 10 quick ways to lift high-fibre fresh or frozen green peas above the ordinary. Each recipe serves 4.

Pea & Potato Salad

Cook 4 medium potatoes just until tender. Cut into bite-size pieces.

Toss warm potatoes with 2 cups frozen peas, 1 chopped carrot, 1/2 cup light Italian dressing and 1/4 tsp pepper.

Serve at room temperature with chicken or sausages. *Makes 6 cups.*

Cool Curried Salad

Stir 2 tbsp mayonnaise with 3 to 4 tbsp milk and generous pinches of curry powder, pepper and cayenne.

Toss with 2 1/2 cups cold cooked peas.

Chunky Soup

Heat 10-oz can condensed green pea soup with 1 soup can water, 1 cup frozen peas and 1 tsp curry powder. *Serves 3 to 4.*

Cashews 'n' Pea Sauté

Cook 2 1/2 cups fresh or frozen peas.

Heat 2 tsp butter in a frying pan.

Add 1/4 cup cashews and sauté until golden. Add peas and stir until hot.

Oriental Peas

Combine 1 sliced onion,
   1 crushed garlic clove
   or 1/4 tsp garlic powder,
   1 tbsp soy sauce and
   2 tbsp water or sherry in a frying pan.

Sauté over medium heat, stirring often, 5 min.

Add 2 to 3 cups frozen peas.

Stir often over high heat until piping hot, about 3 min. *Makes 2 to 3 cups.*

Lemon-Herbed

Toss 2 cups cooked peas
   with 1 tsp butter,
   1/2 tsp finely grated lemon peel,
   squeeze of lemon juice and
   generous pinch of dried oregano.

Classic Mint

Cook 2 1/2 cups peas. Toss with
   1 to 2 tbsp finely chopped fresh mint,
   1 tsp butter and pinch of sugar.

Citrus Peas

Cook 2 1/2 cups fresh or frozen peas.

Heat 2 tsp butter in a frying pan.

Add peas and finely grated peel of 1 orange.

Sauté until hot.

Light 'n' Creamy Peas

Cook 2 cups peas.

Immediately stir in
   2 tbsp plain yogurt and
   pinches of crushed dried mint and pepper.

Colorful Salad Sandwich

Rinse 2 cups frozen peas under hot tap water, 30 sec. Drain well.

Pulse in a food processor until finely chopped.

Then stir with 1 finely chopped celery stalk,
   1 shredded carrot and
   3 thinly sliced green onions.

Stir 1/2 cup light mayonnaise with
   1/4 tsp salt and 1/4 tsp curry powder, then stir in vegetables. Spread on dark bread or stuff into pitas. *Makes 2 cups.*

Peppers

Sweet peppers add more than a blast of color. A green pepper provides as much vitamin C as an orange, a red pepper twice as much. Here's how to roast, stuff or salsa your next peck of peppers.

Red Pepper & Chèvre Dip

In a food processor, purée
    1 cup creamy goat cheese with
    ¼ cup chopped red pepper and
    2 tbsp olive oil.
Serve with fresh vegetables. *Makes 1 cup.*

Pepper, Garlic & Chèvre Pasta Sauce

Sauté 3 garlic cloves in ¼ cup olive oil.
    Add 3 red peppers, cut into thin strips.
Sauté until hot. Toss with cooked pasta,
    ½ cup creamy goat cheese and
    ¼ tsp pepper. *Serves 2 to 3.*

Amazing Microwave Stuffed Peppers

Cut 4 green peppers in half lengthwise.
    Place in a dish with 2 tbsp water.
Microwave, covered, on high, 2 min.
In an 8-cup (2-L) dish, stir
    1 lb (500 g) ground beef with
    1 chopped onion, 2 crushed garlic cloves
    and ¼ cup chopped parsley.
Microwave, uncovered, on high, until beef is
    brown, 5 min. Stir once. Pour off fat.
Stir in 1 cup cooked rice,
    2 lightly beaten eggs,
    ¼ cup chili sauce and
    pinches of salt and pepper.
    Spoon into peppers.
Microwave, covered, on medium, 5 min.
    Let stand, covered, 3 min. *Serves 4.*

Sautéed Sweet 'n' Hot Peppers

Sauté 6 sliced red peppers,
    2 chopped hot banana peppers,
    1 sliced red onion and pinches of salt and
    pepper in 3 tbsp olive oil.
Cook, stirring often, until lightly browned,
    about 7 min. Good as a vegetable or makes
    filling for 16 fajitas.

Salsa Fresca

Stir 2 finely chopped green peppers with
    4 finely chopped seeded tomatoes and
    1 finely chopped onion.
Whisk ⅓ cup vegetable oil with
    1 to 2 tbsp lime juice,
    2 crushed garlic cloves,
    ¼ tsp salt and pinches of dried oregano
    and pepper. Toss with vegetables.
Serve with burgers, steak, grilled fish steaks
    or chicken. *Serves 6.*

Moroccan Pepper Salad

Whisk ⅓ cup olive oil with
    2 tbsp red wine vinegar,
    2 crushed garlic cloves,
    1 tsp ground coriander, 1 tsp paprika,
    ½ tsp cumin, ½ tsp chili powder and
    ¼ tsp salt.
Slice 3 red peppers and 3 green peppers into
    bite-size strips. Stir into dressing.
Serve immediately or cover and refrigerate to
    blend flavors. *Serves 6.*

GREEN & RED PEPPER SALAD

Slice 2 green peppers and
  2 red peppers into bite-size strips.
Whisk ¼ cup olive oil with
  1 tbsp red wine vinegar,
  1 crushed garlic clove and
  generous pinches of dried basil,
  dry mustard, salt and pepper.
Pour over peppers. Let stand half an hour.
  Drain and place in a lettuce-lined bowl.
  Serves 4.

EASY GRILLED PEPPERS

Cut 2 large red peppers into quarters.
Stir 1 tbsp olive oil with 1 tbsp balsamic
  vinegar and generous pinches of salt,
  pepper and cayenne. Brush on peppers.
Barbecue, brushing with oil occasionally,
  until hot and singed around edges, about 6
  min. per side. *Serves 2.*

MICROWAVE "ROASTED" PEPPERS

Pierce 1 whole sweet pepper.
  Place on a microwave-safe plate.
Microwave, uncovered, on full power, 8 min.
  Turn pepper. Microwave 4 more min.
Cover and let sit, 4 min. Remove seeds and
  peel off skin. Use right away or freeze.
(For two peppers, microwave, 16 to 18 min.)

ROASTED RED PEPPERS

Place whole peppers on barbecue or under
  broiler. Turn often until skins blacken,
  12 to 15 min.
Remove and seal in brown paper bag or foil
  so peppers steam in their own heat. Skin,
  core and seed peppers. Pack in their own
  juices in an airtight container and freeze.
Peppers will hold smoky flavor for 1 year. Use
  in steamed rice, risottos and pasta sauces.

AMAZING MICROWAVE STUFFED PEPPERS

PESTO

Pesto is a deep-green sauce made from fresh basil, Parmesan, garlic and olive oil. For a foolproof recipe, see page 23. Use it to add an intense basil taste to steaks, pizza, potatoes, even tuna sandwiches.

PESTO FRENCH BREAD

Cut French stick in half horizontally.
   Spread with ½ cup pesto.
   Generously sprinkle with grated Parmesan.
   Sprinkle with 1 diced seeded tomato and
   2 tbsp chopped black olives.
Grill until piping hot. Slice and serve
   immediately. *Serves 4.*

PESTO PIZZA BITES

Spread a store-bought pizza crust with pesto.
   Generously sprinkle with grated Parmesan
   and a few hot red pepper flakes.
   Cover with grated mozzarella or dot
   with creamy goat cheese.
Bake at 450°F (230°C) until golden, about
   10 min. Cut into triangles and serve as an
   appetizer.

LIGHT 'N' CREAMY LINGUINE TOSS

Cook ½ lb (225 g) linguine until al dente.
Drain and toss with ⅓ cup pesto,
   ⅓ cup sour cream and
   pinches of salt and pepper.
Sprinkle with 2 chopped seeded tomatoes
   and 2 chopped green onions. *Serves 2.*

PESTO STEAK

Stir pesto sauce with an equal amount of
   room-temperature butter.
   Form into a small roll and refrigerate.
Place a slice on grilled steak or burgers.

ITALIAN TUNA SANDWICH

Stir 2 tbsp pesto with 2 tbsp mayonnaise.
   Gently mix in 7-oz can drained tuna and
   2 chopped seeded tomatoes.
Stuff into pitas with shredded lettuce.
   Serves 2 to 4.

ZUCCHINI SIDE STAR

Slice 2 zucchini into julienne strips.
Microwave, covered, on high, until hot,
   about 1½ to 2 min.
Toss with 2 tbsp pesto and
   pinches of salt and pepper. *Serves 4.*

NEW TOMATO GRILL

Slice 2 large tomatoes in half.
   Spread with pesto.
   Dot with creamy goat cheese.
Broil, 8 in. (20 cm) from heat, until hot.
   Serves 4.

PESTO FRENCH BREAD

PESTO BAKED POTATOES

Bake 4 potatoes in oven or microwave.
Slice off top quarter. Scoop out interior
and break up with a fork.
Stir in ¼ cup pesto, ¼ cup light sour cream
and grated Asiago or Parmesan to taste.
Mound in shells. Sprinkle with more cheese.
Broil, 4 in. (10 cm) from heat, until golden.
Serves 4.

PESTO TOMATO SALAD

Slice 2 large tomatoes in half. Spread 1 side
of each slice with 1 tbsp pesto.
Overlap on a bed of shredded lettuce.
Sprinkle with 1 tsp balsamic vinegar.
Serves 4.

PESTO POULET

Sauté 4 skinless boneless chicken breasts
in 2 tsp butter until golden, about 2 min.
per side.
Add ½ cup white wine and 2 tbsp pesto.
Cover and simmer until chicken feels springy
to the touch, about 8 to 12 min.
Turn partway through. *Serves 4.*

PITA

Pita is a sturdy pocket bread used for stuffing, spreading and dipping. Keep a package in the freezer so when a pizza mood hits, simply top a "crust" with whatever you have on hand.

HERB-SCENTED PITA CRISPS

Stir ¼ cup olive oil with ½ tsp curry powder
and ½ tsp cumin.
Brush over both sides of 3 pitas.
Slice into wedges and split. Sprinkle with
pinches of salt and pepper.
Bake on an ungreased baking sheet, 8 to 10
min. *Makes 60 crisps.*

PARTY TUNA PACKETS

Finely flake 7-oz can drained tuna.
Stir in 1 tbsp mayonnaise,
2 tsp lemon juice, ½ tsp curry powder and
1 finely chopped apple.
Cut 10 mini pita breads in half. Fill with tuna
mixture and top with alfalfa sprouts.
Makes 20 appetizer pitas.

QUICK HERBED PITAS

Stir 2 tbsp room-temperature butter with
1 tbsp chopped fresh basil,
1 tbsp chopped parsley,
1 tbsp chopped fresh dill and
generous pinch of pepper.
Split 2 pitas, then brush with butter mixture.
Cut into quarters.
Broil until toasted. *Serves 4.*

QUICK PIZZA

Stir 1 tbsp spaghetti sauce or pizza sauce
with dash of hot pepper sauce.
Lightly spread over 1 pita.
Sprinkle with sliced thin pepperoni,
Italian seasoning, grated Parmesan, then
grated mozzarella. Broil. *Serves 1.*

MICROWAVE MEDITERRANEAN PIZZA

Stir 1 julienned red pepper with
1 chopped onion and 1 crushed garlic
clove in a microwave-safe bowl.
Microwave, on high, 1½ min.
Sprinkle 2 pitas with
½ cup crumbled feta,
2 tbsp chopped black olives,
red pepper mixture and
½ tsp dried oregano.
Microwave on a double thickness of paper
towel, on medium, 3 min. *Serves 2.*

MICROWAVE BACON & TOMATO PIZZA

Sprinkle 2 pitas with
1 cup grated Swiss cheese,
1 chopped seeded tomato,
3 slices crumbled cooked bacon and
2 tbsp chopped fresh basil.
Microwave on a double thickness of paper
towel, on medium, 2 to 3 min.
Drizzle with 1 tsp olive oil. *Serves 2.*

3-CHEESE SALSA PIZZA

Spread ⅓ cup salsa, ¼ cup grated Parmesan, ¼ cup grated cheddar and ¼ cup grated Asiago or Monterey Jack over pita bread.

Bake at 425°F (220°C) until golden, 10 min. *Serves 1.*

MICROWAVE SANTA FE PIZZA

Place 1 chopped onion, 1 crushed garlic clove and ½ tsp olive oil in a bowl.

Microwave, on high, 1 min.

Sprinkle over 2 pitas.

Top with 1 cup grated cheddar, 1 sliced tomato, 1 tbsp chopped jalapeño, ½ tsp dried oregano and ½ tsp cumin.

Microwave, on medium, 2 min. *Serves 2.*

CURRIED PITA POCKET

Mix 1 cup chopped cooked chicken or smoked turkey with ¼ cup sour cream, ¼ to ½ tsp curry powder and pinch of cayenne.

Stir in sliced green onions or finely chopped celery.

Spoon into pita halves and top with chopped cucumber and shredded lettuce. *Serves 1.*

PITA POCKET FILLINGS

Slice pitas in half.

Open up and half fill with your favorite egg, tuna or salmon salad.

Top with chopped tomato or grated carrot, shredded lettuce and/or alfalfa sprouts.

MICROWAVE MEDITERRANEAN PIZZA

POPCORN

Popcorn is a smart low-fat, fibre-filled snack. Count on 25 calories per cup when air-popped and 40 calories when popped in oil. Spice it up with any of the following.

HOT 'N' CHEESY

Melt ¼ cup butter. Stir in 1 tbsp chili powder and 1 tsp garlic powder.

Pour over 8 cups popped corn, along with generous sprinklings of grated cheddar.

Toss well. *Makes 8 cups.*

ITALIAN STYLE

Melt ¼ cup butter. Stir in
    1 tsp dried oregano, 1 tsp dried basil,
    1 tsp garlic powder and 1 tsp salt.

Pour over 8 cups popped corn and toss well.
    Makes 8 cups.

LOW-CAL CURRIED CRUNCH

Combine 1 tsp curry powder,
    1 tsp cumin, 1 tsp paprika and
    ½ tsp salt in a large plastic bag.

Add 8 cups popped corn.
    Close bag and shake to coat.

Add melted butter if you can afford the
    calories. *Makes 8 cups.*

BEST OF BACON

Melt ¼ cup butter. Stir in 1 tbsp bacon bits,
    1 tsp garlic salt and Italian seasoning.

Sprinkle over 8 cups popped corn and toss
    well. *Makes 8 cups.*

SPICY CREOLE POPCORN

Drizzle 16 cups popped corn with
    2 tbsp melted butter.

Stir 1 tsp chili powder with 1 tsp cumin,
    ½ tsp salt and ¼ tsp cayenne.

Toss with popcorn. *Makes 16 cups.*

CURRIED POPCORN & PEANUTS

Melt ½ cup butter. Stir in 1½ tbsp cumin,
    1 tbsp curry powder and ½ tsp salt.

Stir with 10 cups popped corn and
    1 cup salted peanuts. *Makes 11 cups.*

SUGAR & SPICE POPCORN

Melt 2 tbsp butter.

Stir in 3 tbsp brown sugar,
    ½ tsp cinnamon, ½ tsp allspice,
    ¼ tsp nutmeg and ¼ tsp paprika.

Toss with 8 cups popped corn and
    2 cups nuts.

Bake at 350°F (180°C), 5 min., stirring
    partway through. *Makes 10 cups.*

CINNAMON-SCENTED POPCORN

Combine 1 tsp cinnamon with
    ½ tsp allspice,
    ¼ tsp ginger and
    2 tbsp sugar in a large plastic bag.

Add 8 cups butter-coated popcorn.
    Close bag and shake to coat. *Makes 8 cups.*

CARAMEL CORN

Mix **7 cups popped corn** with
  1 cup salted peanuts.
In a saucepan, combine **1 cup butter** with
  ½ cup corn syrup and
  ½ tsp cream of tartar.
Boil until a little of the syrup dropped in cold
  water will form a hard ball
  (250°F/130°C on a candy thermometer).
  Remove from heat.
Carefully stir in **½ tsp baking soda** and
  1 tsp vanilla.
Immediately pour over popcorn and nuts
  and toss with two buttered forks until
  coated. *Makes 8 cups.*

POPCORN BALLS

Lightly sprinkle **15 cups popped corn** with **salt.**
In a small saucepan, heat
  1½ cups granulated sugar with
  ½ cup liquid honey and **1 tsp salt.**
  Stir often, until sugar dissolves.
Boil until a little of the syrup dropped in cold
  water will form a hard ball
  (250°F/130°C on a candy thermometer).
  Remove from heat.
Stir in **3 tbsp butter** and **1 tsp vanilla.**
Immediately pour over popcorn and
  toss until coated.
When cool, butter your hands and shape into
  balls. *Makes 16 (3-in./7.5-cm) balls.*

PORK

*Pork chop and tenderloin specials are a weekly feature in most supermarkets.
Take advantage of the super prices and stock your freezer. Then work your way down our list
of swift sautés and simple simmers.*

LEAN PORK WITH PEAR CHUTNEY

Cut 1 pork tenderloin into 1-in. (2.5-cm)
thick slices. Flatten with palm of hand
until about ⅓ in. (1 cm) thick.
Season with pinches of salt and pepper.
Sauté pork, uncovered, in 2 tsp olive oil until
browned, about 6 min.
Spoon Pear-Cumin Chutney (see recipe
page 138) over top. *Serves 2 to 3.*

PORK TENDERLOIN KEBABS

Cut 1 pork tenderloin into
1-in. (2.5-cm) cubes.
Stir 2 tbsp teriyaki sauce with
1 tbsp red wine vinegar,
1 tbsp vegetable oil, 1 tsp brown sugar
and ¼ tsp hot red pepper flakes.
Toss with pork. Thread on skewers.
Barbecue, with lid closed, or broil, about
7 to 9 min. Turn often. *Serves 2 to 3.*

ORIENTAL TENDERLOIN

Place 1 pork tenderloin on a baking sheet.
Spread with 2 tbsp peanut sauce
or 1 tbsp hoisin sauce.
Roast at 375°F (190°C) for 15 min.
Spread pork with another 2 tbsp peanut
sauce or 1 tbsp hoisin sauce.
Roast 15 min. more. Let sit, covered,
10 min. before slicing.
Great with rice and stir-fried vegetables.
Serves 2 to 3.

HARVEST PORK TENDERLOIN

Heat 1 tsp butter and 1 tsp oil in a frying pan.
Add 1 pork tenderloin.
Turning pork, evenly sprinkle with
1¼ tsp cumin and ¾ tsp curry powder.
Cook over medium heat, turning often, until
lightly browned, about 4 min.
Pour 1 cup apple juice over top.
Cover and simmer for 12 min.,
turning often. Remove and cover.
Boil juice, uncovered, stirring often, until
reduced to ½ cup.
Stir in ¼ cup sour cream.
Pour over sliced tenderloin. *Serves 2 to 3.*

SPICE-SCENTED APPLE CHOPS

Brown 4 to 6 chops.
Add 1 cup apple juice.
Stir in 2 tbsp brown sugar,
¼ tsp cinnamon and
pinches of nutmeg and pepper.
Cover and simmer until tender. Turn once.
Remove chops. Boil sauce until thick enough
to coat meat, then pour over top.
Serves 4 to 6.

CREAMY CURRY CHOPS

Brown 4 to 6 chops in 1 tsp vegetable oil.
Add 10-oz can condensed cream of
mushroom soup and ½ tsp curry powder.
Simmer, covered, until chops are tender.
Stir often and turn chops.
Wonderful over rice. *Serves 4 to 6.*

CURRIED CHOPS & PEAS

Brown 4 chops in 1 tbsp olive oil.
  Remove chops. Add ½ cup water,
  10-oz can cream of celery soup,
  ½ tsp curry powder and ¼ tsp pepper.
Stir until blended. Add ½ cup frozen peas
  and 2 chopped carrots.
Return chops and spoon sauce over top.
  Cover and simmer until tender, 20 min.
  Turn once. *Serves 4.*

MAPLE-MUSTARD CHOPS

Cook 4 pork chops in 2 tbsp vegetable oil
  until almost done. Remove to a platter.
  Drain fat from pan.
Stir ¼ cup maple syrup and
  1 tsp dry mustard into pan drippings.
Return chops to pan. Simmer, uncovered,
  until richly glazed, about 2 min. per side.
  Serves 4.

SOUTHERN ACCENTS

Brown 4 to 6 chops.
Add 7-oz can tomato sauce,
  1 ½ tsp cumin, ¼ tsp garlic powder and
  pinch of cayenne. Stir to mix.
Cover and simmer until tender. Stir often.
  Turn once. *Serves 4 to 6.*

HOT CHILI CHOPS

Heat 10-oz can undiluted tomato soup with
  2 sliced onions, 2 crushed garlic cloves,
  1 tbsp curry powder and
  ½ tsp chili powder until bubbling.
Pour over 4 pork chops in a baking pan just
  large enough to hold them. Cover and
  bake at 375°F (190°C) until tender, 45 min.
Great with Perfect Baked Potatoes
  (see recipe page 150). *Serves 4.*

CURRIED CHOPS & PEAS

POTATOES

We used to regard potatoes as fattening and bland. But no more! In our surge toward homey wholesome food, complex carbohydrate spuds are premier players – and not just as side dishes.

FABULOUS OVEN FRITES

Slice 2 baking potatoes into ½-in. (1-cm) thick rounds, then into ½-in. (1-cm) thick strips. Drizzle with 1 tbsp olive oil.

Generously sprinkle with salt and pepper. Stir to coat. Spread out on a baking sheet.

Bake at 450°F (230°C), turning 2 or 3 times, until browned, 30 to 35 min. *Serves 2.*

GLAMOROUS POTATO SALAD

Cook 10 unpeeled large potatoes in boiling water just until tender, 20 min.

Meanwhile, whisk 1 cup vegetable oil with
    4 tbsp red wine vinegar, 1 tbsp Dijon,
    2 crushed garlic cloves,
    ½ tsp each dried basil,
    dried oregano and salt.

Toss with hot cooked potatoes, cut into cubes,
    1 chopped red onion and
    2 cups thinly sliced celery.

Wonderful warm. *Serves 8.*

PERFECT BAKED POTATOES

Scrub potatoes, then pat dry. Pierce. Bake on oven rack at 400°F (200°C), 45 to 55 min.

CREAMY MASHED POTATOES

Boil 12 peeled potatoes until tender.

Immediately drain and mash in a large bowl with 2 tbsp butter.

Add ½ (8-oz/250-g) pkg cream cheese, cut into squares, ½ to 1 cup sour cream, ½ tsp salt, ¼ tsp pepper and pinch of nutmeg.

Beat with an electric mixer until creamy. *Serves 6 to 8.*

PERFECT MICROWAVE POTATOES

Scrub 2 potatoes. Pat dry. Pierce.

Arrange on a paper towel with thick ends toward outside.

Microwave, uncovered, on high, 7 to 8 min., rearranging after 5 min.

CREAMY GORGONZOLA

Slice 1 hot baked potato in half.

Top with ¼ cup crumbled Gorgonzola, slivers of fresh basil and pinch of ground pepper.

BACON & BLUE CHEESE

Slice 1 hot baked potato in half.

Top with 2 tbsp crumbled blue cheese and 1 slice crumbled cooked bacon.

HOT RED PEPPER CHEDDAR

Slice 1 hot baked potato in half.

Top with ¼ cup freshly grated nippy cheddar and pinch of hot red pepper flakes.

MEDITERRANEAN FETA

Rub 1 split baked potato with olive oil, then red wine vinegar.

Sprinkle with ¼ cup crumbled feta, 1 tsp chopped black olives and pinches of dried oregano and pepper.

MEXICAN SALSA SPUDS

Slice 1 hot baked potato in half.

Spread with salsa.

Dab with sour cream.

Sprinkle with grated cheddar and fresh coriander.

Pumpkin

Don't confine pumpkin to pies. It's a rich source of cancer-inhibiting beta-carotene and fibre. Open a can of purée (not sugary-spiced pie filling) and use in soups, side dishes and more.

Elegant Bisque

Whisk 14-oz can or 2 cups puréed pumpkin
with 2 cups chicken bouillon,
1 cup half-and-half cream,
2 tbsp maple syrup, ¼ tsp cinnamon,
¼ tsp mace and ¼ salt in a saucepan.
Heat, stirring often, until hot. *Makes 4 cups.*

Quick Baked Veggie

Stir 2 (14-oz) cans pumpkin with
2 tbsp butter, 2 tbsp brown sugar and
pinches of ginger and cinnamon.
Bake in a covered casserole at 350°F (180°C),
30 to 40 min. Stir after 15 min.
Great with turkey. *Serves 6 to 8.*

Curried Purée

Add 2 finely chopped onions and
1 crushed garlic clove to
2 tbsp butter in a saucepan.
Sprinkle with 1½ tsp cumin and ¼ tsp cayenne.
Sauté for 5 min., stirring often.
Stir in 14-oz can or 2 cups puréed pumpkin
and heat through, stirring often.
Great with pork or turkey. *Serves 6.*

Pumpkin Pancakes

When making your favorite pancake recipe,
add ½ cup canned pumpkin and
½ tsp sugar for each cup of milk used.

Harvest Bran Muffins

Prepare your favorite bran muffin mix,
reducing water called for by ¼ cup and
stirring in ½ cup canned pumpkin and
½ tsp cinnamon. *Makes 12 muffins.*

Pumpkin Muffins

Stir 1 cup all-purpose flour with
1¼ cups natural bran, 3 tsp baking
powder, 1 tsp cinnamon, ½ tsp salt,
½ tsp allspice and ¼ cup brown sugar.
Make a well in the centre.
Whisk 1 cup canned pumpkin with
1 cup milk, ¼ cup vegetable oil,
2 tbsp molasses and 1 egg. Pour into well.
Mix just until moist. Spoon into 12 greased
muffin cups. Bake at 400°F (200°C), 18 to
20 min. *Makes 12 muffins.*

Light Fall Parfait

Whisk 1 cup plain yogurt with ¼ cup canned
pumpkin, 2 tbsp maple syrup and pinch of
cinnamon. Layer in parfait glasses with
toasted chopped pecans. *Serves 2.*

Butter-Pecan Pumpkin Pie

Spread 2 cups slightly softened butter-pecan
ice cream in graham wafer piecrust.
Stir ½ cup brown sugar with ½ tsp cinnamon,
¼ tsp ginger and 1 cup canned pumpkin.
Beat 1 cup whipping cream and fold in.
Spread over ice cream and freeze. *Serves 10.*

No-Bake Cheesecake

Prepare 11-oz (330-g) pkg no-bake
cheesecake, adding 1 cup canned pumpkin,
pinches of cinnamon, ginger and nutmeg
along with milk. *Serves 8.*

Yogurt Delight

Stir equal quantities of yogurt and canned
pumpkin together. Add brown sugar to taste.

R is for Ribs

This homey MICROWAVE BERRY RHUBARB CRISP (see recipe page 154) is easily made in 15 minutes. It's a wonderful warming dinner finale or a great dish to wake up to.

Rhubarb

*Whether it's fresh or frozen, rhubarb is a smart sauce or dessert choice.
A whole cup contains only 27 calories and lots of calcium and potassium.*

Morning Sauce

Heat 2 cups sliced rhubarb with
　1 tbsp frozen orange juice concentrate
　and 2 tbsp sugar, covered and stirring
　often, over medium-low heat, 5 min.
Uncover and cook, stirring often, 7 min.
　Makes 1 cup.

Rhubarb Muffins

Stir 1 cup finely chopped rhubarb and
　grated peel of 1 orange into
　your favorite muffin batter.
Bake according to recipe. *Makes 12.*

Raspberry-Rhubarb Compote

Heat 2 cups sliced rhubarb with
　$\frac{1}{3}$ cup sugar over medium heat, 5 min.
Then stir in 12-oz (340-g) pkg unsweetened
　frozen raspberries and dash of vanilla.
Stir until hot. *Makes 2 cups.*

Microwave Breakfast Sauce

Stir 2 cups coarsely chopped rhubarb with
　$\frac{1}{3}$ cup granulated sugar and
　pinches of ginger or cinnamon.
Microwave, on high, uncovered, stirring
　once, until bubbly and slightly thickened,
　about 7 min. Spoon over yogurt.
Add sprinkle of granola. *Makes 1 cup.*

Savory Pork Sauce

Stir 2 cups sliced rhubarb with
　$\frac{1}{3}$ cup brown sugar, 1 tbsp cider vinegar
　and $\frac{3}{4}$ tsp grated fresh ginger over
　medium heat, until soft.
Good with pork. *Makes 1½ cups.*

Warm Maple Rhubarb Dessert

Cook 4 cups fresh or frozen rhubarb,
　covered, in a saucepan with 2 tbsp water
　and $\frac{1}{2}$ tsp cinnamon over medium-low
　heat. Stir often, until soft, about 7 min.
Stir in 2 tbsp maple syrup and
　2 tbsp brown sugar. *Serves 3 to 4.*

Bananarama Dessert

Slice 1 banana. Add dash vanilla and stir into
　2 cups stewed rhubarb. *Makes 2½ cups.*

Microwave Berry Rhubarb Crisp

Place 3 cups chopped rhubarb in an 8-cup
　(2-L) microwave-safe dish with
　425-g thawed frozen strawberries and juice.
Blend $\frac{1}{4}$ cup sugar with 2 tsp cornstarch.
　Stir into fruit.
Microwave, covered, on high, 5 min. Stir well.
　Combine $\frac{1}{4}$ cup chilled butter with
　$\frac{1}{4}$ cup brown sugar, $\frac{1}{3}$ cup rolled oats,
　$\frac{1}{3}$ cup all-purpose flour and
　$\frac{1}{2}$ tsp cinnamon until crumbly.
　Sprinkle over fruit.
Microwave, uncovered, on medium, 10 min.
　Let stand, 5 min. *Serves 6.*

Tangy Rhubarb-Apple Crisp

Stir 2 cups sliced rhubarb into
　your favorite apple crisp filling
　(see Classic Apple Crisp page 11). *Serves 6.*

Stewed Rhubarb

Stir 4 cups sliced rhubarb with
　$\frac{2}{3}$ cup sugar over medium heat, until
　tender, 15 min. Stir often. *Makes 2 cups.*

Ribs

For tender ribs, precook before baking or barbecuing. Fold ribs and put in a large pot of boiling water. Cover and simmer until fork-tender, 45 to 55 minutes.

Perfect Barbecued or Baked Ribs

TO BARBECUE: brush precooked ribs with sauce (see recipes below) and place on a greased grill about 6 in. (15 cm) above hot coals.

Barbecue, turning often and basting with sauce until richly glazed, 15 to 20 min.

TO BAKE: brush precooked ribs with sauce (see recipes below) and place on a greased baking pan.

Bake, uncovered, at 375°F (190°C), basting often for 15 to 20 min.

Basting Sauces for 3lbs (1½ kg)

Quick Chili

Stir ½ cup chili sauce with
½ cup vegetable oil and
2 tbsp Worcestershire.

Oriental Mustard

Stir ½ cup soy sauce with
¼ cup brown sugar, ¼ cup vegetable oil,
2 tsp dry mustard and
2 crushed garlic cloves.

Herbed Italian

Stir ½ cup Italian salad dressing with
1 tsp dry mustard, 1 tsp sugar and
1 tsp dried thyme.

Sassy Caesar

Whisk ⅓ cup ketchup with
¾ cup Caesar salad dressing.

Fast 'n' Fiery

Stir ½ cup barbecue sauce with
2 tbsp Worcestershire,
1 tsp hot pepper sauce and
¼ tsp cayenne.

Honey-Garlic

Stir ½ cup vegetable oil with
½ cup liquid honey.
Then stir in ¼ cup prepared mustard and
2 tsp garlic powder.

Hot Texas

Whisk ½ cup vegetable oil with
½ cup ketchup,
2 tbsp chili powder,
2 tbsp Worcestershire,
¼ tsp cayenne and
¼ tsp garlic powder.

Canadian Maple

Whisk ⅔ cup maple syrup with
¼ cup ketchup,
2 crushed garlic cloves,
2 tbsp lemon juice and
½ tsp hot pepper sauce.

Mild Curry

Whisk ½ cup vegetable oil with
½ cup ketchup,
¼ cup liquid honey and
2 tsp curry powder.

Zesty Horseradish

Stir 2 tbsp horseradish into
½ cup barbecue sauce.

Rice

Rice is much more than a bed for stir-fries and curries. With a flick of a spice jar, it becomes bold, spicy and fragrant.

Fast Lemon Tarragon Rice

Sauté 1 chopped onion in 1 tbsp butter
  in a small saucepan, stirring often,
  until soft, about 5 min.
Stir in 1 cup chicken broth or bouillon and
  ¼ tsp dried tarragon.
Cover and bring to a full boil.
Stir in 1 cup instant rice,
  finely grated peel of ½ lemon and
  ¼ tsp salt.
Cover and remove from heat. Let stand for
  5 min. Fluff with a fork. *Serves 4.*

Rice Salad with Asparagus & Peppers

In a large saucepan, bring 3 cups water
  and ½ tsp salt to a boil.
Stir in 1½ cups long-grain rice.
  Cover, reduce heat to low and cook, 15 min.
Meanwhile, slice ½ lb (250 g) trimmed
  asparagus into 1-in. (2.5-cm) pieces.
Julienne 1 sweet pepper and 2 small zucchini.
After rice has cooked, 15 min., stir in
  asparagus and pepper. Cover and cook
  until rice is tender, 5 to 10 min.
Stir in zucchini. Remove from heat.
Stir ¼ cup mayonnaise with
  ¼ cup sour cream,
  then stir into drained rice mixture.
Stir in ¼ cup snipped chives.
Good warm or cold. *Makes 8 cups.*

Curried Coconut Rice

Place 14-oz can unsweetened coconut milk,
  ½ cup water, 1 cup long-grain rice,
  ½ tsp salt, ¼ tsp sugar and
  ¼ tsp curry powder in a medium-size
  saucepan. Stir often over medium heat
  until bubbling.
Reduce heat to low. Simmer, covered and
  stirring often, until rice is tender and
  liquid is absorbed, 20 to 25 min.
  Makes 2 cups.

Spring Rice for Two

In a small casserole dish, combine
  ½ cup long-grain rice with
  1¼ cups chicken broth or bouillon,
  1 chopped green onion, 1 tbsp butter,
  1 tbsp lemon juice, ½ tsp grated lemon peel
  and pinches of salt and pepper. Mix well.
Cover, bake at 375°F (190°C), 35 min. or
  until liquid is absorbed. *Serves 2.*

Party Baked Rice

In a large casserole dish, dissolve 6 chicken
  bouillon cubes in 7 cups boiling water.
Stir in ¼ cup butter,
  3 cups long grain rice and ½ tsp salt.
Cover and bake at 350°F (180°C) for 1 hour
  or until tender. *Makes 10 cups.*

BOLD 'N' SPICY RICE

Sauté 2 chopped onions and
  4 crushed garlic cloves in 3 tbsp butter
  over medium heat, until soft, about 5 min.
Stir in 2 cups long-grain rice,
  5 cups chicken broth or bouillon,
  2 chopped seeded jalapeños,
  ½ tsp cayenne and ½ tsp pepper.
  Bring to a boil.
Cover, reduce heat to low and simmer
  until liquid is absorbed, 20 to 25 min.
  Makes 4 cups.

RICE WITH ORIENTAL VEGETABLES

Place 1 cup long-grain rice,
  1¾ cups chicken broth or bouillon,
  3 tbsp orange juice concentrate and
  ¼ tsp salt in a saucepan. Bring to a boil.
Reduce heat to low and simmer, covered,
  15 min.
Stir in 3 cups Oriental-style stir-fry frozen
  vegetables. Increase heat to medium-low.
  Cover and continue cooking, stirring
  often, until rice is tender, about 10 min.
  Makes 4½ cups.

FRAGRANT RICE

Heat 1 tbsp olive oil in a medium-size
  saucepan.
Add 1 tsp cumin seeds, 3 whole cloves and
  1 broken cinnamon stick and stir for
  1 min. over medium heat.
Stir in 1 cup long-grain or basmati rice
  until coated.
Add 2 cups chicken broth and
  2 bay leaves. Bring to a boil.
Cover, reduce heat to low and simmer until
  liquid is absorbed, about 20 min.
Remove bay leaves. *Makes 2 cups.*

STOVE-TOP RICE STUFFING

In a large saucepan, sauté 2 crushed garlic
  cloves in ¼ cup butter until soft.
Stir in 2 cups long-grain rice.
Add 5 cups chicken bouillon, 1 cup golden
  raisins, 2 tsp poultry seasoning and
  1 tsp curry powder. Bring to a boil.
Cover, reduce heat and simmer until rice is
  tender and liquid is absorbed, about
  30 min.
Stir in 4 chopped green onions. *Makes 8½ cups.*

RICE PUDDING FOR ONE

Bring ¾ cup water to a boil.
Add ¼ cup long-grain rice.
  Cover and simmer, 20 min.
Whisk ¼ cup milk with 1 egg,
  4 tsp sugar and ¼ tsp vanilla.
Stir in hot cooked rice and 2 tbsp raisins.
  Pour into a small greased baking dish.
Bake, uncovered, at 350°F (180°C), 20 min.
  Serve with cream or milk.

Stove-Top Rice Stuffing

Rice ◆ Cooked

Don't pitch that rice left from an order-in Chinese dinner or your own enthusiastic cooking. Instead, whip up Oriental Fried Rice, a lemony mushroom companion for fish or a no-cook yogurt pudding.

Rice Florentine

Cook 12-oz (400-g) pkg frozen spinach.
   Squeeze dry, then chop.
Sauté 1 crushed garlic clove in 1 tbsp butter.
Stir in 2½ cups cooked rice until evenly coated.
Stir in spinach, 2 tbsp lemon juice and
   freshly grated nutmeg. *Makes 3 cups.*

Herbed Rice

In a small frying pan, melt 2 tbsp butter.
Add 2 sliced celery stalks and
   3 green onions. Sauté for 1 min.
Stir in 2 cups cooked rice and generous
   pinches of dried thyme, salt and pepper
   until evenly coated. *Makes 2½ cups.*

Mushroom Rice for Fish

Sauté 1 cup sliced mushrooms in 2 tsp butter.
Stir in 2 cups cooked rice,
   1 tbsp lemon juice, 1 tsp grated lemon peel
   and generous pinch of chervil.
Stir until hot. Good with fish steaks.
   Makes 2½ cups.

Curried Rice 'n' Coconut

Heat 1 tbsp butter with ½ tsp curry powder
   and pinch of garlic powder.
Stir in 2 cups cooked rice and
   2 tbsp shredded coconut.
   Stir 3 min. Add 1 chopped red apple.
Good with chicken or pork. *Makes 2½ cups.*

South Seas Salad

Stir grated peel of 1 lime with
   ¼ cup lime juice, 2 tbsp fish sauce,
   1 tbsp sugar, 1 tsp cumin, ½ tsp hot red
   pepper flakes and ½ tsp salt.
Stir in 6 cups cooked rice, 1 large chopped
   mango and 1 small chopped red onion.
Just before serving stir in 1 cup chopped
   coriander and ½ cup roasted salted
   cashews. *Makes 7 cups.*

Oriental Fried Rice

In a large saucepan, sauté 1 cup sliced celery
   in 2 to 3 tbsp vegetable oil, 2 min.
Stir in 3 cups cooked rice and
   4 sliced green onions. Stir until hot.
Then whisk 1 egg with 1 tbsp soy sauce and
   pinch of cayenne.
Stir with rice until piping hot and evenly
   coated. *Makes 4 cups.*

Mandarin Chicken & Rice Salad

Combine 2 cups diced cooked chicken
   with 2 cups cooked rice,
   ½ chopped red pepper and
   2 sliced green onions.
Stir 10-oz can mandarin oranges and
   2 tbsp of its juice with ⅓ cup mayonnaise
   and ¼ tsp ginger.
Stir with salad.
Good chilled or at room temperature.
   Makes 4 cups.

*SOUTH SEAS
SALAD*

FAST SKILLET STUFFING

In a large frying pan, melt 1 tbsp butter.
Stir in 2 sliced celery stalks and sauté
for 1 min.
Stir in 3 cups cooked rice and
½ tsp poultry seasoning.
Stir until evenly coated.
Serve right away as a side dish with chicken
or turkey. Or use as poultry stuffing.
Makes 3 cups.

YOGURT RICE PUDDING

Stir 1 cup yogurt with
1 tsp liquid honey and dash of vanilla.
Stir in 2 cups cooked rice,
¼ to ½ cup raisins and pinch of nutmeg.
Chill. Serve sprinkled with cinnamon.
Makes 2½ cups.

MUSHROOM & GINGER RICE STUFFING

In a large saucepan, melt ½ cup butter.
Add ¼ cup chopped fresh ginger and
3 crushed garlic cloves.
Stir over low heat, 5 min.
Add 10-oz can drained sliced water
chestnuts, 2 cups sliced mushrooms and
4 sliced green onions. Stir for 2 min.
Stir in 6 cups cooked rice.
Use as a stuffing for duck, chicken and
turkey. *Makes 8 cups.*

ROAST ◆ Leftovers

Roasts always taste great a day, even two, after the big dinner. Reincarnate your next roast beef or chicken into Pronto Puttanesca pasta or Roasted Potato Toss.

FAJITA SALAD

Stir ½ cup chopped cooked roast beef with
 ½ cup chopped green pepper,
 ¼ cup chopped seeded tomato,
 1 sliced green onion,
 2 tbsp light sour cream,
 1 tbsp salsa and
 pinches of chili powder and cayenne.
Roll in warm tortillas. *Serves 1.*

BEEF & RADISH SALAD

Whisk ½ cup vegetable oil with
 2 tbsp red wine vinegar,
 1½ tsp chili powder and
 generous pinches of dry mustard, sugar,
 salt and pepper.
Combine 2 cups julienned cooked roast beef
 with 3 sliced zucchini and
 4 sliced radishes.
Toss with dressing and serve on a bed of
 lettuce. *Serves 4.*

ROAST BEEF WITH RED WINE VINAIGRETTE

Whisk ¼ cup vegetable oil with
 2 tbsp red wine vinegar,
 1 crushed garlic clove and
 pinches of salt and pepper.
Combine ½ lb (250 g) julienned cooked
 roast beef with ½ sliced red onion.
Toss with dressing. Refrigerate until cold.
 Serve on lettuce leaves or drain pieces and
 serve in pita. *Serves 2.*

PRONTO PUTTANESCA

Heat 19-oz can undrained Italian-style
 tomatoes with ⅓ cup sliced
 black or stuffed green olives and
 1 tbsp capers until bubbly.
Boil gently, uncovered and stirring often,
 until thick enough to coat pasta.
Stir in 2 cups roasted chicken strips and heat.
Toss with 8 oz (250 g) cooked spaghetti.
 Serves 2.

LIGHT-SUPPER MEAT SALAD

Combine ½ lb (250 g) julienned cooked
 roast beef with 6 chopped cooked new
 potatoes, ¼ lb (125 g) cooked green beans,
 6 halved cherry tomatoes and
 1 chopped red pepper.
Whisk ⅓ cup olive oil with
 2 tbsp red wine vinegar,
 1 tsp grainy mustard, dash of hot pepper
 sauce and pinches of sugar, salt and
 pepper. Toss with salad. *Serves 4.*

ROAST BEEF DELUXE SANDWICH

Cover whole-grain bread with
 sliced cooked roast beef.
Stir 3 tbsp mayonnaise with
 ½ to 1 tbsp horseradish,
 ½ cup diced apple and
 2 tbsp minced green onion.
Spoon over roast beef.
 Makes ½ cup for 3 sandwiches.

ROQUEFORT & BEEF GRILLED SANDWICH

Lightly spread 1 slice whole wheat bread with mayonnaise or Dijon.

Layer with thinly sliced cooked roast beef.

Sprinkle with 2 tbsp crumbled Roquefort, then broil until cheese begins to melt.

ROASTED POTATO TOSS

Slice enough roasted chicken or beef into bite-size strips to measure 2 cups.

Cube enough roasted potatoes to measure about 2 cups.

Sauté 1 sliced onion and 4 crushed garlic cloves in 1 tbsp olive oil for 3 min.

Add roasted potatoes, $\frac{1}{2}$ tsp salt and $\frac{1}{2}$ tsp Italian seasoning. Stir frequently until hot and crisp, about 3 min.

Stir in meat and 1 cup cooked leftover vegetables, such as carrots or peppers, until hot. *Makes 5 cups.*

RED PEPPER PASTA ENCORE

Saute 1 tbsp minced garlic in 2 tbsp olive oil over low heat, 5 min.

Add 2 cups roast beef or cooked chicken strips and 1 cup roasted red pepper strips. Stir over medium heat until hot.

Sprinkle with 3 to 4 tbsp sliced fresh basil strips.

Toss with cooked pasta, adding pinches of salt, pepper and grated Parmesan. *Serves 1 to 2.*

SPICY BEEF & CHEESE SUPPER SANDWICH

Spread cream cheese over sourdough bread.

Top with dabs of hot pepper jelly, then slices of cooked roast beef and lettuce.

Add a top slice of sourdough bread.

LIGHT-SUPPER MEAT SALAD

S is for Strawberries...

Keep a can of salmon in your cupboard shelf and you always have the basis for these moist SALMON PATTIES (see recipe page 164). Excellent served with lemon and dilled rice or tucked into warm pita bread.

SALMON ◆ Canned

Half a can of salmon provides 20 grams of protein and healthy Omega-3 fatty acids, but less than 150 calories. Here's how to deliciously use a 7½-oz can of drained salmon.

SALMON PATTIES

Stir salmon with 1 beaten egg,
   ½ cup dry bread crumbs,
   ¼ cup sliced green onion,
   1 tsp lemon juice and pinch of pepper.
Form into 6 patties.
Fry in a little oil until golden. *Serves 3.*

SEAFOOD CHOWDER

Sauté 1 sliced leek in 1 tbsp butter until tender.
Stir in 10-oz can Manhattan clam chowder,
   1 cup milk, 1 cup water and salmon.
Cover and heat, stirring occasionally.
   Makes 4 cups.

DEVILED EGGS WITH SALMON

Hard-boil 6 eggs. Halve, mash yolks with
   salmon, 4 tbsp mayonnaise, dash of hot
   sauce and pinches of salt and white
   pepper. Mound into whites. *Makes 12.*

FRENCH FILLING

Stir 2 tbsp sour cream with ½ tsp Dijon
   and ¼ tsp dried tarragon.
Stir in flaked salmon.
Use as a sandwich filling. *Makes ⅔ cup.*

MICROWAVE HOISIN SALMON & RICE

Place 1 sliced celery stalk and 2 sliced green
   onions in a microwave-safe dish.
Add 1 cup bean sprouts,
   1 tbsp hoisin sauce and
   bite-size chunks of salmon.
Microwave, covered, on high until hot,
   about 1½ min. Stir partway through.
Serve on rice. *Serves 2.*

ORIENTAL SALMON PASTA

Sauté 2 sliced green onions and
   2 crushed garlic cloves in 2 tbsp olive oil.
Add 1 cup sliced mushrooms and
   2 sliced celery stalks and sauté 2 min.
Stir in 2 tbsp soy sauce and salmon.
Toss with pasta. *Serves 2.*

PERFECT PASTA SAUCE

Heat 28-oz can plum tomatoes with
   1 chopped green pepper, 2 sliced green
   onions and pinch of hot red pepper flakes.
Break up tomatoes. Boil gently, uncovered,
   until thickened. Stir in salmon.
Spoon over pasta. *Makes 4 cups.*

SALMON STIR-FRY FOR TWO

Heat 1 tbsp vegetable oil over medium-high
   heat. Add 1 julienned red pepper and
   ½ cup sliced celery or 1 cup snow peas.
Stir-fry 2 min. Add salmon and heat through.
   Sprinkle with soy sauce or lemon juice.
Serve over rice.

GINGER SALMON SANDWICH

Stir 3 sliced green onions, 1 tbsp finely
   chopped ginger in syrup and
   2 tbsp mayonnaise into salmon.
Use as sandwich spread. *Makes ¾ cup.*

SALMON TACO

Stir salmon with 2 tbsp chili sauce and
   ½ tsp chili powder. Stir in 1 chopped
   tomato. Spoon into taco shells.
Top with chopped green onion and shredded
   lettuce. *Serves 2.*

Salmon Steaks

Here are 10 fast ways to bring salmon steaks to the table with just enough gilding to compliment the fish's satiny elegance.

Baked, Barbecued or Broiled Salmon

Buy salmon steaks or fillets 1 in. (2.5 cm) thick. Cook 10 min.

Lightly oil. Bake at 450°F (230°C) or barbecue or broil, 10 min., turning after 5 min.

Honey-Ginger Glaze

Heat ½ cup orange juice, 1 tsp liquid honey and 1 tsp grated fresh ginger in a frying pan.

Add 4 salmon steaks. Cover and simmer, 10 min., turning partway through.

Remove salmon. Boil sauce until reduced by half. Pour over salmon.

Oriental Maple Salmon

Whisk 1 tbsp Dijon with 2 tbsp maple syrup and 2 tbsp soy or teriyaki sauce.

Spoon half over 2 salmon steaks placed on a foil-lined dish. Bake, uncovered, at 450°F (230°C), 5 min. Add remaining sauce and bake another 5 min.

Baked Salmon Provençal

Blend ¼ cup white wine with 1 tsp olive oil, 1 large crushed garlic clove, ¼ tsp dried thyme and ¼ tsp dried tarragon.

Pour over 1 or 2 salmon steaks and bake at 450°F (230°C), uncovered, 10 min. Baste often.

Spicy Cajun

Stir 1 tsp chili powder with 1 tsp cumin, ¼ tsp cayenne and ¼ tsp garlic powder.

Brush both sides of 6 steaks with oil. Sprinkle with seasonings.

Broil 5 min. per side.

Salmon with Garlic Butter

Melt 2 tbsp butter in a frying pan.

Add 2 small crushed garlic cloves, then 4 salmon steaks. Cook, covered, over medium-low heat, 5 min. Turn.

Sprinkle with 3 sliced green onions. Continue simmering, uncovered, 5 more min. Squeeze lemon juice over top.

Spinach & Shallots

Thaw, then drain 12-oz (400-g) pkg chopped spinach. Spread over bottom of a 9-in. (23-cm) pie plate. Sprinkle with 1 tbsp finely chopped shallots and pinches of salt and pepper. Top with 2 salmon steaks. Dot steaks with 1 tsp butter.

Bake, covered, at 450°F (230°C), 15 min.

Salmon Steak Dress-Up

Lightly brush salmon steaks with olive oil.

Grill 4 in. (10 cm) from broiler, 8 min. Turn. Broil 2 min. Spread 1 tbsp salsa and 1 tsp sour cream over each. Broil 4 more min.

Fast French Salmon Steaks

Stir 1 chopped jalapeño and ¼ tsp dried dillweed or 2 tbsp chopped fresh dill into 2 tbsp Dijonnaise.

Spread over 2 salmon steaks.

Bake at 450°F (230°C), 12 min.

Dijon-Honey Salmon

Stir 2 tbsp Dijon with 2 tsp liquid honey, ¼ cup sour cream and ½ tsp dried dillweed. Brush over 4 salmon steaks.

Bake at 450°F (230°C), 15 min.

SALSA

Salsa has exceeded ketchup in condiment sales – and no wonder. It's chock-full of hot peppers and onions, instead of sugar and salt, so a whole tablespoon has less than 5 calories.

TUNA-SALSA SALAD

Stir 2 tbsp low-fat mayonnaise with
   3 tbsp salsa.
Mix in 7-oz can drained tuna and
   1 chopped green onion.
Spoon into whole wheat pitas or on sliced
   cucumber. *Makes 1 cup.*

FAST FIERY GUACAMOLE

Stir ¼ cup salsa with 1 diced avocado.
   Use as a dip for tacos or as topping for
   chicken. Serve within 2 to 3 hours.
   Makes 1 cup.

LOW-CAL DIP

Stir equal amounts of salsa and
   light sour cream together.
Excellent with veggies or taco chips or as a
   topping for chicken.

SALSA BRUSCHETTA

Spoon salsa over
   toasted slices of crusty bread.
Sprinkle with
   grated Parmesan or mozzarella.
Broil until melted.

MEXICAN PORK CHOPS

Place 4 pork chops in a baking dish.
   Spread with ⅔ cup salsa.
Cover and bake at 375°F (190°C) until
   tender, 45 min. Baste often.
Sprinkle with 1 cup grated cheddar.
   Broil until golden, 5 min. *Serves 4.*

2-INGREDIENT SALSA BAKE

Remove skin from 4 chicken breasts.
Cover bottom of an 8-in. (2-L) square baking
   dish with ½ cup hot or mild salsa.
Place chicken, bone-side up, in dish.
   Pour ½ cup salsa over chicken.
Bake, uncovered, at 375°F (190°C), 30 min.
   Turn chicken. Continue baking, basting
   occasionally, 25 to 30 min. *Serves 4.*

MANDARIN HOLIDAY SALSA

Peel 4 mandarin oranges or tangerines.
   Remove seeds.
Chop pulp and stir into ½ cup salsa with
   ½ finely chopped green pepper.
Serve with pita crisps or tortilla chips.
   Makes 3 cups.

FIERY BARBECUED STEAKS

Barbecue steaks on 1 side.
Turn and brush browned side generously
   with salsa.
Continue barbecuing until done as you like.

MEXICAN SALSA PASTA

Stir $\frac{1}{2}$ cup hot salsa with
   $\frac{1}{4}$ cup sour cream,
   2 chopped tomatoes and
   2 sliced green onions.
Toss with 4 cups hot cooked pasta and
   lots of grated cheese. *Serves 2 to 4.*

LIGHT SALSA CHICKEN

Brown 4 skinless boneless chicken breasts
   in butter in a frying pan.
Add $\frac{1}{2}$ cup white wine and
   $\frac{1}{4}$ cup mild salsa.
Cover and simmer, turning once, about 10
   min., until chicken is springy to the touch.
   Serves 4.

FIERY BARBECUED STEAKS

Sausage

Sausages – hot, sweet or savory – can always be counted on for an effortless dinner. But think beyond dishing them up with mashed potatoes. Here we offer everything from a gusto pasta sauce to a hot stir-fry.

Italian Pasta Sauce

Slice ½ lb (250 g) sausages into ½-in.
(1-cm) pieces. Sauté in 1 tbsp oil. Drain.
Stir in 1 cup spaghetti sauce,
2 chopped tomatoes and
⅛ tsp cayenne.
Cover and simmer, 5 min., stirring often.
Makes 3 cups.

Italian Ratatouille Sauce

Heat 1 tsp olive oil over medium-high heat.
Stir-fry 2 sliced hot Italian sausages
until cooked.
Add 1 cup sliced zucchini, then
19-oz can undrained tomatoes.
Break up tomatoes and stir often, until sauce
is thickened.
Serve over rice or pasta. *Serves 2.*

Hearty Red Wine Sauce

Slice 1 lb (500 g) sausages into ½-in.
(1-cm) pieces. Brown in a little oil.
Stir in 1 chopped green pepper.
Add ½ cup red wine,
28-oz can diced tomatoes,
1 tsp Italian seasoning and
¼ tsp pepper. Boil gently, uncovered,
5 to 10 min. Stir often.
Serve over pasta or rice. *Makes 5 cups.*

Kid-Pleasing Sweet 'n' Sour

Slice 1 lb (500 g) sausages into bite-size
pieces. Brown in a large frying pan.
Drain off fat.
Stir in 14-oz can pineapple chunks with juice,
¼ cup ketchup and
2 tbsp brown sugar.
Simmer, covered, stirring often, 5 minutes.
Serve over rice or macaroni. *Serves 4.*

Fast BBQ

Brown 4 Italian sausages in 1 tbsp oil.
Drain well.
Add ¼ cup water and
¼ cup barbecue sauce.
Cover and simmer, 10 min.
Uncover and boil, turning sausages often,
until sauce is thickened.
Serve in crusty rolls or with pasta. *Serves 4.*

Mustard-Glazed Sausages

Brown 4 sausages. Drain off fat.
Add ¼ cup white wine.
Cover and simmer for 10 min.
Remove sausages.
Whisk in 2 tbsp Dijon. Boil, stirring often,
until thick enough to coat sausages.
Pour over sausages and serve in toasted
crusty rolls. *Serves 4.*

EGGS RANCHERO

Slice 1 lb (500 g) sausages into bite-size
  pieces. Brown in a large frying pan.
  Drain off all but 1 tbsp fat.
Whisk 8 eggs with 1 tsp chili powder.
Add to sausage with 2 chopped green onions.
  Stir over medium heat until eggs are set.
  Serves 3 to 4.

CURRIED PEPPER STEW

Slice 1 lb (500 g) sausages into bite-size
  pieces.
Brown in a large frying pan in a little oil.
  Drain off fat.
Add 28-oz can undrained tomatoes,
  2 chopped green peppers,
  2 crushed garlic cloves and
  1 tsp curry powder. Simmer, covered,
  stirring often, 10 minutes.
Serve over a bed of rice or with whole wheat
  bread. *Serves 3 to 4.*

PASTA WITH SAUSAGE

In 1 tbsp olive oil, sauté
  1 lb (500 g) sweet Italian sausages, sliced
  into bite-size pieces,
  1 sliced red pepper,
  1 sliced green pepper and
  1 chopped onion, about 10 min.
Stir in 28-oz can undrained plum tomatoes,
  ½ cup red wine,
  1 tsp dried thyme,
  ½ tsp dried oregano and ¼ tsp pepper.
Boil gently, uncovered, stirring often,
  until sauce is thickened, about 15 min.
Toss with hot cooked fusilli. *Serves 4.*

MUSTARD STROGANOFF

Slice 1 lb (500 g) sausages into bite-size
  pieces. Brown in a large saucepan.
Add 10-oz can cream of mushroom soup
  and 1 tbsp Dijon. Stir often over low heat
  until hot, about 5 min.
Toss with noodles. *Serves 4.*

SHRIMP

Shrimp takes no more than 2 or 3 minutes to cook. Capitalize on their sophisticated fresh seafood taste with our exceptionally easy ways to add panache.

SHRIMP SHALLOT PÂTÉ

In a food processor, whirl
   ½ lb (250 g) cooked shrimp with
   ½ (8-oz/250-g) pkg cream cheese,
   2 tbsp butter,
   1 tsp white wine or milk,
   1 tsp chopped shallots and
   pinches of salt and white pepper.
Serve cold. *Makes 1 cup.*

SOUTHERN SHRIMP DIP

Purée 1¼ lb (625 g) cooked shrimp with
   ¼ cup cream cheese, 1 tsp lime juice and
   ½ tsp chopped jalapeño.
Serve with breadsticks or crackers. *Makes ½ cup.*

GARLIC SHRIMP DIP

Stir ½ cup light mayonnaise with
   ½ cup sour cream, 1 tbsp red wine vinegar,
   2 crushed garlic cloves,
   ¼ tsp pepper, ¼ tsp cayenne and
   dash of hot pepper sauce.
Sprinkle with chopped green onions.
Serve with shrimp for dipping. *Makes 1 cup.*

CHILI SHRIMP SALAD

Mix 1 cup coarsely chopped cooked shrimp
   with ½ cup chopped celery,
   2 tbsp light mayonnaise and
   1 tbsp chili sauce.
Serve in whole-grain buns. *Makes 1⅓ cups.*

SUMPTUOUS SEAFOOD MACARONI

Sauté 1 chopped onion and 1 crushed garlic
   clove in 1 tbsp butter until soft.
Add 3 tbsp white wine and
   2 cups shelled fresh or frozen shrimp.
Stir often until shrimp are almost completely
   bright pink, 2 to 4 min.
Add 3 cups cooked macaroni and stir until
   hot. *Serves 4.*

SHRIMP & BROCCOLI TOSS

Sauté 2 crushed garlic cloves with
   1 tbsp chopped ginger in
   2 tbsp vegetable oil for 2 min.
Add ½ cup chicken bouillon,
   2 cups broccoli florets and
   ½ lb (250 g) frozen shrimp.
Cover and simmer, 3 to 5 min. Stir often.
Spoon over rice or couscous. *Serves 2.*

CARIBBEAN HOLIDAY SHRIMP

Stir 1 tbsp vegetable oil with
   2 tbsp finely chopped fresh ginger,
   juice from 2 limes, 2 crushed garlic cloves,
   1 tbsp soy sauce, ½ tsp sugar and
   ½ tsp hot red pepper flakes.
Stir in 2 lbs (1 kg) large, tail-on cooked shrimp
   (defrosted if frozen) and
   ½ cup chopped fresh coriander.
Cover and refrigerate, at least 1 hour or up to
   4 hours. Stir occasionally. Good as appetizer
   or toss with greens. *Makes about 40 shrimp.*

*CARIBBEAN
HOLIDAY SHRIMP*

SHRIMP & VEGGIE STIR-FRY FOR TWO

Beat 1 tbsp cornstarch with 1 egg white.
Stir in 10 shrimp until coated. Set aside.
Combine ¼ lb (125 g) sliced mushrooms
   with 1 cup frozen peas and
   2 sliced green onions.
Sauté 1 crushed garlic clove and
   2 thin slices ginger in 2 tsp vegetable oil
   for 2 min. Add coated shrimp and stir-fry,
   1 min. Add vegetables and stir-fry until
   peas are hot, 3 to 4 min. *Serves 1 or 2.*

CAJUN SHRIMP

Stir 3 tbsp chili sauce with
   1 tbsp vegetable oil, 1 tbsp lemon juice,
   ¼ tsp hot pepper sauce and pinch of salt.
Stir in 1 lb (500 g) cooked shrimp.
   Makes 3 to 6 appetizers.

SHRIMP & GINGER STIR-FRY

Sauté 1 tbsp grated fresh ginger,
   1 tbsp minced garlic and
   ½ tsp hot red pepper flakes in
   1 tbsp vegetable oil for 5 min. over low
   heat. Turn heat to high.
Add 10 cups sliced vegetables,
   such as peppers, red onions, broccoli,
   mushrooms and celery,
   1 lb (500 g) shelled fresh or frozen shrimp
   and ¼ cup sherry.
   Stir-fry for 4 min.
Add ¼ cup teriyaki sauce and stir until hot.
Serve over rice or rice noodles.
   Serves 3 to 4.

SOLE

A slip in and out of the pan is all it takes to cook sole fillets.
As well as having a gentle taste, sole is extremely low in fat and high in protein.
Each recipe serves 3 and calls for ¾ lb (400 g) of thawed or fresh fillets. See also FISH FILLETS.

CORN CHOWDER

Heat 10-oz can condensed cream of
potato soup with ¾ cup water or milk,
stirring until smooth.
Then add 1 cup frozen or canned corn,
sole fillets, cut into bite-size pieces,
3 sliced green onions and
¼ tsp dried dillweed.
Cover and bring to a boil, stirring
occasionally. Simmer, covered, stirring
often, 3 to 5 min. *Makes 3½ cups.*

CHIVES 'N' LEMON

Season fillets with pinches of salt and pepper.
Cook in 2 tsp butter in a frying pan over
medium heat, about 2 to 3 min. per side.
Remove fillets.
Stir 1 tbsp lemon juice and 2 tbsp snipped
chives into pan.
Then spoon over fish.

CLASSY MUSHROOM

Sauté ¼ lb (125 g) sliced mushrooms in
1 tbsp butter, 4 min.
Add ¼ cup white wine, ¼ tsp salt,
¼ tsp pepper and ¼ tsp dried dillweed.
Push mushrooms to side.
Add fillets. Spoon mushrooms over top.
Cover and simmer, 5 to 7 min.
Remove fillets and mushrooms.
Boil liquid until reduced to 3 tbsp.
Pour over fish and mushrooms.

SALSA 'N' WINE

Pour ¼ cup salsa and 2 tbsp white wine
into a wide frying pan.
Add fillets.
Simmer, uncovered, 5 to 7 min., turning once
partway through.

SOUTHERN FILLETS

Heat 1 tsp butter in a large frying pan.
Add ½ tsp minced garlic.
Sprinkle both sides of fish with cumin and
salt. Place in pan. Cook over medium heat,
uncovered, about 2 to 3 min. per side.
Squeeze juice from half a lemon or lime
over top.

DIJON DILL CREAM

Stir ¼ cup yogurt or sour cream with
½ tsp Dijon, ¼ tsp dried dillweed and
pinches of salt and pepper.
Spoon over baked or sautéed fillets.
Makes ¼ cup.

CREAMY HORSERADISH

Season fillets with pinches of salt and pepper.
Cook in 2 batches, in 2 tsp butter, in a large
frying pan over medium heat,
about 2 min. per side. Remove fish.
Add 2 diced fresh tomatoes, 1 tsp horseradish
and 3 tbsp sour cream to pan.
Stir until hot. Spoon over fish.

CRISPY CORNMEAL

Dip fish in 2 beaten eggs.
  Coat with ½ cup cornmeal stirred with
  2 tbsp grated Parmesan,
  ½ tsp dried Italian seasoning and
  pinches of salt and pepper.
Cook in 2 batches, in 2 tsp butter, in a
  frying pan over medium heat, about
  2 min. per side.

CREAMY CURRIED

Cook fillets in 1 to 2 tsp butter in a frying
  pan over medium heat, 2 to 3 min.
  per side. Remove fish.
Add ⅓ cup sour cream,
  ½ tsp curry powder and
  pinches of salt and pepper.
  Stir until it just begins to bubble.
Pour over fillets.

EASY ORIENTAL

Heat 3 tbsp teriyaki sauce,
  3 tbsp water,
  2 tbsp brown sugar and
  2 tsp freshly squeezed lemon juice in
  a large frying pan.
Add fillets.
  Sprinkle with 4 sliced green onions.
Cover and simmer, 5 to 7 min., turning
  partway through.
Remove fish.
  Boil sauce until thickened, stirring often.
Pour over fish. Wonderful with rice.

CRISPY CORNMEAL sole

Soups ◆ Canned

A can of soup has been the inspiration for many a great fast meal.
Here's everything from a chilled party soup to a pasta sauce.

Cucumber-Dill Soup

In a food processor, whirl 1 coarsely
chopped peeled English cucumber with
10-oz can cream of potato soup,
½ cup cold water, 1½ cups yogurt and
½ cup chopped fresh dill.
Refrigerate, covered, until cold. *Makes 5 cups.*

Tomato 'n' Basil Sipping Soup

Heat 10-oz can condensed tomato soup
with 19-oz can vegetable-cocktail juice,
1 tsp dried basil, 1 tsp sugar and grinding
of pepper. Great in mugs for after skating
or with grilled cheese sandwich. *Serves 3.*

Curried Chicken Soup

Gently heat 10-oz can cream of chicken soup
with 2 cups milk and 1 tsp curry powder.
Add 1 cup frozen peas, 1 cup cooked
chopped chicken and ½ cup instant rice.
Simmer, covered, over low heat, 10 min.
Serves 2.

Hearty Scotch Broth

Heat 10-oz can Scotch broth soup with
1 cup water. Add 1 cup fresh sliced carrots
and ½ lb (250 g) ground lamb or beef,
formed into tiny meatballs. Simmer,
covered, 10 min. to cook meatballs. *Serves 2.*

Potato Parmesan Soup

Gently heat 10-oz can cream of potato soup
with soup can of milk, 1 crushed garlic
clove and ½ cup sliced celery.
Serve with grated Parmesan sprinkled over top.
Makes 3 cups.

Quick Skillet Sauce

Sauté 1 chopped onion in 1 tsp butter.
Add 10-oz can tomato soup, 1 tbsp brown
sugar, 2 tbsp lemon juice, dash of hot
pepper sauce and garlic powder and heat.
Pour over cooked turkey. *Makes 1½ cups.*

Fast Curry Soup

Heat 10-oz can cream of celery soup with
½ cup milk, 1 tsp curry powder and
pinches of onion powder and cayenne.
When smooth, add ½ cup frozen peas and
½ cup chopped cooked chicken or tuna.
Simmer, covered, 10 min. *Makes 3 cups.*

Florentine Soup

Heat 10-oz can cream of potato soup
with 1 cup milk and pinches of garlic
powder and nutmeg. When smooth, add
12-oz (400-g) pkg frozen chopped spinach.
Simmer, covered, 5 min. *Makes 3 cups.*

Chic Double Mushroom Soup

Soak 2 cups dried mushrooms, 20 min.
Slice and heat with 10-oz can cream of
mushroom soup, ½ cup milk, 1 tbsp sherry
and ¼ cup chopped chives or fresh
coriander. *Serves 3.*

Fast Dilled Salmon & Pasta

Heat 10-oz can cream of mushroom soup
with ¼ cup milk or white wine.
When smooth add 7-oz can drained salmon,
2 cups frozen peas and ½ tsp dried
dillweed. When hot toss with ½ lb (225 g)
cooked fettucine. *Serves 2.*

Sour Cream

Light sour cream should be a staple in every kitchen. A mere tablespoon can add instant creaminess to pasta sauces, soups, curries and salad dressings, but only 10 calories.

Oriental Dip

Stir ½ cup sour cream with 1 tsp soy sauce, ¼ tsp ginger and ¼ tsp ground coriander.
Sprinkle with chopped green onion or fresh coriander.
Surround with raw vegetables. *Makes ½ cup.*

Garlic Shrimp Dip

Stir ½ cup sour cream with ½ cup light mayonnaise, 1 tbsp red wine vinegar, 2 crushed garlic cloves, ¼ tsp pepper and dash of hot pepper sauce.
Taste and add ¼ tsp hot red pepper flakes if you like.
Sprinkle with chopped green onions.
Use as a dip for shrimp. *Makes 1 cup.*

Leek & Salmon Dip

Stir ½ pkg dry leek soup mix and ¼ cup chopped smoked salmon into 2 cups sour cream. Refrigerate overnight.
Serve with French bread or spoon into centre of hollowed-out crusty bread. *Makes 2¼ cups.*

Curry Sauce

Stir ½ cup sour cream with ½ tsp curry powder and 1 tbsp of your favorite chutney.
Spoon over fish, steak, chicken or turkey. *Makes ½ cup.*

Creamy Dilled Mustard

Stir ½ cup sour cream or mayonnaise with 2 tbsp Dijon and ½ tsp dried dillweed.
Good with ham, salmon, pork or turkey. *Makes ½ cup.*

Light Dijon Dressing

Whisk ½ cup light sour cream with ¼ cup olive oil, 1 tbsp Dijon and ½ tsp dried dillweed or tarragon.
Great with mixed greens, tuna or chicken salad, or as a salmon sauce. *Makes ¾ cup.*

Lime-Peach Salsa

Stir a finely chopped peach with ¼ cup sour cream and finely grated peel of 1 lime.
Spoon over chicken, cold poached salmon or roast pork. *Makes 1 cup.*

Microwave Curried Cream Sauce

In a small microwave-safe bowl, stir ½ cup sour cream with ¼ cup mayonnaise, 1 tsp curry powder, ½ tsp cumin, ½ tsp garlic salt and ¼ tsp pepper.
Microwave, uncovered, on medium, 20 sec. Stir. Continue to microwave, 30 more sec. or until warm. Serve over carrots, peas, fish or chicken. *Makes ¾ cup.*

Tex-Mex Tomato Salad

Blend ¼ cup sour cream with ½ tsp cumin and generous pinches of chili and garlic powder.
Fold in 2 coarsely chopped tomatoes.
Serve over leaf lettuce. *Makes 2 cups.*

Really Easy Potato Salad

Stir ½ cup light sour cream with 1 tbsp grated onion, 1 tbsp cider vinegar and ¼ tsp pepper.
Toss with warm cubed potatoes. *Makes ½ cup.*

SPAGHETTI SAUCE

Some of today's commercially prepared spaghetti sauces are so flavorful you'd think they were homemade. Here we extend their use.

HERBED ITALIAN CHOWDER

In a saucepan, heat 1½ cups spaghetti sauce with 10-oz can cream of potato soup. Stir often until hot.
Add 1 lb (500 g) frozen fish fillets, cut into bite-size pieces, and ½ tsp dried dillweed.
Simmer, covered and stirring occasionally, until fish flakes easily with a fork, about 4 to 6 min. *Serves 3.*

CHEESE 'N' TOMATO FOCACCIA

Spread a focaccia bread, about 9 in. (23 cm) wide, with ½ cup spaghetti sauce.
Sprinkle with 1 tsp Italian seasoning, ¼ tsp hot red pepper flakes (optional) and ½ to 1 cup grated old cheddar cheese.
Bake on bottom rack of oven at 375°F (190°C) until cheese melts, 18 to 22 min. *Makes 12 wedges.*

PASTA-FREE LASAGNA

Simmer 3 cups spaghetti sauce with 2 crushed garlic cloves, 2 chopped onions, ½ tsp dried oregano, ½ tsp dried basil and ½ tsp sugar.
After 5 min., add 5 cups cooked turkey or chicken pieces.
Layer in a casserole dish with mozzarella or cheddar slices.
Sprinkle with grated Parmesan.
Bake at 350°F (180°C), 35 to 45 min.

ITALIAN EGGS

Heat 2 cups spaghetti sauce in a large frying pan.
Break 6 eggs into sauce.
Lightly sprinkle with cheddar.
Cover and simmer until eggs are poached.
Serve on slices of toasted crusty Italian bread. *Serves 3.*

CHEATER PIZZA

Stir 2 cups spaghetti sauce with
1 cup grated mozzarella,
2 crushed garlic cloves and
1 tsp Italian seasoning.
Spread over a store-bought pizza crust.
Sprinkle with 1 cup grated mozzarella.
Bake in 450°F (230°C) oven, 15 min. *Serves 2.*

FAST OLD-FASHIONED SPAGHETTI SAUCE

Brown ½ lb (250 g) lean ground beef or chicken in a frying pan. Cook over medium heat, working with a fork until it loses its pink color, about 4 min.
Add 19-oz can drained Italian-style stewed tomatoes, 1 cup spaghetti sauce and 1 tsp hot red pepper flakes.
Continue simmering, stirring often, 5 min.
Add 1 chopped green pepper. Simmer, uncovered and stirring often, until peppers are done, about 3 min.
Toss with hot pasta. *Makes 4 cups.*

*5-MINUTE
HOT SAUCE*

5-MINUTE HOT SAUCE

In a saucepan, heat 2 cups spaghetti sauce
  with 2 tbsp brown sugar,
  $\frac{1}{2}$ chopped green pepper,
  1 chopped celery stalk,
  2 sliced green onions,
  1 crushed garlic clove and
  $\frac{1}{2}$ tsp hot red pepper flakes.
Boil gently, uncovered and stirring often,
  until thick, about 5 min.
Toss with hot pasta. *Makes 2 cups.*

QUICK CURRY

In a saucepan, heat 2 cups spaghetti sauce
  with 1 tbsp curry powder. Stir often.
When hot, whisk in $\frac{1}{2}$ cup sour cream, then
  add 2 cups bite-size pieces cooked
  chicken, beef or pork. Heat through.
Toss with pasta or spoon over rice. *Serves 2.*

HOT TOMATO FETA DIP

Cover bottom of a small baking dish with
  $\frac{1}{2}$-in. (1-cm) layer of feta cheese.
Top with $1\frac{1}{2}$ to 2 cups spaghetti sauce
  mixed with pinches of oregano, basil
  and garlic powder.
Bake, covered, at 450°F (230°C), until cheese
  is hot, about 7 min.
Use as a dip for shrimp, sliced sweet peppers,
  zucchini sticks or bread sticks.
  Makes 2½ cups.

ITALIAN RAREBIT

In a saucepan, heat $1\frac{1}{2}$ cups spaghetti sauce.
Add 2 cups grated mozzarella or mix of
  grated cheeses and dash of hot pepper
  sauce. Stir constantly until melted.
Serve over toasted crusty bread. *Serves 2 to 4.*

SPINACH

Young tender spinach has a refreshing earthiness without any bitter aftertaste.
It's rich in beta-carotene, low in calories and, combined with a good source of vitamin C,
as in our Spinach Watercress Salad, it provides essential iron.

SPINACH VEGETABLE SOUP

Heat 4 cups chicken or vegetable broth or
   bouillon with 2 chopped celery stalks,
   1 chopped large onion,
   2 crushed garlic cloves and $\frac{1}{2}$ tsp cayenne.
   Simmer for 5 min.
Then stir in 19-oz can rinsed drained lentils
   and heat through.
Just before serving, stir in 2 cups coarsely
   shredded spinach leaves. Serve right away
   with squares of hot corn bread. *Makes 6 cups.*

FAST VEGETABLE SOUP

Heat 2 (10-oz) cans vegetable soup with
   2 cups shredded spinach. Sprinkle each
   serving with grated Parmesan. *Serves 2.*

PARMESAN SPINACH & EGGS

Sauté 10-oz (300-g) pkg fresh spinach,
   about 7 cups, in 2 tbsp butter.
When wilted, season with pinches of nutmeg,
   salt and pepper. Divide between 4 plates.
Top each with 2 poached eggs.
   Sprinkle with grated Parmesan. *Serves 4.*

PEPPER STIR-FRY

Heat 2 tbsp butter in a large frying pan.
Add 1 chopped red pepper and
   3 cups fresh spinach. Stir until hot.
Toss with $\frac{1}{4}$ tsp sesame oil or
   $\frac{1}{2}$ tsp soy sauce. *Serves 2.*

SUMPTUOUS SPINACH

Steam or microwave 2 bunches spinach,
   about 7 cups, just until wilted, 3 min.
   Drain. Squeeze out liquid.
Sauté 1 crushed garlic clove in
   1 tsp butter, 2 min.
Stir in spinach, $\frac{1}{4}$ cup sour cream,
   1 tbsp lemon juice and pinch of salt.
   Stir often until just hot. *Serves 4.*

BASIL, SPINACH & ORANGE SALAD

Combine 1 bunch spinach, torn into large
   pieces, with $\frac{1}{4}$ cup shredded fresh basil,
   $\frac{1}{4}$ cup chopped red onion and
   1 sliced, peeled seedless orange.
Whisk 3 tbsp olive oil with
   1 tbsp red wine vinegar, 1 tsp brown sugar,
   $\frac{1}{2}$ tsp dried oregano and pinches of salt
   and pepper.
Toss with salad. Great for brunch. *Serves 4.*

SPINACH WALDORF SALAD

Whisk grated peel and 3 tbsp juice from
   1 orange with $\frac{1}{4}$ cup olive oil and
   generous pinches of ginger, pepper and salt.
Tear 1 to 2 bunches spinach into large pieces.
   Add 1 chopped apple or pear.
Toss with dressing. Sprinkle with $\frac{1}{4}$ cup
   sliced hazelnuts or unblanched almonds.
   Serves 4.

FRESH DILL SPINACH SALAD

Combine 2 bunches spinach, about 7 cups,
   with ½ cup coarsely chopped fresh dill
   and ½ chopped English cucumber.
Whisk 3 tbsp olive oil with
   2 tbsp lemon juice and
   ¼ tsp salt and toss with salad.
   Serves 4.

SPINACH GORGONZOLA SALAD

Tear 1 bunch spinach into large pieces.
   Scatter with ¼ sliced red onion and
   1 chopped seeded tomato.
Mash 2 tbsp Gorgonzola cheese with
   ¼ cup sour cream and 1 tbsp lemon juice.
Drizzle over salad and grind black pepper
   over top. *Serves 4.*

SPINACH WATERCRESS SALAD

Whisk 3 tbsp olive oil with
   2 tbsp white vinegar,
   1 tsp sugar,
   grated peel from 1 orange and
   pinches of salt and pepper.
Combine 2 bunches spinach, about 7 cups,
   with 1 bunch watercress and
   2 peeled sliced oranges.
Toss with dressing.
   Serves 4.

SPINACH GORGONZOLA SALAD

SQUASH

A highly touted nutritious veggie, squash not only has fibre, it's rich in vitamin A and potassium, with almost no fat and few calories. Spice it up in soups, dice into racy ragouts and cube into curries.

FAST SQUASH SOUP

Heat 12-oz (400-g) pkg frozen puréed squash with 10-oz can chicken broth, 1 cup water, 1 tsp cumin or ½ tsp curry powder.

Stir often, over medium heat, until smooth. Serve topped with chopped roasted red peppers or a crumbling of goat cheese or Stilton. *Makes 4 cups.*

MICROWAVE SQUASH

Pierce a whole squash. Microwave an acorn squash, 8 to 12 min. or a spaghetti squash, 15 to 18 min. Turn once, partway through. Let stand 5 to 10 min. *Serves 2 to 4.*

HERBED SPAGHETTI SQUASH

Slice cooked spaghetti squash in half. Scoop out seeds. Scrape out pulp with a fork.

Toss with 2 tbsp butter, ½ tsp dried thyme, 4 sliced green onions and pinches of salt and pepper. *Serves 3 to 4.*

SPICED SQUASH PURÉE

Cook 12-oz (400-g) pkg frozen puréed squash according to directions.

Stir in 1 tbsp butter, finely grated peel of 1 small orange and pinches of salt, pepper, nutmeg and allspice. *Serves 4.*

SQUASH & WALNUT STIR-FRY

Cut pulp from 1 butternut squash into small bite-size cubes.

Stir-fry in 2 tbsp vegetable oil in a large frying pan until almost tender, about 3 min.

Sprinkle with ¼ cup chopped walnuts or slivered almonds.

Continue to stir-fry until squash is cooked, about 1 min.

Sprinkle with a little lemon juice. *Serves 4.*

GINGER SQUASH

Microwave an acorn squash on high, 3 min.

Peel and thinly slice. Discard seeds. Cut into bite-size pieces.

Sauté in 2 to 3 tsp butter with 1 crushed garlic clove and 3 thin slices fresh ginger. Sprinkle with pinches of salt and pepper. *Serves 2.*

SOUTH SEAS STUFFED SQUASH

Cut 2 cooked acorn squashes in half and scoop out seeds.

Stir 14-oz can crushed pineapple with 1 tbsp brown sugar, 2 tbsp rum, 1 tbsp butter and generous pinches of cinnamon and salt.

Spoon into centres of squashes.

Broil until golden, about 7 min. *Serves 4.*

SOUTH SEAS
STUFFED
SQUASH

TODDLERS' SQUASH 'N' APPLES

In a microwave-safe dish, combine
  ½ mashed cooked squash with
  1 finely chopped apple or
  ½ cup applesauce and
  1 tbsp apple juice or milk.
Microwave, until apple is soft, 3 min. Mash.
  For thinner texture add more juice.
  Makes ¾ cup.

MAPLE-BUTTERNUT PURÉE

Add 1 tbsp butter and 2 tbsp maple syrup to
  2 lbs (1 kg) hot cooked butternut squash.
Mash until smooth. *Serves 4.*

SAVORY MICROWAVE STUFFED SQUASH

Slice 2 cooked small acorn squashes
  (see Microwave Squash page 180) in half
  crosswise. Discard seeds. Scoop out pulp,
  leaving a ½-in. (1-cm) rim next to skin.
In a large bowl, stir pulp with
  2 tbsp butter,
  1 tbsp brown sugar, ¼ tsp pepper,
  ¼ tsp allspice, ¼ tsp cinnamon and
  generous pinch of ginger or nutmeg.
Purée using a fork or potato masher.
  Spoon back into shells.
Serve right away or cover and refrigerate.
  Reheat, uncovered, in a preheated 350°F
  (180°C) oven, about 30 min. *Serves 4.*

Strawberries

There's nothing better than biting into a ripe juicy strawberry. But once you've enjoyed its great taste au naturel, try these quick ways to indulge in summer's top berry.

Beautiful Berry Soup

Purée 4 cups sliced strawberries with
    1 cup sour cream.
    Thin with milk if necessary.
Add squeeze of lime or sprinkle of sugar
    if needed. *Serves 4.*

Creamy Berry Appetizers

Wash large strawberries, leaving hulls on.
    Dry. Slice in half lengthwise.
Dab with spreadable pineapple or raspberry-
    flavored cream cheese.
Gently press halves together so it looks like a
    berry sandwich.
Press finely chopped toasted nuts into edges
    of cream cheese if you wish.

Microwave Classy Camembert Dip

Remove rind from 6-oz (200-g) round of
    Camembert or piece of Brie.
Pack into a microwave-safe dish that
    holds 1 cup.
Microwave, uncovered, on medium, 2½ to
    3 min., just until cheese begins to melt.
Sprinkle with 1 tbsp brown sugar and
    pinch of cinnamon.
Surround with strawberries for dipping.
    Serves 6.

Ginger-Berry Spread

Purée ½ (8-oz/250-g) pkg cream cheese with
    1 tbsp chopped candied ginger.
Add 6 large strawberries.
    Whirl until chopped.
Add pinch of sugar if needed.
Spread on crackers. *Makes enough for 8
    appetizers.*

French Berry Croissant

Stir 2 cups sliced strawberries with
    ¼ cup sugar.
Split 2 croissants lengthwise.
Cover with strawberries.
Top with 1 cup sour cream stirred with
    2 tbsp sieved brown sugar. *Serves 4.*

Glamorous Omelette

Before folding an omelette, cover half with
    sliced strawberries and dabs of sour
    cream or very thin slices of Camembert
    or Brie. *Serves 1.*

Strawberry Yogurt Fool

Turn 2 cups yogurt into a sieve lined with a
    new reusable kitchen cloth or cheesecloth.
    Drain 1 hour at room temperature or
    overnight in refrigerator.
Stir in 2 cups (1 pt) chopped strawberries
    and 3 to 4 tbsp sugar.
Garnish with whole strawberries. *Serves 4.*

*BEAUTIFUL
BERRY SOUP*

SCARLET BERRY SAUCE

Wash and hull 2 cups (1 pt) strawberries.
Whirl in a blender with 2 tbsp sugar and
  ¼ tsp finely grated lime peel.
Spoon over ice cream, pound cake or use in
  daiquiris. *Makes 1 cup.*

YOGURT FRAPPÉ

Purée ½ cup plain yogurt with
  6 large strawberries,
  1 tsp sugar and
  dash of vanilla. *Serves 1.*

PINK COW

In a blender, whirl 1 cup milk with
  6 hulled strawberries and
  2 tbsp frozen orange juice concentrate.
Taste and whirl in 1 to 2 tbsp sugar as needed.
  Serves 1.

Sweet Potatoes

Sweet potatoes are popping up on the most fashionable menus these days as we gain respect for their naturally sweet taste and high beta-carotene content. Ounce for ounce they contain no more calories than white potatoes.

MICROWAVE SWEET POTATOES

Prick **4 sweet potatoes** all over.
Place 1 in. (2.5 cm) apart on a paper towel in a microwave. Microwave, on high, 10 to 15 min., turning potatoes partway through. Let sit for 2 min. before peeling. *Serves 4.*

REAL HOT SWEET POTATO SOUP

Pierce **2 sweet potatoes** and bake at 350°F (180°C) until soft, about 45 min. Or microwave, on high, 10 min. Peel potatoes.
Purée in a food processor with **2 (10-oz) cans** undiluted chicken broth, **1 cup water** and **1 tsp** hot pepper sauce.
Stir often over medium heat until hot.
Top with a dollop of sour cream and a swirl of hot chili-garlic sauce. *Makes 6 cups.*

SWEET POTATO BAKE

Peel **6 sweet potatoes** and slice into ½-in. (1-cm) thick rounds.
Cook in boiling water, 5 min.
Slice **3 peeled apples** into thin wedges.
Combine ½ **cup brown sugar** with ½ **tsp salt** and ¼ **tsp cinnamon**.
Cover a 9x13-in. (3-L) pan with half the potatoes. Top with half the apples.
Sprinkle with half the sugar mixture. Dot with **2 tbsp butter**. Repeat layers.
Bake, uncovered, at 350°F (180°C), until potatoes are tender, about 30 min. *Serves 8 to 10.*

HONEY SWEET POTATO BAKE

Peel **3 sweet potatoes** and slice in half. Place in an 8-cup (2-L) casserole dish.
Stir ½ **cup chicken bouillon** with **2 tbsp liquid honey, 1 tbsp white vinegar** and pinches of nutmeg, salt and pepper.
Drizzle over potatoes.
Cover and bake at 400°F (200°C), until fork-tender, about 50 min. Turn and baste occasionally. *Serves 6.*

CHICKEN & SWEET POTATO STIR-FRY

Stir-fry **2 very thinly sliced sweet potatoes** in **2 tbsp vegetable oil**, 3 min.
Add ¼ **lb (125 g) sliced mushrooms** and **3 sliced green onions**. Stir-fry for 2 min.
Add **2 cups cooked chicken or turkey pieces**, ⅓ **cup orange juice**, ¼ **tsp marjoram** and ¼ **tsp sage**.
Stir often until potatoes are tender-crisp, about 3 min. Great over rice. *Serves 4.*

STUFFED DILL SPUDS

Bake **2 sweet potatoes** until fork-tender, 45 min.
Slice in half lengthwise and remove pulp.
Mash with **1 tbsp unsalted butter**, **2 tbsp sour cream, 2 tbsp chopped fresh dill** and pinches of salt and pepper.
Spoon back into shells.
Bake at 400°F (200°C) until hot, 10 to 12 min., or microwave until hot. *Serves 4.*

SASSY PURÉE

Peel 4 hot cooked sweet potatoes.
Purée in a food processor with 1 tbsp butter,
¼ cup half-and-half cream, 1 tbsp orange
juice concentrate, pinch of ginger and ¼
tsp ground white pepper. *Serves 6.*

GLAZED SWEET POTATOES

Cook 6 sweet potatoes in a saucepan of
boiling water, until partially cooked, about
20 min. Remove skins and slice in half
lengthwise. Place cut-side up in a buttered
9x13-in. (3-L) casserole dish.

Stir ½ cup maple syrup with ⅓ cup orange
juice, 2 tsp grated orange peel and
pinch of pepper. Pour over potatoes.

Bake, uncovered, at 350°F (180°C), until
potatoes are tender, from 30 to 50 min.
Baste often. *Serves 6.*

ZESTY BAKE

Peel and cut 3 sweet potatoes into chunks.
Place in an 8-cup (2-L) casserole dish.

Combine 3 tbsp melted butter with
¼ cup orange juice and pinches of salt
and pepper. Drizzle over potatoes.

Cover and bake at 400°F (200°C), 45 min. or
until fork-tender. Stir often. *Serves 6.*

SWEET POTATOES NOËL

Boil 5 sweet potatoes in salted water until
almost tender, about 30 min. Peel.
Slice potatoes lengthwise into 4 pieces.

Overlap in a buttered 9x13-in. (3-L) dish.
Put 2 sections of mandarin oranges on
each slice. Drizzle with liquid honey, about
½ cup. Dot with ¼ cup butter.

Bake, uncovered, at 350°F (180°C), 30 min.
Baste often. *Serves 4 to 6.*

REAL HOT SWEET POTATO SOUP

T is for Tuna...

Spicy beef and vegetables burst out of warm
tortillas. FIERY FAJITAS *(see recipe page 196)*
are a perfect wrap-and-roll dinner to leisurely
enjoy in front of the TV.

T

TOFU

Wiggly custard-like tofu is made from soy beans, reputed to protect us from cancer and lower our bad cholesterol. High in protein and cheap, tofu takes little preparation. Here's 10 neat ways to fit it into mainstream meals, and all are vegetarian.

MORNING TOFU

Slice ½ (1-lb/454-g) pkg tofu into ½-in. (1-cm) thick bite-size pieces. Generously brush with maple syrup. Sprinkle with cinnamon.

Sauté in 1 tbsp butter over low heat until warm.

Serve drizzled with extra maple syrup and sautéed apples. *Serves 2.*

SPICY MEXICAN TOFU

Sauté 1 large chopped onion and 2 garlic cloves in 1 tsp vegetable oil until soft.

Add 19-oz can undrained Mexican-flavored stewed tomatoes (or 19-oz can stewed tomatoes and 1 tbsp chili powder) and bring to a boil.

Boil vigorously, uncovered and stirring often, until thick, about 8 min.

Stir in 1 cup tofu, cut into small cubes.

Add 1 cup canned kidney beans and just heat through. *Serves 2 to 3.*

MOROCCAN COUSCOUS

Prepare 1 cup couscous following package directions.

Slice ½ (1-lb/454-g) pkg tofu into bite-size strips. Toss tofu with 1 tsp cumin, ½ tsp cinnamon, ¼ tsp cayenne and ¼ tsp salt.

Sauté in 2 tsp olive oil or butter.

When browned, toss with couscous, ½ cup raisins and 1 cup sliced cooked carrots. *Serves 3 to 4.*

BAKED ITALIAN TOFU

Slice tofu lengthwise into ½-in. (1-cm) thick pieces. Drizzle Italian salad dressing over top. Spread to coat.

Bake in a pie plate at 400°F (200°C), 10 min.

Sprinkle with grated cheddar.

Bake until cheese melts, 5 min. Sprinkle with chopped fresh basil leaves and serve hot. *Serves 2.*

HOT 'N' FIERY TOFU

Slice ½ (1-lb/454-g) pkg tofu into ½-in. (1-cm) thick bite-size pieces.

In a frying pan over medium heat, stir 3 crushed garlic cloves and ½ tsp hot red pepper flakes in 1 tbsp vegetable oil. Stir often for 3 min.

Add tofu. Sprinkle with cayenne.

Sauté until golden, adding more oil if necessary. *Serves 2.*

TOFU SALSA SCRAMBLE

Sauté 1 coarsely chopped onion and 1 chopped green pepper in 2 tsp vegetable oil, about 5 min.

Add ½ cup salsa and stir until warm.

Meanwhile, in another frying pan heat 2 tsp butter.

Add 2 cups finely chopped tofu and stir until hot.

Stir in ½ cup grated Parmesan or cheddar.

Serve topped with salsa mixture. *Serves 2.*

*TOFU SALSA
SCRAMBLE*

TOFU QUICHE

Bake a 9-in. (23-cm) pie shell or store-bought
deep pie shell at 400°F (200°C), 10 min.
In a food processor, whirl
I lb (454 g) drained tofu with ½ cup milk,
3 eggs, 3 tbsp all-purpose flour,
½ tsp Worcestershire, ¾ tsp salt,
½ tsp basil, ½ tsp leaf oregano and
grinding of pepper.
Stir in I cup cooked chopped broccoli and 3
sliced green onions. Pour into shell.
Bake at 325°F (160°C) for 35 min. or until set.
Serves 6.

CORN & ROASTED PEPPER CHOWDER

Heat 2 (14-oz) cans cream-style corn with
I ½ cups milk,
3 tbsp diced seeded jalapeños and
½ cup chopped roasted red pepper.
When hot, stir in I lb (454 g) tofu, cut into
bite-size pieces, and just heat. *Makes 5 cups.*

CAESAR SALAD DRESSING

In a food processor, whirl
½ (10-oz/290-g) pkg silken tofu with
2 tbsp lemon juice, 2 tbsp water,
I tbsp olive oil, I tsp anchovy paste,
¼ tsp salt and pinch of pepper.
Add 2 tbsp grated Parmesan and whirl until
mixed.
Toss with romaine lettuce and croutons.
Makes 1 cup.

WARM CAESAR SALAD

Sauté bite-size strips of tofu in
light sesame oil until golden.
Sprinkle with cayenne.
Squeeze lime juice over top.
Toss warm strips with a Caesar salad.

TOMATOES ◆ Fresh

Nothing rivals the taste of tomatoes fresh from the vine. When in season, have your fill. Then use our bushelful of ideas to take advantage of their natural sweetness in a myriad of colorful ways.

FAST GARDEN GAZPACHO

In a food processor, purée
4 peeled tomatoes with
1 small green pepper,
½ coarsely chopped English cucumber and
generous pinches of basil, salt and pepper.
Stir in 2 (5½-oz) cans or
1½ cups vegetable juice cocktail.
Refrigerate until cold. *Makes 6 cups.*

FRESH CORIANDER SALSA

Dice 3 tomatoes and finely chop ½ red onion.
Stir with ¼ cup chopped fresh coriander,
2 tbsp olive oil,
1 tbsp red wine vinegar,
⅛ tsp hot pepper sauce and
pinches of salt and pepper.
Wonderful with steak. *Makes 3 cups.*

FRESH SALSA

Combine 4 chopped seeded tomatoes
with 3 sliced green onions,
¼ cup chopped fresh Italian parsley or
coriander, 3 crushed garlic cloves,
2 tbsp olive oil, 2 tbsp lemon juice,
1 tbsp chopped hot pepper and
pinches of salt and pepper.
Allow flavors to blend, about 1 hour.
Delicious on eggs, steaks and chicken.
Makes 3½ cups.

DEVILED BROIL

Slice 2 tomatoes in half and place on a
baking sheet.
Whisk 2 tbsp melted butter with
1½ tsp Dijon, ½ tsp Worcestershire and
1 crushed garlic clove.
Stir in ½ cup fine dry bread crumbs.
Press on top of tomatoes.
Broil until golden, about 4 to 5 min. Good
with burgers or eggs. *Serves 4.*

SAUTÉED TOMATOES

Sauté 4 thickly sliced tomatoes in 1 tbsp
olive oil, about 1 min. per side. Remove.
Add 2 tbsp red wine to pan.
When reduced by half, stir in
⅓ cup sour cream,
1 tbsp chopped fresh basil and
pinches of salt and pepper.
As soon as sour cream is hot, spoon over
tomatoes. Wonderful with steak,
scrambled eggs or as a burger topping.
Serves 4.

BBQ HERBED FETA TOMATOES

Slice 2 tomatoes into ¼-in. (0.5-cm)
thick slices.
Liberally brush with olive oil.
Generously sprinkle with dried oregano,
basil and pepper.
Barbecue 3 min. per side. Crumble feta over
top and serve with chicken or steak. *Serves 4.*

Frigid Tomatoes

SUN-DRIED TOMATO SALAD

Trim ½ bunch watercress and place
   on a platter.
   Arrange 3 sliced tomatoes over top.
Julienne 3 sun-dried tomatoes, packed in oil,
   and 2 pieces bocconcini cheese.
   Scatter over sliced tomatoes.
Drizzle salad with 1 tbsp olive oil and
   1 tbsp red wine vinegar.
Sprinkle with 1 tbsp chopped fresh basil
   and pinches of salt and pepper. *Serves 4.*

CREOLE SALAD

Coarsely chop 3 tomatoes, 1 green pepper
   and 4 stuffed green olives.
Toss with 2 tbsp olive oil, 1 tbsp vinegar,
   ½ tsp basil, ¼ tsp garlic powder,
   ¼ tsp thyme and ⅛ tsp cayenne.
Makes 3 cups.

TOMATOES WITH BALSAMIC VINAIGRETTE

Slice 4 large tomatoes.
Whisk 2 tbsp olive oil with
   1 tbsp balsamic vinegar and
   pinches of salt and pepper.
Drizzle over tomatoes.
   Sprinkle with coarsely chopped
   fresh basil or coriander.
Serve with grilled chicken or fish. *Serves 4.*

FRIGID TOMATOES

For winter soups and sauces, don't bother
   peeling tomatoes.
Core, then freeze whole in plastic bags.
Plunge frozen tomatoes into simmering
   sauces; burst skins will float to the surface
   for easy removing.

TOMATOES ◆ Stewed

A can of stewed tomatoes is a great year-round buy. High in vitamin C and beta-carotene, not to mention taste, it's ready and waiting to make into a tasty sauce.

MILD OLÉ MEAT SAUCE

Sauté ½ lb (250 g) ground beef in 1 tsp oil.
Add 19-oz can undrained Mexican-stewed
  tomatoes and boil gently, stirring often,
  until thickened.
Toss with 4 to 6 cups cooked pasta shells.
  Serves 2 to 3.

FAST 'N' CREAMY SAUCE

Pour 10-oz can cream of mushroom soup
  into a saucepan with 2 (19-oz) cans
  undrained stewed tomatoes,
  1 tsp basil and ½ tsp leaf oregano.
Set saucepan over medium heat. Break up
  tomatoes.
Stir occasionally, until hot. Toss with pasta.
  Makes about 5 cups.

HEARTY BURGUNDY SAUCE

Combine 19-oz can undrained chunky
  pasta-style stewed tomatoes with
  5½-oz can tomato paste and
  ¼ cup red or white wine in a saucepan
  over medium heat. Break up tomatoes.
Boil gently, uncovered, stirring often, until
  thickened, 5 min.
Add pinch of sugar if needed.
  Toss with pasta. *Makes 3 cups.*

ITALIAN CLAMS

Heat 19-oz can undrained Italian-stewed
  tomatoes with ½ tsp dried basil
  and 1 small crushed garlic clove.
  Break up tomatoes. Bring to a boil.
Reduce heat and simmer, uncovered, stirring
  often, until thick enough to coat pasta.
Stir in 5-oz (142-g) can drained clams.
  Toss with hot spaghetti. *Makes 3 cups.*

PASTA PUTTANESCA

In a large saucepan, combine 2 (19-oz) cans
  undrained Italian-stewed tomatoes
  with ¾ to 1 cup small black olives
  and 1 tbsp capers.
Boil gently, uncovered, stirring often, until
  thick, about 15 min.
Toss with ½ lb (225 g) cooked pasta.
  Top with lots of grated Parmesan. *Serves 2.*

MEXICAN SEASHELLS

Sauté ½ lb (250 g) ground beef or turkey in a
  nonstick frying pan until almost cooked.
  Sprinkle with 2 tsp chili powder.
Add 19-oz can undrained Mexican-stewed
  tomatoes and 1 cup frozen kernel corn.
  Break up tomatoes.
Boil gently, stirring often, until thickened.
  Toss with hot pasta shells. *Makes 6 cups.*

SWANKY LINGUINE

In a wide frying pan, stir 19-oz can undrained Italian-style stewed tomatoes with ¼ cup vermouth or dry red wine and 4 crushed garlic cloves.

Boil gently, stirring often, until thickened, 5 to 7 min.

Pour over ¾ (1-lb/450-g) pkg cooked linguine. Sprinkle with grated Parmesan. *Serves 3 to 4.*

HERBED SPANISH CHOPS

In a wide saucepan, heat 19-oz can undrained stewed tomatoes with ½ cup sliced pimento-stuffed olives, 1 chopped green pepper, ½ tsp dried thyme, ¼ tsp oregano and grinding of pepper. Add 6 pork chops.

Cover and simmer, 30 min. Turn once. Wonderful over rice. *Serves 6.*

FAST CACCIATORE

Combine 28-oz can undrained stewed tomatoes and 2 cups sliced mushrooms in a large saucepan. Bring to a boil.

Add 4 skinless chicken breasts, bone-side up. Reduce heat. Simmer, covered, 30 min.

Turn chicken. Add 2 cups sliced mushrooms. Continue cooking, 10 min.

Remove chicken. Boil sauce, uncovered, until thickened. Pour over chicken. *Serves 4.*

MICROWAVE SPICED-TOMATO HALIBUT

Pour 19-oz can drained spicy stewed tomatoes into 10-in. (25-cm) pie plate.

Place 2 halibut steaks, ¾ in. (2 cm) thick, on top.

Cover and microwave, on medium, 12 min. Turn steaks partway through.

Let stand, covered, 5 min. *Serves 2.*

HERBED SPANISH CHOPS

TUNA ◆ Canned

Stock up on tuna when it's on special. You can always count on it for a high-protein low-cal starter for a fast dinner. Each recipe uses a 7-oz can of water-packed drained tuna.

NEW TUNA MELT

Toast 2 slices whole wheat bread.
Drain tuna and combine with
  1 chopped seeded tomato,
  3 tbsp sour cream and
  ¼ tsp dried basil.
Spread over bread.
  Sprinkle with 2 tbsp grated Parmesan.
Broil until golden and bubbly. *Makes 2.*

INSTANT FISH CHOWDER

Mix 10-oz can Manhattan-style clam
  chowder with a soup can of water.
Add tuna and heat.
When piping hot, stir in 2 tbsp sour cream.
  Makes 2½ cups.

CURRIED ZUCCHINI BOATS

Slice off a cap along the length of
  4 zucchini and scoop out pulp.
Finely chop pulp, then stir with tuna,
  ½ tsp curry and pinches of salt and pepper.
Mound in hollowed-out zucchini.
  Sprinkle with grated Parmesan or
  other grated cheese.
Bake, uncovered, at 350°F (180°C), until hot,
  30 min. *Serves 4.*

FAST ITALIAN

In a saucepan, bring 19-oz can undrained
  stewed tomatoes, 1 chopped zucchini
  and 1 tsp crushed garlic to a boil.
Add tuna and boil gently, uncovered, stirring
  often, until thickened.
Toss with hot spaghetti. *Serves 2.*

TATER-TOPPER DINNER

Stir tuna with ½ cup sour cream,
  ¼ tsp basil, 3 sliced green onions and
  pinches of salt and pepper.
Spoon over 4 baked potato halves.
  Makes 4 halves.

PESTO TOSS

Stir 2 coarsely chopped tomatoes with tuna,
  1 tbsp pesto and
  2 tbsp mayonnaise or sour cream.
Serve on a bed of romaine lettuce or whole
  wheat rolls. *Serves 1 to 2.*

FAST NIÇOISE FETTUCCINE

Sauté 1 large crushed garlic clove in
  3 tbsp olive oil over low heat, 3 min.
Add 4 chopped drained tomatoes,
  1 tbsp capers, 1 tsp basil and tuna.
  Stir gently until hot.
Toss with ½ (1-lb/450-g) pkg cooked
  fettuccine. *Serves 2.*

TUNA CAESAR SALAD

Break half a head of romaine lettuce
    into bite-size pieces.
    Sprinkle with tuna and
    2 whole sliced green onions.
Stir squeeze of lemon juice and
    dash of hot sauce into
    $\frac{1}{4}$ cup creamy Caesar dressing.
Toss with salad. *Serves 2.*

LIGHT CURRIED PITAS

Mix tuna with $\frac{1}{4}$ cup light sour cream,
    $\frac{1}{2}$ tsp curry and chopped green onion.
Use as filling for pitas or serve on lettuce with
    sliced cucumber. *Makes 1 cup.*

MEDITERRANEAN PIZZA

Stir tuna with
    2 chopped seeded tomatoes and
    $\frac{1}{4}$ cup sliced black olives and
    $\frac{1}{2}$ cup Caesar salad dressing.
Spread over a store-bought pizza crust.
    Sprinkle with
    2 cups grated mozzarella cheese.
Bake at 450°F (230°C) for 15 min.
    Serves 4.

FAST NIÇOISE FETTUCCINE

TURKEY LEFTOVERS

Many people prefer their turkey the second time around. After the big event, when what you do with the turkey and trimmings are predictable, try these new twists.

CURRIED TURKEY DIP

In a food processor, whirl
   2 cups chopped cooked turkey with
   ½ (8-oz/250-g) pkg cream cheese,
   ½ cup sour cream,
   1 chopped green onion and
   ¼ tsp curry powder until nearly smooth.
Add more sour cream if needed. Serve with slices of apple, pear or colorful pepper strips. *Makes 2¼ cups.*

SUPPER OMELETTE

Before folding omelette, fill with
   chopped cooked turkey moistened with
   yogurt, chopped green onion and
   pinch of curry.

QUICK DINNER

Gently heat 10-oz can condensed cream
   of potato soup with 1 cup chopped
   cooked turkey, 2 cups frozen peas and
   ½ tsp poultry seasoning.
Stir often until hot.
Serve over toasted muffins. *Serves 1 to 2.*

FRENCH SAUTÉ

Sandwich thin slices of turkey and
   mild-flavored cheese between slices
   of crusty bread that have been lightly
   spread with Dijon.
Dip in an egg-and-milk mixture, then
   pan-fry in butter.

QUICK DEEP-DISH PIE

For filling, heat condensed cream
   of mushroom soup with pinches of
   curry powder.
Stir in chopped cooked turkey and frozen
   vegetables.
When hot, turn into a casserole dish.
For topping, use refrigerator crescent rolls
   or frozen puff pastry.
Bake at 375°F (190°C) until topping is golden.

ITALIAN CUTLETS

Cover bottom of a small casserole dish
   with thick slices of cooked turkey.
Spread with a thick layer of
   seasoned spaghetti sauce.
Cover with mozzarella slices.
Bake, uncovered, at 350°F (180°C) until
   cheese melts.

CURRIED TURKEY

Fry several chopped onions sprinkled
   with curry, cumin and cayenne in a
   little butter.
Add canned tomatoes and
   cooked turkey pieces.
Cover and simmer for 30 min., stirring often.
   Serve over rice.

French Sauté

UPDATED TURKEY SANDWICH DELUXE

Spread 2 pieces of focaccia bread with
    creamy goat cheese.
    Cover one piece with sliced cooked turkey.
Top with roasted red pepper (see page 141)
    or pimento strips, then turn other focaccia
    piece over top.

FESTIVE LIGHT TURKEY PÂTÉ

In a food processor, whirl
    2 cups bite-size pieces cooked turkey with
    $\frac{1}{2}$ (8-oz/250-g) pkg cream cheese,
    $\frac{1}{4}$ cup unsalted butter,
    $1\frac{1}{2}$ tsp Dijon and
    generous pinches of salt and cayenne.
Serve with tiny rounds of French bread.
    Covered and refrigerated, pâté will keep
    refrigerated for 2 days. *Makes 2 cups.*

CURRIED SALAD

Season mayonnaise with
    pinches of curry and cayenne.
Add chopped cooked turkey,
    small green grapes and
    toasted chopped almonds.
Hollow out small rolls or brioches and fill
    with salad mixture.

Y is for Yogurt...

Brown sugar and cinnamon create a golden topping for our light YOGURT STREUSEL BISCUITS *(see recipe page 204). Yogurt contributes not only incredible creaminess, but a pleasant natural tang.*

Yogurt

*Yogurt packs more than tangy refreshment. A cup of 2% has more calcium than
a cup of 2% milk and there's a multitude of ways to use it.
When heating in a sauce, use a 5% butterfat yogurt, since low-fat may separate when heated.*

Mint 'n' Honey

Stir 1 cup yogurt with 2 tbsp chopped
fresh mint and squeeze of lemon juice.
Stir in 2 tbsp liquid honey.
Taste and add more if you wish.
Spoon over fruit salad or berries.
Makes 1¼ cups.

Very Berry Sauce

Crush 1 cup strawberries, raspberries
or blueberries. Stir in 1 cup yogurt and
3 tbsp granulated sugar.
Taste and add more sugar if you wish.
Spoon over pancakes or waffles. *Makes 1⅔ cups.*

Yogurt Streusel Biscuits

Stir 2¼ cups all-purpose flour with
2 tsp baking powder, ½ tsp salt and
½ tsp baking soda.
Cut in ¼ cup cold shortening with
2 knives until crumbly.
Stir in 1¼ cups plain yogurt.
Gather dough into a ball. Place on a lightly
floured surface. Knead gently 8 times.
Pat to ½-in. (1-cm) thickness.
Cut with 2-in. (5-cm) floured cookie cutter.
Stir ¼ cup brown sugar with
1 tsp cinnamon and ¼ tsp nutmeg.
Press a little on top of each biscuit.
Bake biscuits on an ungreased baking sheet at
400°F (200°C), 15 to 18 min.
Makes 20 biscuits.

Hollandaise

Whisk 1 cup yogurt with 4 egg yolks,
1 tbsp freshly squeezed lemon juice,
¼ tsp salt and dash of hot pepper sauce
in a small frying pan.
Whisk constantly over medium heat until
thickened.
Whisk in 1 tbsp butter if you wish.
Spoon over eggs or salmon. *Makes 1¼ cups.*

Light Béarnaise

Simmer ¼ cup white wine with
2 tbsp lemon juice or white vinegar,
1 minced large shallot and
¼ tsp dried tarragon in a small pan over
medium heat. Stir often.
Whisk 4 egg yolks with ¾ cup yogurt.
When wine has almost evaporated, slowly
whisk in yogurt mixture. Whisk constantly
just until thickened.
Immediately serve over steaks or burgers.
Makes 1 cup.

Curry Yogurt Sauce

Melt 1 tbsp butter in a small frying pan
over medium heat.
Stir in 2 tsp curry and 1 crushed garlic clove.
Stir 1 min.
Whisk in 1 cup yogurt and ¼ tsp salt.
When hot, stir in
1 to 2 finely sliced green onions and pour
over chicken or vegetables. *Makes 1 cup.*

RICH LEMON SAUCE

Whisk I cup yogurt with 3 egg yolks,
   3 tbsp granulated sugar and
   finely grated peel of I lemon.
Pour into a small saucepan.
Whisk constantly over medium heat
   until thickened and hot.
Drizzle over chocolate cake or pound cake.
   Makes 1 cup.

UPTOWN TARTAR SAUCE

Stir I cup yogurt with
   ¼ cup finely chopped dill pickle,
   2 sliced green onions,
   2 tbsp chopped parsley and
   pinches of salt, pepper and paprika.
Serve with fish, broccoli or cauliflower.
   Makes 1¼ cups.

REFRESHING YOGURT DRESSING

Blend ½ cup plain yogurt with
   ½ cup sour cream,
   I tsp liquid honey and
   ½ tsp lemon juice.
Great dressing for spinach salad. *Makes 1 cup.*

TANGY ROQUEFORT YOGURT DRESSING

Mash 2 tbsp Roquefort cheese with a fork.
Stir in I cup yogurt and
   pinches of salt and pepper.
Toss with a salad or use as a dip for veggies.
   Makes 1 cup.

UPTOWN TARTAR SAUCE ON FISH

Z is for Zucchini...

FAST MEDITERRANEAN ZUCCHINI CHOWDER (see recipe page 209) has delicate pieces of fish and mild zucchini slices in a luxurious herb-scented tomato broth. What a fabulous way to serve up a low-cal dinner. Pass a basket of oven-toasted garlicky baguettes and enjoy.

Z

ZUCCHINI

Zucchini is consistently one of the best buys in the produce section.
Here are new ways to barbecue, sauté, microwave and scramble.

ZUCCHINI NACHOS APPETIZERS

Place 2 zucchini, cut into ¼-in. (0.5-cm)
   rounds, on a baking sheet.
Top with ¾ cup grated Gouda, Asiago or
   cheddar. Sprinkle with generous pinches
   of hot red pepper flakes.
Broil until cheese is bubbly, 2 min. *Serves 4.*

BARBECUED CURRIED ZUCCHINI

Slice 4 zucchini lengthwise into
   ½-in. (1-cm) strips.
Stir ¼ cup vegetable oil with 1½ tsp curry,
   1 tsp cumin, ¼ tsp salt and generous
   pinches of ginger, cayenne and sugar.
Brush on both sides of slices.
Grill, turning and basting often, about 4 min.
   Serves 4.

ZUCCHINI & PEPPER SAUTÉ

Sauté 1 crushed garlic clove in 1 tbsp olive oil.
Stir in 1 sliced zucchini and 1 sliced red
   pepper. Sprinkle with generous pinches of
   salt, pepper and dried thyme.
Cook, stirring often, until tender-crisp, about
   3 to 5 min. *Serves 2 to 4.*

SIMPLE SESAME ZUCCHINI

In a wide frying pan, melt 2 tsp butter.
Add 1 tbsp sesame seeds and stir until golden.
Add 2 sliced zucchini and stir-fry for 1 min.
Stir in 1 tbsp soy sauce and pinch of pepper.
   Serves 2 to 4.

LEMON CHICKEN ZUCCHINI BURGERS

Whisk together 1 egg, grated peel of
   ½ lemon, ½ tsp salt and ¼ tsp pepper.
Add 1 grated zucchini,
   1 lb (500 g) lean ground chicken or turkey,
   ¼ cup dry bread crumbs and
   1 sliced green onion. Form into 4 patties.
Barbecue, broil or sauté until well done, 6 to
   8 min. per side. Serve in rolls. *Makes 4.*

ZUCCHINI CARAWAY CARROT SALAD

Boil 2 julienned carrots until barely tender,
   about 1 min. Drain.
Julienne 8 small zucchini.
Whisk 2 tbsp olive oil with
   1 tbsp white vinegar,
   1 crushed garlic clove, ¼ tsp salt
   and pinch of cayenne.
Crush ½ tsp caraway seeds and stir in.
   Stir in zucchini and carrots.
Wonderful with grilled chicken or steaks.
   Makes 7 cups.

ZUCCHINI 'N' TOMATO GRATIN

Slice 2 zucchini and 2 to 3 small tomatoes
   into ¼-in. (0.5-cm) thick slices.
Overlap slices alternately in concentric circles
   in a greased pie plate. Sprinkle with
   1 tsp dried leaf thyme, 3 tbsp grated
   Parmesan and pinches of salt and pepper.
Broil until lightly browned, about 6 to 8 min.
   Serves 4 to 6.

*LEMON
CHICKEN
ZUCCHINI
BURGERS*

GREEN CHILI SCRAMBLE

Sauté 1 chopped zucchini with
   1 chopped seeded jalapeño in
   1 tbsp butter.
Whisk 6 eggs with ¼ cup sour cream and
   ¼ tsp salt.
Pour over vegetables.
   Stir until partially set, about 2 min.
Add 1 sliced green onion and ¼ cup grated
   cheddar cheese.
   Stir until set, 4 to 5 min. *Serves 3.*

ZUCCHINI-GARLIC RELISH

In a frying pan, melt 2 tbsp butter.
Add 3 grated zucchini, 1 crushed garlic clove
   and pinches of curry and pepper.
   Stir over medium heat, 5 min.
Remove from heat.
Stir in 1 to 2 tbsp chopped pimento or
   roasted red pepper.
Refrigerate. *Makes ½ cup.*

FAST MEDITERRANEAN ZUCCHINI CHOWDER

Heat 28-oz can undrained tomatoes with
   10-oz can chicken broth,
   ½ cup red wine,
   1 chopped green pepper,
   2 crushed garlic cloves,
   ½ tsp anchovy paste,
   ½ tsp dried oregano and
   ¼ tsp chili powder.
   Boil gently, uncovered, stirring often, 5 min.
Add ¾ lb (400 g) fish fillets, cut into bite-size
   pieces, and 2 to 3 sliced small zucchini.
   Continue simmering, uncovered, stirring
   occasionally, 5 min. *Serves 2 to 4.*

SURVIVAL GUIDE

As well as fresh fruits and vegetables and the other 100 ingredients categorized alphabetically throughout this book, keep your freezer, refrigerator and kitchen shelves stocked with the following items; you'll be well on your way to whipping together a quick dinner.

IN THE CUPBOARD

*Refrigerate after opening

FOR BAKING
All-purpose flour
Brown sugar
Baking powder
Baking soda
Chocolate squares,
   semisweet
Cocoa
Coconut, flaked
Oats, rolled
Sugar, granulated
Vanilla extract
Whole wheat flour

CANS
Artichokes
Carrots
Chicken bouillon
Chicken broth
Chickpeas
Corn niblets
Cream of mushroom soup
Cream of potato soup
Green chilies
Kidney beans
Mandarin oranges
Pinto beans
Plum tomatoes
Pumpkin
Romano beans
Spaghetti sauce
Tomatoes
Tomato paste
Tomato sauce

GRAINS
Bran
Bulgur

Cornmeal
Couscous
Instant rice
Quinoa
Rice
Wild rice

JARS
*Capers
*Chopped garlic
*Chopped ginger

MISCELLANEOUS
Almonds
*Apple jelly
Chicken bouillon cubes
Cornstarch
Croutons
*Dijon mustard
Dried apricots
Dry bread crumbs
Dry mustard
Instant coffee
Liquid honey
*Mango chutney
Pasta
Raisins
Taco chips

MIXES
Cake mix
Cookie mix
Muffin mix
Pancake mix
Soup mix
Variety biscuit mix

OIL
Olive oil
*Sesame oil
Vegetable oil

SAUCES
*Barbecue sauce
*Garlic-chili sauce
*Hoisin sauce
*Peanut sauce
Soy sauce
Tabasco sauce
Teriyaki sauce
Worcestershire sauce

SPICES & HERBS
Basil
Black pepper
Cayenne
Chili
Cinnamon
Cumin
Curry powder
Dillweed
Ground coriander
Ground ginger
Hot red pepper flakes
Italian seasoning
Nutmeg
Oregano
Paprika
Sage
Savory
Tarragon
Thyme
White pepper

VINEGAR & WINE
Balsamic vinegar
*Red wine
Red wine vinegar
White vinegar
*White wine

REFRIGERATOR

Bacon
Butter
Cucumbers
Eggs
Garlic butter
Green onions
Horseradish
Ketchup
Lettuce
Mayonnaise
Milk
Parmesan cheese
Pesto

DRESSINGS
Caesar salad dressing
Italian salad dressing
Roquefort salad dressing
Vinaigrette salad dressing

FRESH SPICES
Basil
Coriander
Dill
Ginger
Parsley

JUICE
Apple juice
Orange juice
Tomato juice
Vegetable cocktail juice

FREEZER

FISH
Fillets
Fish sticks·
Steaks

MEATS
Chicken (all cuts)
Ground beef
Ground chicken

Ground pork
Ground veal
Pork tenderloins
Quick-fry pork chops
Steakettes

MISCELLANEOUS
Berries
Bread
Ice cream
Piecrust
Pizza crust
Walnuts

VEGETABLES
Broccoli
Carrots
Cauliflower
Green beans
Peas
Pumpkin
Spinach
Squash

FRESH VS DRIED HERBS

Use fresh herbs whenever you have them. However, we know it's not always possible to have fresh herbs on hand. Here's a rough estimate on how to substitute fresh for dry. Always err on the "too-little side," then taste and sprinkle in more if needed.

FRESH	DRIED
2 to 4 tbsp fresh basil	1 tsp basil
1 tbsp finely chopped fresh oregano	1 tsp dried oregano or ½ tsp ground oregano
1 tbsp chopped fresh thyme	1 tsp leaf thyme
1 tbsp chopped fresh rosemary	1 tsp crushed rosemary
1 tsp grated fresh ginger	½ tsp ground ginger
1 tbsp chopped fresh sage	1 tsp dried sage or ½ tsp ground sage

ITALIAN SEASONING
If you don't have pre-mixed Italian seasoning, make your own:

¾ tsp dried basil and
¼ tsp dried oregano
or
2 tbsp chopped fresh basil and
1 tsp chopped fresh oregano

D

Desserts

Dips. *See also* Appetizers.

Dressings

E

Entrées

Side Dishes

CHATELAINE food express
Quickies

FOR SMITH SHERMAN BOOKS INC.

EDITORIAL DIRECTOR
Carol Sherman

ART DIRECTOR
Andrew Smith

SENIOR COPY EDITOR
Bernice Eisenstein

EDITORIAL ASSISTANCE
Lolita Osorio, Debra Sherman

DESIGN ASSISTANCE
Joseph Gisini

COLOR SEPARATIONS
Compeer Prepress Services Ltd., Scarborough

PRINTING
Kromar Printing Ltd., Winnipeg

SMITH SHERMAN BOOKS INC.
657 Davenport Road, Toronto, Canada M5R 1L3
e-mail: bloke@astral.magic.ca

FOR CHATELAINE

FOOD EDITOR
Monda Rosenberg

PROJECT MANAGER
Lucie Cousineau

TEST KITCHEN STAFF
Marilyn Crowley, Trudy Patterson

CHATELAINE ADVISORY BOARD
Rona Maynard, Lee Simpson, Anita Draycott

CHATELAINE, MACLEAN HUNTER PUBLISHING LIMITED
777 Bay Street, Toronto, Canada M5W 1A7
e-mail: letters@chatelaine.com

ILLUSTRATIONS by Jeff Jackson

PHOTOGRAPHS
Michael Mahovlich: pages 2, 13, 23, 25, 53, 65, 67, 71, 73, 83, 85, 89, 107, 113, 127, 129, 135, 141, 145, 153, 161, 163, 177, 179, 185, 187, 189, 199, 203, 205, 207, back cover inset.

Ed O'Neil: front cover and pages 9, 11, 17, 27, 37, 43, 45, 61, 77, 91, 93, 99, 117, 119, 123, 125, 143, 149, 159, 167, 171, 173, 179, 181, 191, 195, 209.

Lorella Zanetti: pages 19, 33, 41, 51.   Michael Lant: page 103.   Michael Visser: page 59.

Back cover photograph of Monda Rosenberg and the
Chatelaine Test Kitchen staff by Susan Dobson.